THE ETHICS OF COACHING SPORTS

THE ETHICS OF COACHING SPORTS

Moral, Social, and Legal Issues

Edited by

ROBERT L. SIMON

HAMILTON COLLEGE

Routledge
Taylor & Francis Group
New York London

First published 2013 by Westview Press

Published 2019 by Routledge
52 Vanderbilt Avenue, New York, NY 10017
2 Park Square, Milton Park, Abingdon, Oxon OX14 4RN

First issued in hardback 2019

Routledge is an imprint of the Taylor & Francis Group, an informa business

Designed by Cynthia Young

Library of Congress Cataloging-in-Publication Data

The ethics of coaching sports : moral social and legal issues / edited by Robert L. Simon.
p. cm.
Includes bibliographical references and index.
ISBN 978-0-8133-4608-3 (pbk. : alk. paper)—ISBN 978-0-8133-4609-0 (e-book)
1. Coaching (Athletics)—Moral and ethical aspects. 2. Sports—Moral and ethical aspects. I. Simon, Robert L., 1941–
GV711.E82 2013
796.07'7—dc23
2012045429

ISBN 13: 978-0-367-09753-0 (hbk)
ISBN 13: 978-0-8133-4608-3 (pbk)

To my brother David—
A great companion in sports and in life

Contents

Preface

The coach is a major figure in the sports world and even in the general culture, as shown by the success of such television series as *Coach* and *Friday Night Lights*. Legendary coaches such as Knute Rockne and Vince Lombardi are virtual icons, and giants of the coaching profession ranging from Dean Smith to Bill Belichick to Pat Summit seem better known than their star players. Moreover, thousands of coaches at different levels of sports, ranging from youth sports to high school and college to the professional level, have had a positive effect on their athletes and often are positive role models for their communities and beyond. However, there also is a less positive side to coaching represented by a win at all costs mentality, the use of bullying and intimidation, and even participation in academic fraud at some colleges and universities.

In light of the complexity of the decisions involved in coaching and the moral conundrums faced by coaches at all levels of sports, it is surprising that sports philosophers have not paid more attention to the ethical conundrums involved in coaching sports. To my knowledge, the only other volume by philosophers examining the role of the coach and the ethics of coaching (the similarly named *Ethics of Sports Coaching*) was published first in the UK and is cited in several chapters in this book. The present volume, *The Ethics of Coaching Sports*, which I believe to be the first book of its kind published in the United States, is broad in scope and examines the role and responsibility of the coach and ethical issues that arise in the practice of coaching, as well as some of the legal issues.

These chapters, which are designed to be accessible to nonspecialists, raise important questions about various aspects of the coaching role, offer a reasoned approach to arriving at answers, and attempt to add to the critical discussion of sports ethics in the existing scholarly literature. Each selection is followed by Questions for Review and Discussion, which should be useful to students using the book as a text, and a list of references for further reading (supplementing the sources cited in the notes). As editor, I hope the breadth of the topics covered and the accessibility of the discussion to nonspecialists, coaches, and students will allow the book to have a significant impact on coaching practice as well as the philosophy of sports.

There are a number of ways readers may approach this book. Let me suggest two that may be useful, especially to instructors of college and university courses but also to coaches and readers.

What I think of as the default approach is represented by the table of contents. The chapters proceed from general and perhaps abstract analysis of the role of the coach at various levels of sports to the ethical considerations that apply to specific ethical and legal issues that arise in coaching. The order presented in the table of contents encourages development of a broad conception of the role of the coach and the rights, duties, and virtues associated with coaching that can provide a foundation for assessing the chapters in Parts 2–3, which focus on specific ethical and legal issues that arise in coaching. This approach also has the virtue of introducing general issues in the ethics of coaching before confronting controversies about hot-button issues, thereby allowing for reflection on broader principles and values in a cool moment.

Alternately, readers might begin with a chapter that focuses on a problem of special interest to them, for example, John Russell's provocative chapter claiming that coaches have strong moral reasons to help correct officiating errors that significantly benefit their teams, Scott Kretchmar's discussion of coaches' obligations to benchwarmers, or Matthew Mitten's discussion of the legal responsibilities of coaches to protect the health and safety of their athletes. These chapters, like the others in this volume, lead to broader questions about the role of the coach and the ethics of coaching covered in the chapters in Part 1. Some instructors may be able to involve their classes in discussion more quickly by proceeding along this route. However, both paths will lead readers into philosophical analysis of coaching and judicious discussion of the ethical and legal ramifications of issues that arise in coaching practice.

AS THIS BOOK GOES TO PRESS, I owe a great debt to many people. My wife, Joy, remains a proofreader extraordinaire as well as my greatest (and perhaps only) golf fan. She has been a constant source of encouragement and good cheer even in the face of medical difficulties over the past few years.

I am also grateful to my colleagues in the Philosophy Department at Hamilton College for providing a friendly, supportive, and intellectually challenging atmosphere; I couldn't ask for a better teaching and writing environment. I am also grateful to Hamilton College for supporting my research over the years and for granting me a faculty research fellowship that freed me up in the spring of 2012 to complete this project.

I would be remiss if I did not thank a trio of athletic directors at Hamilton College—Tom Murphy, David Thompson, and Jon Hind. Tom Murphy encouraged me to become head coach of men's golf in 1987 and then after I retired as coach in 2001 to continue working with the team as a volunteer assistant.

I also am grateful to the coaches at Hamilton College for their goodwill and support and for their dedication to the athletic and overall educational development of our student athletes. Much of what is right in college sports goes on in Division III of the NCAA. The coaches at small liberal arts colleges such as Hamilton do at least as good a job as any coaches in practicing the ideals of ethical coaching as developed by the contributors to this book. Thanks as well to the players I coached on Hamilton's men's golf team from 1987 to 2001, when I served as head coach and since then while I have also served as a volunteer assistant coach for providing a laboratory for field research on coaching and always showing good humor while I was learning on the job. (The informal rule on one of our highly ranked teams was that I was not allowed to touch a player's clubs because if I did so, magic might take over and reverse his playing ability.)

As always, the editorial team at Westview was wonderful. My initial editor, Kelsey Mitchell, persuaded me to undertake this project after an informal discussion about it and steered me through a number of editorial decisions with tact, grace, and good judgment. When Kelsey left Westview to pursue a career in teaching, Priscilla McGeehon stepped in and, along with editorial assistant Brooke Smith, helped me complete the project without a hitch. Sandra Beris and her production team guided me through the production process with great care, good judgment, and understanding. Thanks and good wishes to everyone at Westview.

I also am indebted to the external reviewers who examined an earlier version of the manuscript. I appreciate their conscientious reading of the text. Their acute comments and suggestions helped me and the other contributors to make improvements that are far too numerous to list.

Finally, I wouldn't have embarked on this project if I did not believe in the importance of ethical coaching at all levels of sport. Of course, significant ethical issues arise in coaching, as in every other significant human endeavor. But in my view, the vast majority of coaches from youth sports to elite levels of athletic competition fulfill their duties with dignity and honor. I hope the chapters in this collection not only shed light on moral and related legal issues in coaching but also help coaches to analyze, understand, and react appropriately to the many ethical issues that arise in their coaching endeavors.

PART 1

Introduction

One

The Ethics of Coaching

ROBERT L. SIMON

The television program *Friday Night Lights* was an especially thoughtful, well-acted series that explored the role of high school football in a small Texas town while following the lives of local young people and adults over several football seasons.[1] The central character, Coach Eric Taylor (played by actor Kyle Chandler), while not without faults, was not only a good father and husband, a leading educator in the area, but a great coach and, most importantly, a role model for his players. Although he sometimes made bad decisions, both in his family life and on the field, he could be counted on by his family members and his players, who came from a variety of backgrounds and economic circumstances and often confronted major personal and social crises.

In the real world, many issues facing the coaching profession, particularly in high profile sports, raise significant ethical questions about the behavior of coaches. Joe Paterno's fall from grace at Penn State, due to the allegations of sexual abuse leveled against former assistant Jerry Sandusky, is a case in point. Some have argued that Paterno fulfilled his moral obligations by informing the university athletic director about the problem and that the scandal was external to football. However, the devastating report by former FBI director Louis Freeh alleges that Paterno contributed to the cover-up of sexual abuse of children and that fear of going up against the renowned Penn

State football program deterred some university employees from reporting the abuse. The Paterno case did not directly involve his coaching practices; by all accounts Coach Paterno ran a clean program, made sure his players graduated, and used funds raised by Penn State football to support the academic mission of the university. However, Paterno's legacy has been significantly tarnished as the Freeh report, released in July 2012, charged that Penn State officials, including Paterno, showed "total and consistent disregard by the most senior leaders at Penn State for the safety and welfare of Sandusky's child victims."[2] On July 23, 2012, the National Collegiate Athletic Association (NCAA) announced unprecedented penalties against Penn State, imposing a $60 million fine (to be used to help victims of child abuse), vacating Penn State football victories from 1998 to 2011, and reducing the number of football scholarships the program can offer.

Moreover, a significant number of NCAA Division I intercollegiate programs were involved in serious rule violations, apparently with the knowledge and even support of the coaching staff. These range from NCAA violations committed in the Ohio State football program under Coach Jim Tressel (which led to his firing) to cases of academic fraud, such as the University of Minnesota case where an NCAA investigation found that tutors did academic work for some basketball players with the knowledge of their coaches. Recently NFL investigators have charged that players on the New Orleans Saints football team were awarded bonuses for hard hits against rival players that resulted in the targets being removed from the game, all with the knowledge and possible support of some members of the coaching staff.[3]

While coaches in youth sports are mostly volunteers and high school coaches who put in enormous amounts of time for little financial reward, men's basketball and football coaches at elite high profile intercollegiate programs make huge incomes, some earning more than the presidents of their institutions. In 2011 Rick Pitino, the basketball coach at Louisville, had a total pay of well over $7 million. Mike Krzyzewski, the basketball coach at Duke, had a reported total payout of over $4 million, and John Calipari, whose teams at different institutions have been cited for violating NCAA rules, made nearly $4 million at Kentucky. Salaries for top collegiate football coaches are comparable.[4] While some argue that huge compensation packages are justifiable as the result of free market bargaining, others have raised questions about whether this reward structure is economically sustainable and whether it is appropriate to pay coaches so much more than top faculty members.

On the other hand, many coaches (perhaps most coaches) at both the collegiate and the interscholastic level not only play by the rules but, like Coach Taylor, play a positive role in the athletic development of their athletes as well as in their educational and personal growth. It is important to look past the negative publicity surrounding some high profile coaches and understand that coaching is a practice that takes place in a wide variety of contexts ranging from professional to youth sports. These good coaches often don't get the attention the media bestow on bad behavior in high profile sports.

Nonetheless, many ethical dilemmas arise among coaches who labor in youth, high school, and college sports and in various low profile clubs and leagues, perhaps *especially* in such cases. For example, is winning the coach's primary goal? Which value takes precedence when winning clashes with other goals, such as showing loyalty to experienced players who are less skilled than newcomers, allowing all the players on the roster to participate, protecting the athletes' health, and showing good sportsmanship when doing so hurts the team's chances at winning? Should coaches tolerate gamesmanship by their players and should they set rules or codes of conduct that apply to the behavior of their players off the field or during the off-season? Is it permissible for coaches to "work" officials, even to the point of intimidation, or bully players in an attempt to improve their performance? To what degree, if any, should coaches stress competition, as opposed to developing skills or just having fun, in youth sports?

The chapters in this book deal with some of the most significant ethical issues facing coaches. They also explore the role of the coach and the duties, responsibilities, and even ideals that apply to coaching behavior, in both ethics and law. In particular, they explore the reasoning that may be used to support different positions on the issues being examined and so provide an analytical as well as a moral perspective on the role of the coach and the practice of coaching.

Sports, Coaching, and Philosophical Analysis

Sports attract attention around the world. The World Cup and the Olympic Games enjoy the greatest visibility, but many sports such as basketball and golf are becoming increasingly international in scope, with Asian as well as American and European players making a major impact. Soccer (elsewhere called football) is arguably the most popular sport worldwide. Children are becoming increasingly involved in youth sports and developmental programs. In the United States, college and high school athletic competitions attract huge audiences throughout the country. Sports are the subject of major films such as the award-winning *Chariots of Fire, Hoosiers,* and *Million Dollar Baby.*

Increasingly, sports are receiving attention from various academic disciplines. Psychologists, economists, and sociologists study empirical questions, for example, investigating what mental qualities tend to contribute to success in athletic competition (sports psychology), or whether highly visible Division I college sports actually bring in revenue for their institutions rather than operate deep in the red (economics).

However, many questions about sports go beyond the ordinary parameters of the natural and social sciences. Social scientists can describe the effects of competitive sports on participants, but can they tell us whether competition is good or bad, ethically permissible, desirable, or morally reprehensible? Whether a high school coach should give significant playing time to the less skilled players on the team, what responsibilities coaches should be expected to meet in protecting the safety of their players, or how much they should involve their players in making strategic decisions (a democratic vs. authoritarian style of coaching) raises ethical issues that are beyond the scope of the natural and social sciences.

Philosophy can help us approach such evaluative issues in part by helping to clarify key concepts and assessing arguments that attempt to justify answers to questions such as, What counts as fair play in sports?

Before turning directly to coaching, however, we need to view the practice of coaching in the broader context of sports and athletic competition. Ethical issues involving such concerns as athletes' use of performance enhancing drugs, questions of gender equity in university athletic programs, and misbehavior by elite athletes are widely discussed in the media, by fans, and even by casual observers. Some behaviors, such as doping to achieve a competitive advantage, are alleged to be violations of the ethics that should govern sports. But even if that claim is true, it presupposes that we have some idea of what that ethic should be. Criticizing a practice as unethical suggests that we have some notion of what is ethical.[5] But while we all have intuitive ideas about, for example, what counts as fair play, it is not easy to articulate the principles that justify our intuitions, defend them, or apply them to hard cases where our principles may appear to conflict.

This suggests a deeper set of questions that go beyond current headlines. Is athletic competition a good thing? Are competitive sports valuable activities? If so, why? Does their value depend on circumstances or context? What circumstances are important or relevant to moral evaluation? Are sports purely recreational or do they also have an educational function, especially in youth sports but perhaps also at the interscholastic, intercollegiate, and professional levels?

In developing responses to such questions, we may ask about the role coaches do play and should play at the different levels of sports. Are coaches purely technical advisers who help their athletes develop better techniques, like a swing coach in golf? Or are they more like generals or CEOs who develop and maintain a "program" as at elite Division I colleges and in professional sports? Or are coaches more like teachers or professors, educating their players about the sport and even about the kind of character needed to play well? Should they aim at developing personal virtues among their charges? Or does that take them beyond their proper role? Does the coach's role depend on context? For example, perhaps different ethical guidelines apply to coaches in youth sports than to coaches in intercollegiate athletics. But even if that is true, are there some universal principles that apply to coaching in all contexts?

Indeed, the role and moral duties of the coach not only change significantly from one context to another (e.g., professional vs. youth sports) but arguably from one cultural context to another. At times in ancient Greece, as well as in nineteenth- and early-twentieth-century England, athletes were expected to succeed on their own; working with a coach was considered unsporting. Part of the charm and interest of the movie *Chariots of Fire*, which tells the story of two contenders for the 1924 Olympics, is that it illustrates the British aristocratic ethics of the time, which frowned on the use of a coach by one of the characters, Harold Abrahams, thereby showing how people's beliefs about sports ethics can be influenced by existing social practices and cultural norms. (Of course, whether the views are defensible depends on the soundness of justifying arguments, not merely on what people at a given time believe is ethical.)[6]

The prevailing attitude throughout most of the world today is very different, but to what extent can the attitude prevalent at a given time and place be justified? What ethical rules, principles, and ideals apply to coaching? Should coaching as we now know it be regarded as purely instrumental, designed only to promote winning, or is it a multifaceted activity subject to moral standards? If the latter, which moral standards apply? How can we *justify* the moral considerations we believe apply?

The contributors to this book attempt to clarify, explore, and in some cases resolve ethical and related legal questions about coaching, including some of those raised above. They look beyond the daily sports headlines and analyze in depth the ethical issues that arise in coaching as most of us experience it; in such contexts as youth sports, high schools, colleges and universities, clubs and other informal organizations, as well as professional and elite teams and institutions. All the contributors hope to advance our theoretical and philosophical understanding of coaching. However, just as important, they also present well-reasoned examinations of issues that coaches face in carrying out their duties and suggest recommendations for coaching practices that can be explored and debated by students, coaches, sports administrators, and fans.

Each chapter, other than the two introduction chapters, is followed by a series of review questions designed to bring the main theses and potential lines of criticism of them into focus. A short list of suggested readings also follows, which may include works cited in the footnotes if the author regards them as especially deserving of attention. Those interested in exploring the issues raised even further should consult the sources cited in the endnotes.

Two

The Coach as Moral Exemplar

JAN BOXILL

Unquestionably, sports play a significant role in our society. Just consider the enthusiasm generated by March Madness, the Olympic Games, the Super Bowl, and the World Series. But perhaps their greatest significance is the moral role sports play for both the participants and society in general. I have argued that given their nature and design, sports provide a unique model for understanding our society, for seeing who we are, our values, and our ethics.[1]

Americans recognize the potential for sports to build character and promote necessary virtues for a greater cause. As a society, Americans value sports and what they can offer. But Americans also believe that an overemphasis on winning threatens sports, possibly by motivating rule breaking and by taking the fun out of it for too many people. Role models, particularly coaches, can play an important part in maintaining the integrity and value of sports. Coaches often function as surrogate parents, bonding strongly with the people they coach. A study by the U.S. Anti-Doping Agency (USADA), in partnership with Discovery Education, concluded that coaches, more than parents, teachers, peers, religion, and school, have the greatest influence on youth sport participants.[2]

> Sport can be great fun to play and entertaining to watch. However, it offers something more important. The lessons it provides—taught properly—apply directly to life. Many of those lessons are usually taught first by a good mother and father, but sports can help make them stick and add a few more.[3]

Given the results of the study, the people entrusted to teach these lessons must be the coaches. Like parents they teach skills, but they also teach life lessons, including morals, ethics, tolerance, and most of all respect, both for themselves and for others. So coaches must be good teachers as well as good role models.

A recent USADA survey showed that more than three-fifths of US adults, approximately 162 million Americans, claim some relationship to sports-related activities. Thus, given the engagement and power of sports and more importantly the power of coaches, ethics and sports must be integrated in the coaches who influence those they coach. But this cannot happen unless coaches possess character and integrity, and intentionally teach and model these values. Since sports play a significant moral role in society, coaches have a greater responsibility in how sports fulfill this role. Of course coaches are not the only ones who bear this responsibility; others, particularly well-known athletes, bear some responsibility as well. However, "coaches have an . . . unparalleled power and platform in young people's lives."[4] This is an awesome and sometimes frightening platform for transforming people's lives. What makes it so is that this is a role they have freely chosen. With that choice comes great responsibility, not just to teach what they know and how to perform and behave, but to model this behavior as well. "There are at least five million coaches with the potential to become one of the most influential adults in a young person's life. Forever."[5] This is a tremendous challenge that requires coaches to serve as moral exemplars.

Coaches are teachers, and coaching, like teaching, takes skill, art, and knowledge. It is a skill that helps young people become stronger athletes and stronger individuals. The hope is to produce excellence in those they coach. We see many examples of this, but unfortunately we see the opposite as well. Part of this has to do with professing one thing while doing another. In the survey coaches responded that teaching self-discipline, doing one's best, having fun, building self-esteem, and respecting others are among the most important values children will learn from playing sports; they ranked playing fairly and winning as the least important.

But while winning seemed least important to the coaches, study participants responded that winning was what they viewed their coach as promoting, that winning was much more important than other values. And according to a summary in *USA Today*, a new NCAA study of college athletes reveals the following:

- Only 39 percent of Division I women's basketball players said their head coach "defines success by not only winning, but winning fairly." Also, just 39 percent said their head coach can be trusted.

- Only half of all Division I men's basketball players said they felt their coaches were as interested in fairness as in winning. In baseball, it was 43 percent. Football coaches scored highest, a still modest 57 percent. The proportion of players who trusted their coaches ran much the same: 50 percent in men's basketball, 52 percent in baseball, 56 percent in football.[6]

These findings lead us to examine why so many athletes lack trust in their coaches, the people entrusted to teach fair play, sportsmanship, and winning within the structure of the rules that define and regulate the games we play. Two possible conclusions may be drawn. Either this lack of trust is a result of misperceptions among athletes or it is evidence that many coaches are deceived about their own teachings. The USADA research revealed a disconnect between what coaches profess and what the participants perceive to be the case.

Sports constitute a secular religion and coaches are its ministers. They hold the same power and we expect the same qualities in our coaches as we do our clergy—trustworthy people who exemplify dignity, empathy, integrity, respect, and virtue. Players, like parishioners, evaluate coaches and learn their values by watching how they treat their players, their opponents, and other coaches. They gauge coaches' values by observing their actions. Given the hypercompetitive atmosphere present in athletic programs at every level, plus the countless documented cases of cheating and malpractice by coaches, it is not unreasonable to conclude that many athletes have good reason not to trust their coaches.

These findings present a sad statement about college sports, which justify their nonprofit status by claiming to teach sportsmanship and character. And this carries over to youth sports as well. However, as a sports enthusiast, ex-coach, and teacher, I argue that the nature and design of sports play a significant moral role in society by *reflecting* and *affecting* changes in our society, and those involved in sports play a significant role in these changes. Sports provide the model for the changes, both positively and negatively. And if the research is correct, coaches play a significant and exalted role, and if change is to be positive, it is a role that coaches must embrace.

Though I have discussed the nature and design of a sports model elsewhere,[7] I will briefly describe it and the obstacles to its implementation here.

Nature and Design of Sports

Here I want to present a paradigm or model of sports to illumine their moral significance. (This model is normative in that it presents a morally defensible conception of sports; see especially the chapters by Simon, Russell, and Torres and Hager for fuller discussion of such normative conceptions. It also describes sports at their best.) I identify four features as essential to the model.

First, in its paradigmatic form, sports participation is a freely chosen, voluntary activity, designed with no end outside itself. Though people may participate in sports for many different reasons, sports are designed to be ends in themselves. Whatever reasons people have for engaging in sports, they are designed to have a constant result, which is sufficient to justify the sport. Even if I play for money, the excellence displayed is sufficient to justify the sport.

For example, you may play basketball for money, but basketball itself is designed to develop and display excellence even if that is not your reason for playing it. Thus in order to make money playing the game you will have to display certain excellences. Further, given human nature, you are likely to respond positively to these excellences and to make them your ends. In this way the game is an unalienated activity. Further participation in the many different sports is an expression of the individual's creativity and his or her freedom to choose which of these various excellences to develop.

Second, sports are governed by constitutive rules and regulative rules. Constitutive rules define the game and the permissible moves allowed within it. These rules define the activity and are usually designed to develop and exhibit sets of skills and talents. Some sports have more rules than others, and the rules may change over time. But whatever the constitutive rules, their existence comes from their acceptance.

Regulative rules complement the constitutive rules. These rules govern fair play, decency, and safety. Rules of fair play include penalties for infractions of the constitutive rules and for moves of strategy within the game. For example, in football the defense wants to rush the passer, but according to the constitutive rules no one can cross the line of scrimmage before the ball is snapped. Regulative rules require that a team that violates this off-sides rule be penalized to restore the competitive balance. Rules of decency reflect basic moral standards. For example, after a great tackle, the tackler should not stand over the tackled player and taunt or gyrate. Rules of safety are designed to protect the participants as they play according to the constitutive rules. For example, no one can tackle a player by grabbing his face mask. In combination, the constitutive and regulative rules impose discipline and create a safe and moral framework for self-expression and self-development. Both sets of rules are regularly evaluated and often revised to promote a competitive, safe, and moral framework.

Third, sports must be physically challenging within the designated framework and rules. This feature contrasts sports to games. Games need not be physically challenging. Again, the constitutive rules are continually evaluated to keep the sports physically challenging.

Fourth, sports involve competition as a mutual challenge to achieve or strive for excellence[8] within the framework set by the constitutive rules and the regulative rules of fair play and decency. The struggle involves both the process and the product, a desire to win, and a desire to be tested.

The mental and the physical come together in competition. Each participant must develop strategies to counter another competitor's skills and strategies. Competition can lead to respect, friendship, or combat—opponents can be viewed either as partners in the struggle or enemies to be conquered. Here coaches play a significant role as skilled strategists. They work with the athletes in practice and discuss the mental aspects of the sport in the locker room. What the athletes learn from their coaches they carry onto the playing field. They must make quick calculations and decisions based on what they have learned. So it is vital that coaches understand and promote the model.

Obviously this is a model and, like any model, is subject to deviations in practice. Nonetheless, it is the model we should use to evaluate how sports are taught, coached, and played out in society. Given the high status of sports, we need to carefully examine the issues that tear at the fabric of the model in order to ensure the integrity and value of sports and allow us to embrace the role that sports plays in our society. But this is a shared responsibility.

Obstacles

What deviations occur from the model? Here I will briefly discuss three of them: the emphasis on winning, the lack of moral courage, and relativism.

Emphasis on Winning in Competition

There are those who place winning above all else and are willing to cheat to achieve this goal. The high stakes involved in winning factor into this orientation.

The desire to win is fundamental to competition, but this does not entail winning at all costs. People desire to win for different reasons. But as noted above, sports are designed so that in order to win, participants will have their skills challenged and tested, and the results of the tests are displayed in winnings and rankings. This is not unlike the tests we give our students in classes. We challenge our students to learn new material. To meet the challenge they strive to do well on exams that require them to learn the skills. But some place winning (e.g., getting an A) above all else and are willing to cheat for the sake of this goal. It is up to the teacher to promote the desire to do well, but not at all costs. Consider a teacher who said, "Here are the rules, and here are the ways to break those rules and avoid getting caught, so that you can get an A." If everyone were given the ways to break the rules, they would become rules unto themselves and cheating would no longer be cheating. It would be cheating if we provided the information to a few who then kept it to themselves to gain an edge. Maintaining the integrity of the academic endeavor requires that while teachers may give students strategies to help them prepare for the exam, they must challenge students to strive to achieve excellence, not just an A.

Sports are no different. If we are to maintain the integrity of sports, while coaches give strategies to help participants prepare for competitions, they must abide by both the constitutive and regulative rules. They should challenge the participants to strive to achieve excellence, not just to win. In this way coaches must serve as exemplars who uphold the integrity of sports. (Critiques of overemphasis on winning are found in chapters by Reid, Simon, and Russell, among others.)

All of us, participants, spectators, administrators, parents, journalists, and coaches, share responsibility for instilling a culture of honor and integrity in sports. But given the power and influence coaches command, they bear a greater responsibility. The pressures are great, including those posed by the excessive public attention to sports and exaggerated monetary rewards at elite levels of competition, but the willingness to prioritize winning, at the sacrifice of ethics and health, erodes our trust in the inherent value of sports. As a nation, we should embrace the positive role that sports can play in our society, as well as the issues now facing sports, in order to determine how to ensure their enduring integrity and value.

Lack of Moral Courage

My colleague Kim Strom-Gottfried has pointed out, quoting Edward Kidder, that "the key to ethical action is moral courage. . . . When we uphold ethical principles, . . . we are acting with moral courage."[9]

It has been said that we all know right from wrong but lack the moral courage to do the right thing or act when we see others doing wrong. Opportunities for ethical action are plentiful, but so too are the reasons not to act. Strom-Gottfried offers five obstacles to moral courage: discomfort, futility, socialization, bystander effect or diffusion theory, and personal cost.[10] These obstacles apply to all aspects of life and are dramatized in sport. Although participants may know what the right thing to do is, they find it difficult to go against what is actually being asked of them; and if they did, they would be criticized for not being a team player or would find themselves ostracized. Participants get their cues from coaches who either reward or condemn rule breaking and unsportsmanlike behavior. So again coaches must serve as moral exemplars for the athletes they coach. However, coaches face these obstacles as well.

It is equally uncomfortable for them to go against the actual demands of the position. And although they might like to do the right thing, they may see it as a no-win situation. Perhaps no one cares or "everyone is doing it," or they believe that ethical appeals will fall on deaf ears. Moral courage may be too expensive if it costs the coach his or her position or professional standing. But those who worry about the cost of action fail to consider the cost of inaction.

"Ethical action often is not easy, but it can be practiced. It can be taught and can be reinforced when we see it in others. . . . As individuals we can support those around us who do the right thing. We can also demand that our society do the same."[11] This is the essence of fair play, sportsmanship, and following the rules for achieving excellence. In this lies the moral significance of sports, the duties of those involved, and their relationship to society. And coaches face even greater demands.

Relativism

People attack moral standards they don't find convenient by making relativistic arguments. Their argument goes something like this: since different societies or institutions in society have differing moral codes, it follows that there is no objective standard that can be used to judge the relative merits of particular codes. But is this argument *sound*? Does the conclusion logically follow from the premise? The premise is about belief systems or what people believe, while the conclusion is about what really is the case.

Because belief systems may have disagreements, does it *logically follow* that there is no objective truth in the matter? Certainly not. The fact that people once disagreed about whether the earth is flat does not mean that there was no objective truth about its shape. Further, it is a mistake to overestimate the extent of the differences. We need to consider underlying goals and principles. I do not deny that we allow some things in sports that we would not allow in society; the hits that we allow in football we would not allow on the street, for example. It does not follow, however, that society and sports do not share common goals and principles.

The constitutive and regulative rules that govern each sport are designed to challenge participants to develop their skills. But there are also descriptive and moral rules necessary for sports to even exist and must be embraced by all. Deliberate harm and cheating are two examples. These rules are in force in all sports and in all cultures. Sports may differ in what they regard as legitimate exceptions to the rules, but those differences exist against a broad background of agreement. And sports exist within a society that shares this broader agreement. So it is a mistake to overemphasize the differences at the expense of the broader background of agreement, whether in our society or in any society. As Robert Simon so aptly puts it, "Sport . . . provides an arena which illustrates a framework of universal values within which the competition takes place."[12] (But see Chapter 5 for William J. Morgan's defense of the importance of historical and social context, which might lead him to dissent from the idea of universal values.)

Given the great impact of sports on society, it is critical that they exemplify this broader moral agreement. Sports both reflect and actively affect society. This is one reason for their moral significance. Sports teach us what is acceptable and what is unacceptable, what is condoned and what is shunned.

Understanding the place of sports in our society and our role in perpetuating it requires us to understand the paradigm and how it is applied. Those who coach and administer sports bear the burden of upholding the integrity of sports. It isn't easy; there is no algorithm to plug in the variables, no simple recipe to follow. Sports display excellence and moral courage, as well the undermining of excellence and the lack of moral courage. We expect our teachers, our coaches, to promote the best displays and serve as exemplars. We cannot expect them to be perfect. Coaches are human and fallible, but in accepting the role of coach, they accept the responsibility of developing excellence in those they teach.

Conclusion

The chapters that follow discuss the moral and legal responsibilities of coaches, examine issues of coaching policy such as allocation of playing time among team members, and the proper emphasis on competition in youth sports. They also explore issues in ethical justification that investigate the logical grounds that might be offered in developing and supporting decisions by coaches. Coaching, far from being a purely technical or strategic activity, is permeated by ethical and related educational concerns. I hope this book contributes to our philosophical and intellectual understanding of the complexities of coaching and to better coaching as well.

Sports provide a unique model for understanding who we are and what we want to achieve. In this way sports serve a significant moral function and as an exemplar for public ethics. Everyone bears responsibility to uphold honor in our society and in sports, but coaches, given their power, bear a greater responsibility. Understanding this is important for all of us, because *the death of ethics is the sabotage of excellence.*

PART 2

The Coach's Role: Conceptions of Coaching

ROBERT L. SIMON

The chapters in Part 2 explore a set of related questions concerning what function coaches should play in sports. What is the best way of understanding the role of the coach? What are a coach's duties, responsibilities, and rights? By what criteria should a coach's performance be evaluated? How should coaches themselves think of their roles and functions?

A quick answer is that the coach's job is to teach the relevant physical skills, with due allowances for the age and physical development of those receiving the coaching—technical coaching about the mechanics of the sport, for example, a pure swing coach in golf who only works on making a player's physical movements as efficient and technically sound as possible.[1]

Is it the coach's job simply to win? I examine and reject this suggestion in my own contribution to this section. For now, it is perhaps enough to say, first, that winning should not be the only goal of coaches in youth and children's sports and, second, that a win in a sloppily played game against an inferior opponent is not necessarily anything to be proud of.

Indeed, a moment's reflection will suggest that in most sporting contexts, these accounts of the coach's role are simplistic. For example, we normally expect the coach to teach not just the physical skills but also the mental skills necessary for good play. Coaches should help players make smart decisions in game situations as well as understand the strategies best employed in contests. Many people also would maintain that coaches, perhaps particularly in youth sports but elsewhere as well, should teach respect for officials and opponents, promote the ideals of fair competition and being a good sport, and generate enthusiasm for the sport among the players.

Should we also expect coaches to have a positive effect on the character of the athletes? If so, what do we mean by "positive effect"? Is it reasonable or fair to expect coaches to have expertise at character building as well as teaching skills relevant to the sport? Do coaches have ethical responsibilities that go beyond building character, such as upholding standards of fair play and respecting the rights of all competitors including opponents?

The contributors to this section address issues such as these as they explore the role of the coach. Heather Reid considers the purpose of athletic competition and its implications for the role of the coach relative to its roots in ancient Greek philosophy. In particular, as Reid explains, Plato saw training in athletics as a major part of a good education designed to produce virtuous people. While many critics of intercollegiate sports regard athletics as an intrusion on the true mission of educational institutions, Reid suggests that on the contrary, when properly carried out, athletics and academics can be integrated elements of an educational process aimed at producing good citizens. The coach, on this view, is in the broadest sense a teacher of virtue.

Theorists who stress the virtues can be divided into those who regard the virtues as fundamental ethical values, not derivable from any more fundamental ones, and those who see them as derivative. For example, utilitarians, who ethically evaluate actions or general practices solely by their consequences, striving for the best ratio of good to bad effects, might regard virtues as those traits of character which incline the bearer toward actions that have good consequences.

Virtue theorists influenced by the writings of Plato and Aristotle regard the virtues as basic; right actions are the ones virtuous people would choose. Virtuous individuals exercise practical wisdom and good judgment that they develop through experience, rather than follow a set of mechanical rules. Wise coaches, on this view, make good judgments that reflect their own virtues and promote the growth of good character in their players. Thus wise coaches know which play to call at which moment, how to motivate players, and how to balance such values as competitive success and broad participation, not through the application of rigid rules but through habits of good judgment they have developed through years of experience. By exhibiting the virtues, they are excellent role models for others and help their players to develop as virtuous persons.

Critics of virtue theory raise a number of concerns. Critics can question whether what counts as a virtue changes from one historical context to another. For example, did the ancient Greeks or medieval knights value honor more than we do? Other critics ask if claims made by virtuous coaches and other sports figures based largely on their personal experience can be justified to others in public discourse. More generally, what would be the nature of justification of ethical claims in sport?

In my own contribution to this section, I explore the question of how ethical and other evaluative claims made in sports can be justified or supported by reason. I first reject what I regard as some crude ideas about sports, such as the view that they should be thought of primarily as a means of discharging aggression, and some equally crude views about the function of the coach, such as the claim that the coach's only obligation is to win. I then argue for what has been called a broad internalist or intepretivist approach to the ethics of sport. According to this approach, similar to the account of law advanced by legal theorist Ronald Dworkin and applied to sports by a number of thinkers, we best understand the value of sports, and why so many find it fascinating, by interpreting the activity in a way that makes sense of its key features and presents it in its ethically best light.[2] For example, why do sports, or at least such paradigm cases as baseball, basketball, soccer, field hockey, and golf, have rules that create artificial challenges to what otherwise would be a relatively easy task, such as simply placing a small ball in a hole compared to holing one's shot according to the established rules of golf? This feature is best explained, as I and other broad internalists argue, by the idea that sports are constructed to provide challenges and that the pursuit of challenge is fundamental to understanding sports and making moral judgments about them. Of course, other areas (e.g., doing well on the SAT exam or in a job) also involve challenges, but we do not normally take the SAT or go to work just for the challenge; we need a decent SAT score to get into college and we need a job to earn a living.[3] Of course, we play sports for other reasons too, for example, to make friends or get exercise, but we make the friends and get the exercise by trying to meet the challenge of the sport. That is what makes challenge so fundamental. (See Jan Boxill's chapter on the idea that a sports contest normally is freely chosen by all parties who wish to challenge themselves in what has been called a "mutual quest for excellence.") Of course, the pursuit of excellence through challenge does not imply an isolated morality of sports separate from more general ethical considerations; such pursuit is constrained by a number of moral considerations, including principles of fairness and respect for others.

As broad internalists and legal interpretivists have developed the idea, a theory of sports includes broad principles that sometimes must be weighed against one another, not simply rules such as "three strikes and you are out," that apply in an all-or-nothing manner. Thus J. S. Russell has suggested as a basic principle of sports that we interpret the rules of a sport "in such a manner that the excellences embodied in achieving the lusory goals of the game are not undermined but are maintained and fostered."[4] Russell cites an 1887 major league baseball game where a runner crossed home plate; according to the then rules of the game he was no longer a base runner and hence not governed by rules prohibiting interference with fielders. He then wrestled the opposing catcher to the ground, enabling a teammate to score. The umpire, however, ruled correctly that the rule about noninterference should be interpreted to prohibit such behavior. This ruling can be justified according to Russell's principle, since wrestling is not a skill baseball was designed to test.

My own version of broad internalism suggests that sports are in significant part an educative activity; we learn about ourselves and others and can develop ethically through our attempt to meet the challenges of sports, especially when carried out as broad internalism recommends. Coaches, on this view, are educators who, particularly in youth sports and educational institutions, should be charged with teaching the physical, mental, and moral skills required to meet the challenges of their sport, which often are closely related to those required for success in the classroom as well.

In my chapter, I briefly suggest, and have argued more fully elsewhere, that a broad internalist theory which survives extended criticism from diverse perspectives might achieve universal assent and might be regarded as justifiable for all reasonable people. More modestly, it would not be unreasonable to believe that the best explanation of why such a theory has survived such critical scrutiny is that it is truly the best interpretive theory applying to the areas of sports in question and accordingly ought to be accepted by all sporting communities.

In his chapter, William J. Morgan endorses many of the ethical recommendations in my chapter and adopts many of the features of interpretivism. However, he rejects the universalism implicit in my development of the approach. Rather, he suggests, any consensus about justification in sports applies to specific social and historical contexts. Thus, to take his example, the role of the coach was viewed very differently among the upper classes in nineteenth- and early-twentieth-century England. Sports were understood as gentlemanly activities characterized by amateurism and generosity, rather than in the "winning comes first" atmosphere of elite sports today. On his view, proponents of these different views would be unable to engage in discussion with one another or reach a consensus based on reason since they lack the common premises with which to argue. (I would question whether different historical and social contexts are as discrete and isolated from one another as he suggests and point to sports such as top amateur and professional golf, which combine fierce competition with respect for and generosity toward opponents as an example of how dialogue and discussion might lead to an improved blend of the two traditions.)

Be that as it may, Morgan forcefully argues that even if interpretations of sports are historically relative, they still can have critical force. We do not have to accept the superficial views of sports prominent in our own culture but through rational critique identify the deep basic principles and values that are most justified within our own cultural tradition and use them to criticize popular but shallow social understandings that cannot pass critical scrutiny.

What is the relevance or practical significance of broad internalism, and the debate over whether or not interpretations of sports are historically relative? Why does this rather abstract debate matter to coaches and those interested in the ethics of coaching?

Let me offer two suggestions. First, if the other contributors and I are correct in maintaining that coaches have ethical responsibilities, coaches need to be able to make sound ethical judgments as well as sound strategic ones. Surely a defensible overall theory of the moral aspects of sports, along with a specific account that makes sense of their own sports and views them in a morally supportable manner, is crucial to such an endeavor. As Doug Hochstetler argues in the concluding chapter of this section, coaches always have a philosophy even if it is never fully articulated. Making that philosophy explicit can help make the individual coach's judgments more consistent with one another and also allow for critical examination of and consequent improvement of it.

Second, on both Morgan's view and my own, coaches need to look beyond a shallow popular consensus on what is ethical in sports.[5] What is popular or widely accepted may not necessarily be supported by good reasons. On Morgan's view, we need to look for the deeper values implicit in our own cultural practices, while on mine, even those are subject to critical scrutiny that through discourse and debate can potentially yield a justifiable universal consensus. But either way, coaches carry out their ethical responsibilities best by being able to distance themselves from widely accepted but not necessarily well-grounded views of sports and examine them with a critical eye.

Doug Hochstetler agrees that coaches need a philosophy and implicitly suggests that coaches need not engage in abstract philosophical theorizing to the extent that my own and Morgan's conceptions of broad internalism seem to require. Hochstetler draws on his own experiences as an athlete and on the approach to pragmatism of American philosopher Henry Bugbee to stress the pragmatic function of the coach's approach to the game.

Pragmatism emphasizes that ideas are tools and are evaluated by how they help us solve specific problems. Hochstetler suggests the coach frequently functions as a problem solver. While he does not deny the need for justification and validation of the coach's approach to problems that arise in sporting contexts, Hochstetler stresses the role of sensitivity and openness to change that characterize good coaching. Coaches, on this view, draw on their experience and judgment and their sensitivity to what is at stake, rather than an elaborate philosophical theory (which still might be useful is assessing coaching decisions after they are made) in order to make good decisions under the pressure of competition. As leaders of their teams, they need to project confidence but also show humility and be open to change and growth as they learn through experience.

In spite of differences in approach, which sometimes run deep, the contributors to Part 2 agree on some main themes that are worth reviewing. First, they all agree that there is a significant moral dimension to coaching and reject the idea that the coach's main function is entirely technical (teaching mechanics of the sport) or purely strategic, let alone simply to win contests. Second, they also agree on the need for development of a moral perspective or theory that can be used not only by coaches themselves but also by those who assess or evaluate their performance. Disagreement among contributors may arise, however, over what moral perspective is most applicable to coaching: for example, whether a virtue-centered approach, a pragmatic one, or one that focuses more on the respect for the challenge of the sport and its implications for fairness and the rights and duties of participants.[6] The other contributors and I hope that the following chapters will stimulate readers to test the ideas proposed and use them to develop their own philosophy of coaching.

Three

Coaching for Virtue in Plato's Academy*

HEATHER REID

The power to learn is present in everyone's soul [but] the instrument with which each learns is like an eye that cannot be turned around from darkness to light without turning the whole body.

—PLATO

Conventional wisdom holds that sports build character. Many social scientists contend that the opposite is true: sports actually degrade moral character. Purists shun the question entirely, believing that sports, as a form of play, require no broader justification. Sports' inclusion in schools and universities, however, does deserve some sort of justification. Recreation and health promotion are only part of the story, and out of proportion to the emphasis placed on competitive athletics. If sports can indeed function as a form of moral education, then their place in the academy would be clearly warranted—not least because classroom presentation of ethical theories has very limited potential for improving moral behavior. Because sports

*Originally published in *Sport Ethics and Philosophy* 4:1 (2010): 16–26.

involve physical activity and interpersonal interaction in a rule-governed environment, they may indeed be an excellent medium through which to habituate good moral character. This was the role of sports in ancient Greek education: the cultivation of a kind of moral and personal excellence known as *aretē*.[1]

But as suggested by some modern social science data, good moral character is not an automatic outcome of athletic participation.[2] Coaches who put character first, or at least near the top of their educational goals, need to be thoughtful and intentional about achieving it. They may have to distance themselves from the conventions and reward systems common in sports today. Since moral education is such an important social task, however, coaches who strive to achieve it are fighting the good fight. I am one of a group of scholars who believe that the cultivation of *aretē* is the highest social good that sports can bring and should therefore be the guiding principle of sports participation and promotion—an approach we call aretism.[3] A better understanding of the relationship among *aretē*, athletics, and education in ancient Greek thought may inspire the modern coach who puts character first to find creative ways to fight that good fight and to become a coach of virtue.

The History of Sports and *Aretē*

A link with *aretē* exists at the very origin of sports. The earliest evidence comes from ancient Sumerian, Egyptian, and Minoan societies in which royal displays of athleticism were offered to the populace as evidence of their leaders' divine favor and worthiness to lead. Of course these were not open competitions; most often they were uncontested displays, or even unwitnessed feats that gained legendary status in their poetic retelling. Whether Gilgamesh actually out-wrestled Enkidu, or whether the Sumerian Shulgi in fact ran the length of his kingdom (over 100 miles) and back in a single day was immaterial.[4] The point was not so much to prove the leader's worth to a skeptical public, but rather to provide comforting and inspiring tales of strength and virtue, not unlike the myths of Heracles or Theseus.[5] What remains most interesting to us is that athleticism was taken to be a sign of virtue and civic worth so many millennia ago. Somehow the link between sports and moral character has endured, despite immense changes in human life and society, up to this day. Although the nature of polities and conceptions of virtue vary with time and place, there seems to be a fundamental link between virtue and sports that transcends those differences.

We can see this variation in ancient Greek literature. Originally the *aretē* associated with athleticism was understood to be something inborn:

the product of divine ancestry or natural aristocracy. Heracles' moral and physical strength comes from his divine father, Zeus, and is displayed immediately when he saves his brother by strangling two snakes as an infant in his crib—there are no ancient stories about him training.[6] Homer's heroes Achilles and Odysseus seem naturally athletic as well. When Odysseus washes up on the island of the Phaeacians and a young man makes the insulting insinuation that he is a tradesman rather than a nobleman, Odysseus puts the matter to rest by grabbing a discus and hurling it (without training or even a practice throw) farther than all the local athletes.[7] Later, upon returning to his kingdom disguised as a beggar, he proves his *aretē* again through athletic feats—defeating even the noblemen courting his wife, Penelope.[8] In ancient Greece athleticism and virtue were thought of as gifts inherited through noble bloodlines rather than earned through training.[9]

In real athletic contests, of course, ancient Greek athletes hired coaches and trained regularly. But the lingering idea that the *aretē* associated with athleticism was inborn rather than acquired is evidenced by early efforts to hide the use of coaches and training. In early poetic and monumental celebrations Olympic victory is attributed to divine favor and the glory of one's family; coaches, instruction, and systematic training programs are almost never mentioned.[10] But as the popularity of athletics and the prestige associated with victory grew (in no small part because of its association with *aretē*), the use of coaches and the success of athletes from humble origins became impossible to hide. The evidence that athletic success could be achieved through training, combined with the traditional link between athleticism and *aretē*, generated the revolutionary idea that virtue could be trained and was not just a matter of birth.

This belief that virtue is trainable underpins the whole concept of higher education—education that goes beyond teaching skills like writing and arithmetic and actually seeks to produce excellent human beings. In the aretic context this concept implies good citizenship.[11] This idea had special appeal in the Greek west (i.e., southern Italy and Sicily), where émigrés seem to have used athletic games, especially the Olympic Games, to prove their *aretē* on the mainland. Indeed the fifth century BCE Sicilian Epicharmus of Syracuse was among the first to suggest that training or practice was more important to virtue than heredity.[12] He may have gotten the idea from Pythagoras, whose sixth century BCE school in southern Italy was among the first institutions to train virtue. It was not mere coincidence that Pythagoras recruited students in the gymnasium,[13] nor does it seem mere coincidence that Plato, after visiting the area in the fourth century BCE, opened his own school in an Athenian gymnasium called the Academy.

Plato likely included athletic exercises in the Academy's program, partly because of tradition but more precisely because he embraced the idea they could contribute to moral education.[14] In a letter describing his experiences in Italy, Plato laments his failure to transform Dionysios, the young tyrant of Syracuse, into "a man who was just and courageous and temperate and wisdom-loving [and therefore able to live] in subjection to justice combined with wisdom."[15] The educational program he outlined in Plato's *Republic,* meanwhile, uses athletic games to select and train leaders with the very qualities that Dionysios lacked: the ability to strive for excellence while resisting temptation, to subject themselves to common laws, and to toil not for individual glory but rather for the benefit of the larger community. Perhaps we can call Plato the first coach of virtue since he used sport to develop self-controlled, hardworking, law-abiding team players—much like many modern coaches. The interesting question is, How?

Winners Versus Wins

The first characteristic of coaching for virtue is that its overarching goal is *aretē*. All other athletic goals, including victories, championships, and equipment contracts, must be subordinated to that. The objective is to produce winners—people with dispositional virtues such as respect, discipline, courage, justice, and wisdom—and not necessarily wins. Although a good win-loss record may provide some evidence of a coach's ability to cultivate *aretē*, it is hardly a reliable measure in and of itself. This is because athletic victory is not a fail-safe indicator of virtue, and defeat is not always caused by the lack of virtue. Sometimes victory doesn't even indicate athletic superiority. Competitors who win by cheating, bribery, or other illicit means fail to be winners in both the moral and the athletic sense. But even in legitimate victories, virtue-irrelevant factors such as brute strength, superior equipment, good luck, or bad officiating can be the deciding factor.[16] Only in closely fought contests where athletes are challenged to bring out their best can we say that victory indicates *aretē*—but in those cases the losers likely demonstrated virtue as well. *Aretē* is not a zero-sum game, and coaches aimed at virtue cannot judge their success strictly in terms of wins and losses.

This is not to say that winning doesn't matter. Striving to win fairly in close competition is a manifestation of virtue in sport. It is victory without virtue that is worthless because it is *aretē* that gives winning its value in the first place. The athletic skills that lead to victory have little value beyond sport. It is not the ability to put a ball in a net or to overtake an adversary that is admirable in champion athletes—after all, machines and vehicles are more efficient than athletes at completing such tasks. Rather, we value these skills and the wins that go along with them because of the virtues we perceive to be embedded therein.[17] Courage is valuable not because it is needed to complete a marathon race, but because it is useful in more important human endeavors like battling disease or searching for truth. In events such as the Susan G. Komen Race for the Cure, which benefits cancer research, the efforts of all the runners, not just the winners, celebrate the kinds of virtues needed to fight disease. In this sense they resemble ancient funeral games, like those held for Patroklos described in Book 23 of Homer's *Iliad,* which celebrated the *aretē* of the deceased. The winner in such events becomes a symbol of those virtues. Without the association with *aretē,* however, he is just a guy who had the skills to make it across the finish line first; he hasn't done anything to benefit mankind.[18]

Plato artfully illustrates the distinction between skill (*technē*) and virtue (*aretē*) with the example of telling falsehoods.[19] Being a good liar certainly does not equate with being a good person, but the skill of lying may be put to good use if the liar also has *aretē.* For example, a liar may use her skill to extort money from innocent victims in a Ponzi scheme, or she may use it to protect innocent victims from injustice—perhaps by lying to Nazi soldiers about the presence of Jews in her basement. The skill of lying is morally neutral; it is a person's *aretē* that makes it potentially valuable. Likewise athletic skills are morally neutral; their value depends on *aretē.* In Plato's dialogues, Socrates is the symbol of *aretē.* He sometimes gets tripped up by the sophists, whose intellectual skills in rhetoric and *eristic* argument were designed not to discover truth, but rather to trick opponents or win over audiences. Their lives are dedicated to short-term success, whereas Socrates' is dedicated to the cultivation of *aretē,* which is the real source of happiness.[20] Athletic skill may lead to victory, but it is virtue that makes victory worthwhile.

Unfortunately, virtue is harder to measure than victory, and reward systems for coaches and athletes alike are calibrated toward the latter. This is not a problem unique to sports. In society more generally, both ancient and modern, the extrinsic rewards of fame and fortune draw people away from the intrinsic goods connected to happiness. Chastising the citizens of Athens in 399 BCE, Socrates said, "Wealth does not bring about *aretē,* but *aretē* makes wealth and everything else good for men, both individually and collectively."[21] For some reason, legions of depressed millionaires and suicidal superstars are not evidence enough to deter young people from pursuing fame and fortune at a very high cost. Athletic paths to stardom are particularly risky. Any other college program with such a low professional placement rate would be considered a failure.[22] We may decry young athletes who are motivated by money, but we have to ask ourselves what values they are supposed to learn from coaching staffs preoccupied with salaries and institutions that see athletics primarily as a means to generate revenue and court alumni donors. Coaching for virtue means not only exhorting athletes to put *aretē* first; it also requires coaches to model this priority personally in their own choices and attitudes—despite an incentive and reward structure that often works against that.

In discussing the educational value of athletics, Plato's *Republic* never mentions wins or losses. Students are to be subjected to "labors [*ponous*], pains, and contests [*agōnas*]" so that they may be tested "more thoroughly than gold is tested by fire."[23] They are to be selected for advancement based on their performance in these contests, but not necessarily by whether they win, and certainly not by whether they have the physical size and strength to achieve Olympic victory.[24] Socrates distinguishes these students from "all other athletes" on the grounds that their goal is psychic rather than muscular strength.[25] Platonic educators are therefore looking for spiritual qualities that can be developed into virtues: the willingness to confront imperfection, the desire to work hard without promise of immediate reward, the discipline to resist laziness and temptation, and the ability to subject oneself to rules as an equal with others. These, at least, are the kinds of traits that Plato describes in relation to the cardinal virtues in his ethical philosophy—virtues still widely valued today: respect (*eusebia*), courage (*andreia*), moderation (*sophrosynē*), justice (*dikaiosynē*), and wisdom (*sophia*). Let us imagine how a coach in Plato's Academy might have used sport to help develop these virtues.

Respect (*Eusebia*)

The foundation of education for *aretē* in the Platonic scheme is summed up in Socrates' famous declaration that his wisdom lies precisely in the awareness that he is not wise.[26] Not unlike a twelve-step program, in which you must admit that you have a problem before you can begin to solve it, the Socratic admission of imperfection initiates and motivates the self-improvement process. Socrates explains his avowal of ignorance as a kind of religious humility. Having been declared by the oracle at Delphi (and therefore by the god Apollo) to be the wisest of men,[27] Socrates sets out to investigate the matter by questioning poets, politicians, and craftsmen who seem to him to be wise. What he discovers is that these men *think* themselves wiser than they really are, and so he concludes that the oracle has declared Socrates wisest because he, unlike these others, admits that he doesn't have knowledge. Furthermore, he spends his days questioning others in search of the truth, as a kind of mission to the god. In other words, Socrates regards it as a kind of piety, first, to acknowledge his imperfection with respect to the gods' perfection, and, second, to work tirelessly to bring himself and others around him closer to perfection through inquiry. In short, he is exercising the virtue of respect: respect for the excellence of the gods, respect for himself in striving for improvement, and respect for others in striving to help them improve.

Long before Socrates, athletics was a milieu that symbolized this conception of respect. The gulf between perfection and imperfection was understood in terms of the contrast between gods and human beings. Respect demands that we humbly acknowledge the gods' superiority—failure to do so amounts to the vice of *hubris*, the characteristic source of dreadful consequences in Greek tragedy. Ancient athletes showed their humility partly by competing in the nude, stripped of the trappings of their worldly ties and status. Athletes were anointed with olive oil and victors were symbolically dedicated to the gods, wearing the same cloth fillets and crowns of vegetation used to adorn sacrificial animals.[28] In the *Republic,* it is likewise said that a man must be "stripped" of his worldly reputation, honors, and rewards in order to be tested for the virtue of justice.[29] Even when we compete in clothes, athletic competition symbolically strips athletes of their social rank and demands that they respect not just the rules of the games they play, but also one another as imperfect equals under those rules. Just as Socratic questioning demonstrates respect by admitting imperfection and encouraging others to improve themselves, athletic competition demands that we admit our imperfection and encourage our competitors (by challenging them) also to improve themselves.

Coaching for respect means, first, admitting one's imperfection and helping others to come to terms with their own. Sports make us aware of our limitations, but in cases of dominant athletes or lack of good competition, may need a little help. When the goal is an ideal of excellence rather than mere superiority to others, there is room for criticism even in a runaway victory. Plato recognizes that flattery, which can come in the form of easy victory as well as verbal approbation, undermines the natural desire for improvement and replaces it with the desire for—and expectation of—constant praise.[30] Coaches talk a lot about being respected, which is important, but showing respect for rules, officials, superiors, and especially inferiors, is the best way to teach respect to others.

As Socrates understood, our individual differences in excellence are negligible compared with our collective distance from the ideal of excellence, as symbolized by the gods. Individual sports have their own "gods," namely, the great athletes, coaches, and officials who have built the history of our sports, and these too deserve recognition and respect from athletes and coaches alike. Beating Jesse Owens's time in the 100 meters does not mean you have achieved the same level of excellence or made the same social impact. Clearly not everyone deserves the same level of respect, but everyone deserves a basic level of respect—even people we neither like nor admire.[31] As human beings, we all fall short of perfection, and our struggle for improvement should be shared. Opponents, officials, sponsors, and staff all contribute to an athlete's personal improvement by making sports possible in the first place. Teaching respect means giving respect, and giving respect appropriately results in earning respect.

Courage (*Andreia*)

The respectful admission of imperfection provides a basis from which the passionate pursuit of excellence can be launched. The next thing Platonic educators look to be revealed through sports is an athlete's courage, as evidenced primarily by *philoponon*, literally the love of hard work.[32] They are looking for souls that do not give up easily, even when there is little hope of immediate reward. It isn't hard to imagine how athletic competition might reveal such a quality; as the proverb says, you can learn a lot about people by watching them play a game.[33] The reason Platonic educators are looking for courageous souls in sports has nothing to do with athletic championships, however. They want to find students who will courageously pursue knowledge because, as Socrates says, "people's souls give up much more easily in hard study than in physical training."[34] In short, they are looking for future philosopher-kings, people willing to "take the longer road and put as much effort into learning as into physical training, for otherwise, as we were just saying, he will never reach the goal of the most important subject and the most appropriate one for him to learn."[35] In short, the courage a student shows in sports is expected to apply as well in academic studies.

A plausible response to this idea of selecting students through sports is that Plato has no idea what he is talking about because in the real world (or at least the modern world), athletes who train and play with outstanding effort and courage rarely employ those qualities in academic pursuits. Plato does seem to have been aware of this problem. In *Republic*, Socrates says that athletes training and competing at the highest levels have little interest in anything else but sleeping.[36] The period in which students are examined and selected on the basis of their athletic performance is accordingly limited to two years devoted strictly to physical training. The study of difficult mathematical and philosophical subjects comes after that.[37] It is never expected of individuals that they dedicate themselves to the highest levels of sport and study simultaneously. It is expected, however, that virtues like courage, which are revealed and rewarded by sports, will be applied to the more important tasks of learning and leadership. Plato's educational philosophy is not aimed at producing star athletes or even commercial titans (although both existed in his day).The goal is to create excellent individuals who apply their virtues for the benefit of the larger community—something similar to the stated aims of most modern colleges and universities.

So what would it mean to coach for courage and other virtues that will be expressed beyond athletics? First, recognize that human beings cannot perform their very best at both athletics and academics simultaneously.[38] Second, incentives and accolades should be structured (within athletic and academic programs) to reward the cultivation of virtue and especially its application in activities that benefit the larger community. In the typical high school or college, standards of excellence for participating in sports are much higher than those for academics. Student athletes are required to make only minimal academic progress toward graduation, while they must train and compete at a very high level to earn a place on a team. Community celebration and reward of top athletes, furthermore, usually outstrips that given to top students. Is it any wonder that individuals tend to "spend" their virtues on sport in this environment? As in the case of win-loss records, coaches need to swim upstream to encourage the application of virtues beyond the athletic field. They need to demand that students always put virtue first and never neglect their obligations to other worthwhile activities and relationships, not that students always put sports first in their lives.[39] Plato's dialogue *Laches* argues that courage requires not just endurance but also the wisdom to direct it toward good causes. Bravery shown only and exclusively in sport is not a virtue at all; those who coach for virtues promote their expression beyond athletics as well.

Moderation (*Sophrosynē*)

Plato's Socrates explicitly rejects the idea that physical training is primarily for the benefit of the body, while the rest of education serves the soul (*psychē*). Rather, he argues that both physical and academic training are primarily for the benefit of the soul.[40] To make sense of this, we must first understand that the Greek word *psychē* is more expansive than many modern ideas of soul. In Plato's philosophy, the soul encompasses three parts: the wisdom-loving intellect, the honor-loving spirit, and the appetitive part associated with desires for food, drink, and sex. *Aretē* on Plato's scheme is explicitly described as a harmony among these three parts of the soul, a harmony that is compared (but not equated) with physical health. Indeed, even physical health has its origin in the soul, for as Socrates says, a fit body does not produce *aretē*, but rather that the soul's virtue makes the body as good as possible.[41] In fact, Socrates says that physical training in isolation risks squelching the soul's native love of learning, creating a person who "bulls his way through every situation by force and savagery like a wild animal."[42] A person pursuing *aretē*, even through the medium of sport, explains Socrates, will not "assign first place to being strong, healthy, and beautiful, unless he happens to acquire moderation (*sophrosynē*) as a result. Rather it's clear that he will always cultivate the harmony of his body for the sake of the consonance of his soul."[43]

This virtue of moderation (*sophrosynē*) may be described in the context of modern sports as a kind of self-discipline. It combines the power to resist appetitive temptations ranging from laziness to greed, with the ability to discern and pursue noble goals with enthusiasm. In the dialogue *Phaedrus* the virtuous soul is illustrated with the metaphor of a two-horse chariot. The driver represents the intellectual part of the soul, the obedient horse represents the spirited or honor-loving part, and the disobedient horse represents the appetitive part of the soul. In order for the chariot to perform well, the spirited and appetitive parts have to be trained to obey the rational part.[44] I don't think it is just by coincidence that Plato uses an athletic metaphor here (chariot racing was an important Olympic event in ancient Greece). Even today athletes must train themselves to resist destructive appetitive desires. The temptations to indulge in unhealthy food or alcohol, to stay out late or leave practice early, must be overcome to maximize athletic potential. Because the game tends to punish those who fail to control such appetites—sometimes in the humiliating form of a poor public performance—sports can help us to follow through in action with what the intellect discerns to be right. Socrates claims that athletic training helps to harmonize the three parts of the soul; to keep appetites in check and to pursue with enthusiasm the well-chosen goals of the intellect.[45]

Coaching for moderation means letting that process take place. Athletes must develop not only the intellectual capacity to make wise choices, but also the moral capacity to follow through with those choices in action. On one level, this requires coaches to allow the space for athletes to make mistakes and suffer the consequences. For example, athletes should come to practice because they know it is the right thing to do and they are following through, as a matter of honor or pride, with what they know to be right. If they come to practice simply to avoid punishment, they will be learning to obey the appetitive fear of pain rather than the intellectual conviction of purpose. This is nothing more than doing what feels good, a habit that can lead to all kinds of troubling behaviors. If, on the other hand, the athlete learns to do what is right because she understands its importance, she will have acquired an important moral skill. As in the case of winning and losing, however, sports do not reliably reward the virtue of moderation and punish the vice of immoderation. For this reason, coaches might create rules and rewards designed to guide rather than force athletes toward virtuous behavior. For example, they might prohibit potentially dangerous supplements so that athletes may come to appreciate the joy of achieving goals without the "help" of shortcuts. Coaches might bench even top-performing players who behave immoderately as a public way of putting virtue first. But restrictions on athlete behavior should be aimed at the goal of self-regulation. Like training wheels on a bike, their purpose is to make themselves unnecessary.

Justice (*Dikaiosynē*)

In using athletics to train and select the rulers of his ideal city, Plato was looking for outstanding individuals who, despite their personal excellence, could see themselves as equal with others before the law and ultimately understood their welfare to be inextricably connected with the good of the whole community. This social virtue was called justice (*dikaiosynē*), and it was learned through sports, on a foundational level, by the simple act of following rules. In the *Republic* it is stipulated that children's games be strictly governed by rules so they could develop the habit of respecting and following laws.[46] Ultimately, the model is of guardians and rulers completely devoted to the state; they are not allowed to have private property or even private families.[47] Their decisions are expected to serve the greater good of the community, disregarding personal concerns or desires. Athletics formed part of the training and selection process through which "they must show themselves to be lovers of their city when tested by pleasure and pain and that they must hold on to their resolve through labors, fears, and all other adversities."[48] To be a just person in Plato's Academy meant not only to have the three parts of your soul in harmony with one another, but also to be in harmony with your community, understanding your particular role within it, and regarding yourself as equal with others before the law.

Obviously the sociopolitical context of Plato's Academy is different from ours today. His understanding of the social virtue of justice, however, is as relevant as ever. In fact, the (relatively) modern invention of team sports seems to be a particularly good tool for promoting the understanding of individuals' dependence on the larger group. Paradoxically, much of the selfish and immoderate behavior seen today comes from athletes in high profile team sports. Like the ancient tyrants who plagued Greece in Plato's day, some superstar athletes are driven by their appetites to regard themselves as above the rules and to disregard the deleterious effects of their selfish actions on their teams. Coaches too behave like tyrants when they use their teams to satisfy their appetite for fame and fortune. These coaches are more dangerous than tyrannical players since they generally have more power. Fortunately, most team sports are structured in ways that penalize selfish behavior. Individual superstars may command big salaries, but they can win only with the cooperation of their team.

Meanwhile, players who put team harmony before personal desire tend to be rewarded by the game.

However, sports do not reliably reward the virtue of justice and so Platonic coaches need to promote it separately. As Socrates says in the *Republic,* "It isn't the law's concern to make any one class in the city outstandingly happy but to contrive to spread happiness throughout the city by bringing the citizens into harmony with each other."[49] The same could be said for the structure of a team. The basis of justice, it will be remembered, is equality before the law. In addition to treating players equitably, coaches should set an example of respect for rules, officials, opposing players, and coaches. Just as players should be smart enough to see the connection between their own success and that of the team, coaches should be smart enough to see the connection between their own success and that of the larger athletic and academic community. Coaches who bend rules or try to manipulate the system for the competitive benefit of the team may believe they are teaching loyalty and dedication to a purpose. But in fact, they are teaching their players to selfishly indulge their own desires at the expense of the community. Furthermore, coaches should penalize players who fail to exercise the virtue of justice—even if doing so hurts the team competitively. These actions reinforce sports' ability to cultivate the virtue of justice and may spur the other players to work more closely together rather than relying on a selfish star. As Socrates says of the guardians, just people are even happier than Olympians because their victory is shared by the entire community.[50]

Wisdom (*Sophia*)

The last of the key Platonic virtues is wisdom (*sophia*). Unlike the other virtues discussed above, he dedicates none of his dialogues to it. I can think of two good reasons for this. First, wisdom is a kind of crowning virtue—the culmination of the harmonious acquisition of all the other virtues. Each virtue depends for its value on some level of wisdom: justice requires the understanding of one's relationship to the community, moderation demands the subjection of appetites and honor to a discerning intellect, courage entails not just the will to take risks, but the ability to understand which risks are worth taking, and respect is based on the wisdom of knowing that one doesn't know. This brings us to the second reason Plato never explicates wisdom: like Socrates he probably would deny that he has it. The Academy educates philosophers, lovers of wisdom who believe themselves to be in perpetual pursuit of it, rather than sophists, people who believe that they possess it.

Wisdom and the virtues that Plato connects with it are strongly intellectual. But they derive their worth precisely from our ability to act in accordance with them. Aristotle defines human happiness as activity in accordance with virtue.[51] So athletics has its place in the Academy because it is an activity, something that requires us to act. Sports, insofar as they reward virtuous action and penalize the opposite, are an important part of training for *aretē* and the wisdom that is essential to it. Coaches, insofar as they promote virtue and penalize its opposite, are accordingly educators of virtue and as such they have an important place not only in Plato's ancient Academy but in modern schools, colleges, and universities. Athletics is not merely an add-on to education; it is wrapped up in its roots, and its link with virtue gives it a foundational role in education.

Questions for Review and Discussion

1. Aretism asserts that cultivation of virtue is the highest social good that sports can achieve. What other goods might coaches seek through sports? Would you argue that any of these is more important than virtue?

2. In ancient times athleticism was associated with moral virtue and leadership ability. Would you say that this is true today? Why or why not?

3. Some ancient philosophers like Plato and Aristotle believed that virtue, like athletic ability, is more a matter of training than of birth. Do you think good athletic performance is more a product of birth or training? What about good moral behavior?

4. Drawing on your athletic experience, compare a hard-earned victory with an easy victory. Which was more meaningful and valuable to you? Have you ever had a meaningful athletic experience that ended in defeat?

5. Plato suggests that athletes who exhibit courage and hard work in sports will apply the same virtues in academic study—an idea that contradicts the stereotype of the modern student athlete. Do you think the problem is more with Plato's theory or with the modern stereotype? Why don't more student athletes show the same virtues in the classroom and on the field or court?

6. The chapter discusses five ancient virtues that might be cultivated through sport: respect, courage, moderation, justice, and wisdom. How have your coaches, or your experience in sports more generally, helped you to cultivate these virtues? Can you think of an experience in sports that worked against one of these virtues?

7. Try to name three specific actions that high schools and universities could take to better facilitate the cultivation of virtue through sports. Now name three things coaches could do.

Suggestions for Further Reading

Arnold, Peter. "Sport and Moral Education." *Journal of Moral Education* 23:1 (1994): 75–90.

Bäck, Allan. "The *Way* to Virtue in Sport." *Journal of the Philosophy of Sport* 36 (2009): 217–237.

Bradley, Bill. *Values of the Game.* New York: Broadway Books, 1998.

Dombrowski, Daniel. *Contemporary Athletics and Ancient Greek Ideals.* Chicago: University of Chicago Press, 2009.

Jones, Carwyn. "Character, Virtue, and Physical Education." *European Physical Education Review* 11:2 (2005): 140–142.

Kennell, Nigel M. *The Gymnasium of Virtue: Education and Culture in Ancient Sparta.* Chapel Hill: University of North Carolina Press, 1995.

McNamee, Mike. *Sports, Virtues, and Vices: Morality Plays.* London: Routledge, 2008.

Reid, Heather L. "Athletic Virtue: Between East and West." In *The Ethics of Sports: A Reader,* 340–347. Edited by M. McNamee. London: Routledge, 2010.

Four

The Ethical Coach: An Interpretive Account of the Ethics of Coaching

ROBERT L. SIMON

I certainly wanted to have great field hockey players, but I wanted them to have character, to be responsible, mature and successful women in whatever they choose.

—Vernon-Verona-Sherill High School coach Wendy Seifried upon her retirement

I never wanted to do anything that would disappoint you.

—Former VVS field hockey player referring to Coach Seifried[1]

A number of years ago, I attended a symposium on college athletics and its problems. One of the speakers coached a highly successful men's program at an athletically elite university. He started his remarks by claiming, "My job is to make money for university X."

While some may regard that as an accurate description of his major responsibility, others may doubt that it captures all the issues, even at the level of big-time college sports. After all, his team wouldn't make money if it didn't win consistently. And to achieve that, the coach would have to be good at tasks that lead to winning, such as recruiting, teaching, motivating, selecting strategies, and persuading players to buy into them. These tasks may conflict with one another, necessitating difficult choices. For example, should a star player who violates the team's code of conduct be benched or suspended even if that means losing games that otherwise would be won? Should the coach berate competent game officials in order to arouse the home crowd and give his team an emotional lift?

These examples suggest that there is a normative or ethical side of coaching. Perhaps a big-time college coach is expected to generate revenues for the institution and hence has a strong imperative to win. Such coaches might resolve conflicts between competing goals simply by estimating which choice will most likely lead to winning. But is winning to be achieved at all costs? Are there constraints on the pursuit of victory, such as good sportsmanship? Aren't there other important goals, such as developing players' skills, ensuring they get a good education, protecting their safety, and perhaps even helping them grow as persons of good character?

Coaches, then, often face ethical choices. The decision to override ethics in pursuit of victory may trigger extensive criticism of the coach, as in 2012, when some New Orleans Saints coaches were found complicit in the team's bounty system that in effect rewarded defensive players for making hard hits intended to injure rival players and remove them from the game. What ethical requirements apply to them? How should coaches be evaluated ethically? How might coaches ethically evaluate their own behavior? In what follows, we will explore three different approaches to understanding the ethical requirements that might apply to coaching. First, however, we need to clarify some issues that might affect our inquiry.

The preceding examples suggest that coaching involves far more than teaching techniques and strategies closely related to the sport. Indeed, even apparently strategic choices may have a subtle evaluational dimension, as, for example, when a basketball coach decides to play a man-to-man defense rather than a zone in part because he thinks it teaches players to show great intensity, concentration, and commitment.

What ethical requirements apply to coaches? The requirements that apply to any competent adult? Or are there special requirements or exemptions for coaches, based on special rights and duties arising from the coaching role? For example, may coaches lie to their players to motivate them to achieve? May a coach exaggerate the extent of injuries to a star player in the hope that opponents will become overconfident and fail to prepare for the challenge of keeping the fully recovered star from dominating the game? May a coach intimidate or even bully players, an issue discussed by Mark Hamilton later in this volume, if the coach believes that is the best way to get them to play harder? What about more subtle forms of manipulation?

Suppose a college coach tells a freshman player that she has a chance to start on the soccer team but does this to get her to play hard enough to challenge the veteran starters in her position to also work hard in practice. If the coach actually has no intention of playing the newcomer over the veterans, is that technique good coaching, even if dishonest?[2]

Suppose we conclude that being an ethical coach is "a many splendored thing," with a variety of factors contributing to our evaluation that must be weighed but without any clear scale on which to do the weighing. How should these factors be weighed? How should a winning coach who uses techniques that are morally questionable but not egregiously so be evaluated? If there is no formula for balancing one factor against another, doesn't this make our evaluation of coaches subjective? Is one person's good coach another's coaching disaster?

Objectivity and Relativism in the Evaluation of Coaching

What does it mean to say a judgment, claim, principle, or even process is objective? There are many ways of distinguishing between the objective and the subjective. I suggest that there is a common concept of objectivity that applies at least to the paradigm cases where the concept of objectivity of judgment applies—there are rationally defensible constraints that we must satisfy in order to be warranted in our beliefs. These include the constraint of not being swayed by prejudice and the constraint of using logically sound methods for evaluating evidence. A judgment or conclusion is not justified just because everyone agrees to it but rather a consensus on a conclusion is justified because of the soundness of the reasons that support it.[3]

In our inquiry, we will consider criteria for the moral evaluation of coaches. The conclusions we arrive at, while tentative and fallible, will claim to be objective in the sense that they can be defended by sound reasoning and survive criticism in extended discussion and debate. Alternately, if further inquiry shows they are incorrect or at least questionable, such a conclusion will be the result of reasoning that, if sound, also makes a claim to be objective. Thus, if we have good reasons for believing Coach X is an unethical coach, we can be correct—Coach X really is unethical—and someone who believes Coach X is ethical can be wrong or in error. Therefore, because we are dealing with subject matter that allows of correct and incorrect evaluations, we are in the realm of objectivity and not mere personal opinion, let alone bias and prejudice.[4] Sometimes it may be difficult to arrive at well-grounded conclusions, as when we debate hard cases in sport such as whether pitchers in baseball ought to retaliate for brush back pitches thrown at their teammates or whether a hard foul from behind to prevent a layup in a basketball game is simply good strategy or unfairly deprives an opponent of an advantage gained by superior play. (See William J. Morgan's discussion of different views of strategic fouling in Chapter 5.)

What counts as an ethical coach may vary with context. That is, the ethical requirements that apply to coaches at one level, such as professional sports, may vary in significant ways from those that apply at another, such as high school or children's sports. This does not make judgments subjective, as we can still have good reasons for judgments such as "Jones is a great college coach but doesn't have the patience to be a good coach with young children."

Keeping these points in mind, let us turn to substantive issues about the moral evaluation of coaches.

Winning as the Only Thing

According to what might be called the instrumental view, a good coach is someone who achieves the goals of coaching. Similarly, a good knife is one that cuts. However, as simple as this formula sounds, it raises at least two significant questions. First, what are the goals of coaching? Second, are there requirements that set moral limits or constraints on what the coach may do while attempting to achieve those goals?

One way of answering the first question is to reply that a good coach is one who wins. Winning is the goal of athletic competition. A coach who consistently loses is a failure as a coach. And indeed, there is something to this proposal. As writers such as Scott Kretchmar have pointed out, winning requires that players learn skills such as how to hold a lead, how to maintain poise when the opposition is making a run, how to mount a run from behind when the opponents take the lead, and how to excel under pressure, especially when a tight game comes down to the wire.[5]

Consider the extreme view, one not held by Kretchmar, that the only ethical obligation of the coach is to win. Coaches and players develop skills, select strategies, and make decisions in game situations that are designed to help them win; as winning is the common instrumental goal of sports, the job of the coach is and only is to promote victory.

However, cursory critical scrutiny suggests that winning is not the only ethical obligation of the coach. At many levels of sport it may not even be a primary one. For example, when coaching young children, it surely is more important to teach fundamental physical skills, teach age-appropriate strategies and game awareness (how to react appropriately to game situations), and arouse enthusiasm and a love of the game that might carry over for a lifetime. (However, as Torres and Hager argue later in this volume, competition still may be a valuable part of youth sports.) Winning may take on increased significance at the levels of professional and elite amateur sports. But don't those coaches also have a responsibility to protect the health of athletes, treat them with respect, and, at schools and colleges, promote their academic success?

A coach may have a winning record but not be a very good coach or satisfy the ethical requirements applicable to coaching. Winning records can be achieved by scheduling weak opponents, for example, or by employing hidden techniques that tilt the playing field. For example, when Bill Belichick's New England Patriots were accused of gaining illegal access to the play calling of rival coaches, critics charged that his teams won, not necessarily because they were better but because of "insider information" that gave them an advantage having nothing to do with their athletic or strategic skills. Or suppose a coach wins because he rewards his players for injuring opponents, as was alleged of the NFL New Orleans Saints in March 2012?

Winning, then, is not the sole criterion by which coaches should be evaluated. Winning does not exhaust the ethical responsibilities of the coach and, indeed, is to the coach's ethical credit only if achieved by ethically justifiable means. But what criteria should be applied to the moral evaluation of coaching?

A Kantian Approach: Athletes Should Not be Used as Mere Means to a Goal

The distinguished eighteenth-century philosopher Immanuel Kant defended an approach to ethics that is generally understood to lay down rationally defensible restraints on the pursuit of our goals, even our personal happiness, based on the intrinsic values of persons. Kant called what he regarded as the fundamental ethical principle the Categorical Imperative, which he expressed in several ways that he apparently regarded as equivalent. Perhaps the most morally influential formulation maintains that we should never treat others only as means to attaining a goal but as ends; as persons rather than as things. A related and perhaps equally influential formulation, which Kant himself might have thought equivalent, requires that it be possible or logically coherent for the point or motive of our act to be made a universal rule. Thus it would be logically incoherent for everyone to cheat in a golf tournament since there would be no golf tournament if the rules of golf were not followed. Also, cheating another reduces the victim to a thing or means to our own success rather than a person who is trying to compete with us under an agreed upon set of conditions for contesting the golf tournament. Thus cheating opponents in a golf tournament violates both versions of the Categorical Imperative.

The central basis for Kant's claim goes something like this. None of us does or even can regard ourselves as mere things. None of us want or even can want to simply be used to achieve the goals of others that we do not share. And so if we are to be consistent we must regard all others who also function as persons as ends in themselves as well. As philosopher and legal theorist Ronald Dworkin suggests, "We cannot consistently treat our own lives as objectively important unless we accept that everyone's life has the same objective importance."[6]

What does it mean to be treated a mere means? On one view, the key implication is that we should not be treated in ways we do not or would not (if reasonable and fully informed) consent to be treated. On a related view, we should not be exploited or taken advantage of. On a third view, which draws on Kant's emphasis on our status as rational choosing beings, we should be valued or cherished as persons (as intrinsically valuable beings) and not just units who might be traded off against other units in a cost-benefit analysis to achiever the greatest overall good or profit.

How does this abstract discussion apply to coaching? The most obvious application is that there is a Kantian requirement on coaches—coaches are not to use others, particularly the athletes they coach, as mere means.

In a consideration of coaching ethics, Jeffrey Fry provides several examples of how Kant's Categorical Imperative might apply. We already have considered two illustrations based on Fry's scenarios. In the first, a coach during preseason tells a promising rookie and a veteran that they are competing for a starting position on the team even though he already has decided to go with the rookie. The coach's motive is to get both players to work harder in practice, thus better preparing them for the season ahead. In the second case, the coach orders a player to make an especially hard hit on the opponent's key player in order to get the opposing star out of the game. The coach brushes off his player's moral qualms by telling him, "It's all part of the game."[7]

Fry goes on to give a very plausible Kantian analysis of why the coach's behavior in the first case probably is unethical and why it is clearly unethical in the second. In the first case, the coach is deceiving the veteran, especially if he had indicated earlier that the veteran would get a chance to start. Moreover, as Fry points out, if told the truth, the veteran might select another sport to play, decide to play at the professional level, or ask to be traded or, if in college, transfer to another school. The coach, in Fry's view, is reducing the athlete to a mere means to the team's success.[8]

Moreover, the coach's behavior violates the universality version of the Categorical Imperative: it is doubtful the coach's behavior can be made into a universal law of a public code of conduct for coaches. For if it was publicly known that coaches deceive in this sort of situation, no one would believe them in the first place and their deception wouldn't work.[9]

If the coach's behavior is dubious in the first case, it is clearly unethical in the second. By instructing his player to injure an opponent, the opposing player is not viewed as a person to be valued and respected, but as an obstacle standing in the way of victory. Indeed, as Fry notes, the coach's own player is also being used as a mere means since the coach disregards the player's moral qualms about carrying out the instruction.[10]

Should we conclude, then, that the coach's whole range of ethical responsibilities is captured by Kantian ethics, suitably interpreted and applied? A major difficulty with regarding the Kantian approach as the whole story of coaching ethics is illustrated by a third example of Fry's. In this case, a basketball team is nearing the end of a mediocre season, and a high school coach is faced with the decision of benching her seniors, who have all played for years in the program, in order to develop the potential of currently less skilled younger players so the team will be more competitive the following year. Should the coach show loyalty to the veterans who have worked hard for the program and continue to play them or focus on building a championship contender in the future? Fry comments,

> Even though her actions may promote the greatest overall utility, she has not taken the seniors' ends—i.e. goals for the season—seriously enough. . . . Instead, . . . coach is only committed to the players as long as they fulfill a narrowly defined role. Given that, she has lost sight of their humanity.[11]

While Fry's analysis seems correct as applied to his description of the case, the coach, as Fry might agree, has a number of options in slightly altered versions of this scenario. For example, the coach can be open with her players, tell them that she has a responsibility to build for the future as well as work as hard as possible for success this season, and inform the team that for the remaining games, she will try to give the younger athletes more playing time than previously. She can enlist the help of her seniors in building for the future. In this approach, the seniors are not totally ignored, but their playing time is reduced so that younger players can be prepared to replace them next season. However, this is done in an open way, with, one would hope, the cooperation of the seniors. Indeed, the coach arguably has responsibilities to future teams as well as to the present one.[12]

The point is not identifying one best solution to this coach's dilemma but rather achieving ethically acceptable results. What's needed is good judgment in balancing a variety of factors rather than simply applying an abstract injunction not to treat players as mere means to someone else's end. The Kantian injunction against treating others as mere means may set a moral baseline below which the coach must not fall, and perhaps may even be a necessary condition of moral acceptability. But above that baseline, good judgment might lead to a variety of solutions, some of which balance the competing values at stake.

We can think of a great many coaching situations that have ethical dimensions and call for good judgment in balancing a number of competing values in ways not easily captured by rules or formulas. How should a coach distribute playing time among team members? (Scott Kretchmar considers this question in Chapter 8.) Is it permissible for a coach to "work" the officials and, if so, how far may a coach go? (Mark Hamilton considers the ethics of intimidation in Chapter 9.) May a coach lay down rules for player conduct off the field and, if so, how far may the coach go? How much of a voice should players have in framing team rules or even in helping formulate team strategies?

To take a final example, how a coach addresses her team may call for good judgment that is sensitive to moral factors that are hard to codify under a rule. Thus a coach who encourages players to make suggestions about strategy, use of practice time, and decision making during games is making a different moral choice than a more directive coach who does not involve players in decision making. Both may avoid treating their players as mere means but surely there are different moral values involved in their approaches.

Clearly coaching is a complex activity that involves a network of strategic, technical, personal, and moral dimensions, all of which may be interrelated in particular cases. While I agree with Fry that there are important moral side constraints, perhaps Kantian in character, that may prohibit certain coaching decisions, such as telling a team member to deliberately injure an opponent, these side constraints are not always determinative in the complex situations that arise in coaching. These complexities may lead many to conclude that the ethical coach is not primarily a person who follows well defined moral rules or avoids violating Kantian prohibitions. Rather, the ethical coach is a person who makes good judgments in particular sporting contexts. Similarly, in evaluating coaches, the evaluators are not bound by a rule book but must look at the variety of virtues the coach exhibits and the judgment the coach makes in a variety of contexts.

The Ethical Coach as a Person of Practical Wisdom

In a high school basketball game I witnessed many years ago, two strong teams were taking each other down to the wire in a hotly contested game. Most of the starters on one team fouled out, and as the clock wound down, the outcome depended on foul shots by a rarely used substitute. In a time-out called by the opponents to "ice" the foul shooter, his coach looked him in the eye and, according to reports, said, "These are the most important shots you will ever have in your life!" In retrospect, this was probably not the best thing to have said, as the nervous substitute didn't even hit the rim in two attempts.

While the coach may not have said anything unethical, he may have used poor judgment in how he addressed the player. Perhaps the shooter would have done better if the coach had simply told him to take deep breaths and relax and reassured him about his value to the team regardless of the outcome.

Similarly, good judgment might be called for in other sorts of cases more directly involving ethics. For example, a high school golf coach sees that an inexperienced player on an opposing team inadvertently teed her last shot a few inches in front of the tee markers, a rule violation that calls for a penalty. Should the coach call for a penalty to be assessed? Or in light of the player's inexperience, the fact that her playing partners failed to notice and hence warn her in advance of the possible infraction, and that virtually no advantage was gained, should the coach simply advise the violator to check where she teed her ball more carefully in the future? Should the coach remind the other players of their obligation, recognized by golfers, to warn their competitors in advance of possible rules infractions? Clearly a lot will depend on contextual factors such as how inexperienced the player actually was (was it her first competitive match?), the type of match (a scrimmage versus a state championship), the attitude of the other players in the group (did they deliberately fail to warn the violator or were they simply inattentive)? If no precise rule or formula covers this case, the coach must simply exercise good judgment.[13]

Proponents of the view just articulated rightly point out that the coach must be a master of "spontaneous response."[14] Making just the right substitution, for example, at just the right time, or changing the defense just at the moment when the opponent is least likely to adjust to the change, call for good judgment in response to complex situations, not automatic application of strategic rules. Similarly, when the ethical dimension of decision making is paramount, good judgment rather than mastery of the rules is key. For example, knowing how to motivate a player whose play has been halfhearted may involve walking a fine line between intense criticism and verbal abuse. To take another example, consider a high school coach trying to choose between (or perhaps blend) two offensive strategies, one that emphasizes the talents of a star player and another that emphasizes cohesive team play that will develop the talents of all the players but perhaps result in less competitive success. This coach may need to strike a balance between two extremes that is not dictated by a rule book but requires sensitivity to the particular characteristics of the team.

Advocates of such a view maintain that the good coach is a person of practical wisdom; one who is adept at making the right judgment in particular contexts. Such a coach applies a variety of virtues, such as sensitivity, passion, and fairness, as dictated by the situation. Aristotle called such a quality *phronesis*, emphasizing that it, rather than rules, is fundamental in ethics. The ethical coach, then, is not simply a Kantian who avoids treating players as mere means but has the practical wisdom to make the decision most appropriate to the case at hand. On this view, the good coach does not need a philosophy in the sense of a general rule book for how to make decisions. Rather, a good philosophy of coaching may just summarize how wise and virtuous coaches decide. (See also the chapters by Reid and Hochstetler for discussion of the importance of good judgment in specific contexts.)

This account may well be perspicuous in describing what good coaches actually do, but questions can be raised about whether it is a complete account of the ethics of coaching. Although no manual of rules could be complete or fine-tuned enough to allow coaches to deduce good decisions from its pages, it does not follow that making good intuitive judgments is all there is to good coaching. Consider three criticisms of this approach.

First, coaches may be called on to *justify* their decisions in public forums (or to themselves when they second-guess their own actions). If the decision is questionable, people will want to know more about the reasons for the decision other than it just seemed right to the coach in the situation. Coaches may need to provide reasons, not just to themselves or to fans, but to their own players, to parents, to the press, and in educational institutions to the athletic director and other administrators, such as a principal or dean. Just as judges in higher courts need to defend their decisions in written opinions available for public scrutiny, coaches also may need to defend their decisions by presenting justifications for them and answering criticism in various forums.

Second, coaches need to assess not just single decisions but also whether the set of their decisions over time is internally consistent and coherent. Coaches who decide in one way at one time but then handle a relevantly similar case differently need to either explain why the cases are relevantly different or else acknowledge that they were inconsistent, and thus made a mistake or were unfair. (Perhaps they learned from experience and corrected an earlier error, but they cannot be correct in treating two cases that do not differ in any relevant respect differently.)

Finally, coaches are not infallible. They are most likely to avoid mistakes in complex cases if they test their judgments about specific cases by seeing if they cohere with a larger framework, including rules and principles, that might help justify them. For example, a coach is torn between suspending a star player for missing a practice without a good excuse but also needing that player in the next game that might decide the league championship. The coach leans toward allowing the player to participate because a loss would harm the other players on the team, who have done no wrong, but also questions whether she is placing too much importance on winning and whether it is unfair to exempt the star from team rules that apply to everyone else.

In cases where intuition is not determinative, appealing to a more general theory about the purposes of competitive sport and the role of the coach in achieving such goals might be helpful. Ideally, we should try to reflect over time so as to harmonize our judgments about particular cases with an overall theory that explains and justifies them, a state philosophers call "reflective equilibrium."[15]

Of course, such criticisms are not decisive. For one thing, advocates of the coach as a person of practical wisdom might emphasize that on their view, the best coaching decisions, especially ethical ones, are not based on hunches or intuitions but on deep-seated traits of character that enable the coach to act virtuously. Moreover, they would argue, if a situation is so complex that even a person of practical wisdom has difficulty deciding what to do, it is unlikely a more general philosophical theory will help either. Let me suggest, however, that before assessing the role of *phronesis* or practical wisdom in coaching, we consider one more alternative.[16]

Broad Internalism: An Interpretive Approach to Coaching

Consider the following example. You are playing in an important soccer game and the opposing team, through clever passing and dribbling, is in position to have a breakaway attempt at the goal. A rival player inadvertently bumps you. If you pretend to be injured and writhe on the ground as if in pain, the opposition, known for its sportsmanlike conduct, will follow the convention of soccer and kick the ball out of bounds, thereby losing its opportunity to score, so that your "injury" can be treated. Should you pretend to be injured?

Surely you should not. Faking an injury is not a fundamental skill in soccer. (Thus it would be absurd to claim that A is a better player than B because even though B is more skilled at passing, dribbling, shooting, and defense, A is much better at faking injuries.) The point of competitive athletics is to see whether your team is more skilled than its opponents. Negating the other team's skills through trickery changes the contest from one where the skills of soccer are being tested to one where deception irrelevant to soccer skills may become decisive.

Surely a major point of competitive sports is to test our relative abilities against worthy opponents and to learn from meeting challenges. Arguably, a good competitor should want to meet the challenge presented by the rules of the sport, not avoid the challenge by turning the contest into something other than a test of soccer skills.

This analysis rests on a broad theory about the purpose and value of competitive sport. I have elsewhere described this account as "a mutual quest for excellence," the idea being that in a sports contest, opponents voluntarily challenge each other so as to bring out the best in each participant.[17] On this view, competitive sports are an educational activity in which competitors are tested by the challenges of the sport and the play of opponents, and learn from the experience of competing. Winning a game, especially against a worthy opponent, is a sign of success. However, as noted earlier, one can meet the challenge of the sport without winning, as when one pushes a vastly superior opponent to the limit or plays an excellent game only to lose to a nearly equal opponent.

This approach to understanding and evaluating sports has been called broad internalism because it suggests that a broad interpretation of sport that makes sense of its internal features is crucial both to understanding and ethically assessing competitive athletics. Interpretations are to be assessed by their ability to explain the different key features of sports, such as explaining which primary skills the rules are designed to test, by their coherence or internal consistency, and by their ability to present sports in their morally best light.[18] Thus the crude theory that winning is everything fails to explain why winning is cheapened or lacks significance when it is achieved in spite of sloppy play against a vastly overmatched opponent.

Broad internalists, following legal theorist Ronald Dworkin, emphasize the role of principles as well as rules in interpreting sport. Unlike a rule such as "three strikes and you are out," principles have weight and need to be balanced against other considerations. How they apply to a situation requires seeing how they fit in an overall theory of the sport at issue, and perhaps the point of athletic competition itself (the mutual quest for excellence) in which the principle is embedded.

How does this apply to the ethics of coaching? First, the coach should apply a defensible interpretation of sports in making hard coaching decisions, especially those with an ethical dimension. Not only should the coach have a philosophy (as Doug Hochstetler argues in Chapter 6), but it should be interpretive or broad internalist in character.

This theory may (and in my view does) include the sort of Kantian side constraints discussed by Fry but goes beyond them in applying to complex cases that require the use of a broad set of principles of interpretation. For example, the judgment that the soccer player should not fake the injury might be based on a principle that enjoins players to seek out competitive challenges based on skill rather than avoid them through trickery.[19]

Second, I also suggest that a broad internalist theory is needed in order to *evaluate* the performance of coaches. Such a theory would provide an account of the role of the coach and how it is embedded in a broader account of the point and value of athletic competition. For example, if a coach achieves a winning record by avoiding worthy opponents, the behavior normally would be open to criticism on the grounds that under the theory of the mutual quest for excellence, athletes should welcome competitive challenges and be prepared to learn from their successes and failures in attempting to meet them.

Thus if we interpret sport as a mutual quest for excellence in meeting challenges for their own sake, we explain and justify major features of sport relevant to coaching. Winning, as we have seen, is important, since it often is a sign that the challenge of the contest has been met, but it is not everything since the challenge sometimes can be met without winning. This explains why coaches at most levels of sport should not act as if winning is everything and also justifies their emphasizing other values, such as playing one's best, trying to improve, and respecting opponents. Indeed, since opponents are not mere obstacles to be overcome but rather facilitators who freely enter into a mutually acceptable activity (the contest) in order to create a challenge, the coach should emphasize respect for the opponent and not teach viewing opponents as mortal enemies.

In hard cases, however, theories or broad interpretations of sports may only issue debatable guidelines for coaches rather than decisive answers. For example, let us consider the case discussed earlier where a high school coach seems forced to choose between showing loyalty to senior players who most likely will lose as many games as they win or bench the seniors and play currently less experienced and somewhat less talented younger players in order to give them experience and build a top team for the following season.

In this sort of case, coaches may need to use practical judgment in deciding how to deal with the team, but also need a rationale to justify their response should it be questioned. My own view is the situation calls for compromising competing values. I suggested earlier that the coach should be open with the team and point out the variety of challenges involved. Thus the team has an obligation to challenge opponents to the best of its abilities, but the coach also has a duty to help all the players develop their capacities to meet the challenges of the sport. Moreover, the coach arguably has a duty, although perhaps a less weighty one than others, to think not only about the next contest or even the present season alone but also to consider the players who will be on the team in later seasons.

As I suggested earlier, in view of the complexity of the situation the coach might explain the situation to the team, challenge the seniors to help develop the abilities of the younger ones during practice, and gradually move the younger players into the lineup through judicious substitution and variation in the starting lineup so that the younger players can gain experience by being in the game at the same time as the more experienced older players. Such a strategy might involve compromising, say, loyalty to the seniors by adding playing time for the others. But the seniors would not be relegated to the bench and would be involved as "assistant coaches," helping the less experienced athletes to improve. In this way, the coach would be acting as an educator by involving all members of the team in a quest to improve but still seeking to put a lineup in the game that vigorously challenges opponents. Although all these values may not be maximally implemented, none are disregarded either.

However, some may well dissent from the compromise proposed above, perhaps with good reason. But this is where the beauty of the interpretivist (broad internalist) approach shines through. Coaches and other members of the sporting community can engage each other in reasoned discourse to evaluate the soundness of different approaches in an attempt to reach reflective equilibrium. Such discourse may show that a number of approaches are equally defensible, although one resolution may emerge as correct or at least as more justifiable than others. What surely will not be the case is that any approach will turn out to be as reasonable as any other. Thus a coach who angrily tells the seniors that they lack ability, that he will no longer help them improve, and that their only future role on the team will be as practice players not only is cruel to the older players but is unfair to opponents by not giving any weight to the duty to create a meaningful challenge in actual contests.

What I have suggested, then, is that the ethical evaluation of coaching decisions and behavior is best understood as requiring a broad interpretation of the point of competitive sport and its moral justification. Such an interpretation is debatable and revisable but also is objective in that the arguments in its favor may or may not stand up to critical scrutiny. In hard cases, sometimes a plurality of approaches may be equally reasonable, but all should be subject to critical scrutiny. I have proposed that one broad internalist theory—the idea of sport as a mutual quest for excellence through challenge—is a strong candidate for the ethical and explanatory framework required by the internalist approach.

The exact form such a theory should take might vary according to the level and type of sport. Winning may play a much weightier role at the professional or Olympic level than in youth sports, for example. Thus in professional sports, the coach may be more justified in benching or even cutting a veteran player in favor of promising rookies than would a high school coach in cutting seniors who are not quite as good as younger players. But according to the idea of the mutual quest for excellence, even the professional coach would not be justified in acting as if winning was the only goal, overriding such other legitimate objectives as the safety of players and respect for the deepest values of the game.

To summarize, a broad theory can be useful not only to the coach in decision making, for after all the coach sometimes may need to make quick decisions and rely on practical wisdom as suggested by those who emphasize the role of *phronesis*, but also in the practice of justifying decisions once they are made, and in the critical scrutiny of sports by administrators and supervisors, as well as commentators and fans.

Evaluating Coaches in Educational Institutions

Let us conclude with a brief examination of the implications of this discussion for assessing the performance of coaches in educational institutions, particularly secondary schools and colleges and universities. When competitive sports are viewed as a mutual quest for excellence through challenge, sports clearly have an educational component. Athletes need to learn to meet the challenges of competition, to improve, to overcome failure, to value the ideas of a contest with a worthy opponent, and to respect the fundamental values of their sport. This requires critical scrutiny of one's own performance and that of others, willingness to learn from criticism and to work hard to perfect skills, ability to analyze decisions made in the heat of competition, and respect for truth in evaluating one's own performance and that of fellow competitors.

These values have a clear affinity with many values presupposed in academic pursuits such as the importance of critical scrutiny, respect for evidence and truth, and willingness to test one's ideas by exposing them to critiques in such contexts as classes, papers, artistic exhibitions and performances, and published books and articles. Seen in this light, academics and athletics not only can be compatible but actually might be mutually reinforcing in the right circumstances.[20]

This suggests that a crucial role of coaches in educational institutions is to educate. While they have many responsibilities, such as scheduling, recruiting, and representing their programs to alumni and the broader community, they are primarily teachers. If they are thought of in this way, their work helps to harmonize athletics and academics and affirms the view that athletics contribute to the academic enterprise rather than constitute an alien intrusion on the life of the mind.[21]

Critics might reply that perhaps such a model applies best to many secondary schools, colleges and universities in Division III of the NCAA (who explicitly endorse the integration of athletics and academics in the Division III mission statement), and NAIA institutions, as well as the Ivy League in Division I but add that the model has no application to high visibility sports at the athletically elite levels of Division I. Coaches at that level enjoy national prestige and often make more than the presidents of their institutions. Surely the major function of big-time collegiate athletic programs is providing entertainment and raising money for their institutions.[22]

However, the pursuit of revenue and the national publicity that goes with winning is a root cause of the scandals, low graduation rates in some programs, and charges of exploitation of athletes that have plagued big-time college sports and have led critics to call for their radical reform and even abolition. Perhaps a greater emphasis on evaluating coaches as educators would be part of a multifaceted program that emphasizes the educational benefits of competitive athletics, for both participants and spectators.

While the way to best achieve such a goal will vary with the kind of institution and the level at which it competes, I suggest that a major component of reform should require colleges and universities to include a formal recommendation by a faculty committee, independent of the athletic department, that evaluates coaches on how they contribute to the educational mission of the university. This already is the case in many colleges in Division III, including Hamilton College, where I teach. Here coaches normally hold faculty appointments. Also requiring a formal faculty review, Division I institutions would promote greater oversight of athletics by educators and take a step toward implementing respect for athletics as a legitimate program within academic institutions, over and above whatever entertainment value they provide. A coach who wins but runs a program that undermines the educational values of the institution may be successful in one sense. But it is doubtful at best if such a program can be defended on ethical grounds. In other words, coaches at educational institutions should be evaluated, in part, in ways parallel to the evaluation of faculty and other educators at their school.

Moreover, institutional oversight of big-time college athletic programs is crucial. The 2012 report on the Jerry Sandusky scandal at Penn State by former FBI director Louis Freeh claims to have found "total and consistent disregard by the most senior leaders at Penn State for the safety and welfare of Sandusky's child victims."[23] If true, this finding may indicate that the prestige and influence of top coaches and the natural desire to protect elite programs can overwhelm important values and overriding moral concerns.

Indeed, the Freeh report alleges that the desire to protect the prestige (and the financial benefits that accrued from it) of Penn State football kept high Penn State officials from reporting what they knew of Sandusky's crimes to the police. Less powerful employees allegedly felt powerless to challenge what amounted to a cover-up of Sandusky's activities. As a result of the Freeh report, the NCAA imposed unprecedented penalties on Penn State, including a $60 million fine (to be used to help the victims of child abuse), loss of football scholarships, and a four-year ban on Penn State participation in postseason bowl appearances.[24]

On the other hand, if we accept the twin ideas that athletics should be integrated with academics and that a primary task of coaches is to function as educators, a strong case can be made for my proposal for the academic evaluation of coaches and their programs.[25] A fuller examination of coaching at athletically elite colleges and universities would also examine the compensation of powerful coaches and perhaps, most important, their influence over other areas of the university. Fuller institutional and faulty oversight of athletics should be considered a primary goal of reform of big-time college sports.

Conclusion

Coaching has a major ethical component. An unethical coach, or one who coaches in an unethical way, normally is not a good coach. The major argument for this view is that the goals of competitive sports should not be understood only in terms of winning but more broadly in a way involving important moral norms.

These norms are partially captured by Kantian, contextualist, and virtue oriented accounts of sports. However, I have suggested that an interpretive or broad internalist approach, especially one that regards competitive sport as a mutual quest for excellence through challenge, provides a defensible overall account of the value of athletic competition. It brings out the educational aspects of competitive sport as an activity that values overcoming challenge for its own sake but also helps promote and illustrate the values and the self-knowledge that enable us to succeed in such a mission.

On such a view, the role of the coach is interpretive; on the broad internalist view, the best theory of the coach's role is the one we ought to adopt. The best theory is the one that makes the most sense of paradigmatic coaching practices and presents them in their morally best light. Consequently I have suggested that the coach is primarily an educator in the context of viewing athletic competition as a mutual quest for excellence. Coaches, especially in educational institutions, should be treated and evaluated under such a heading.

The test of such proposals is continuing critical examination, which contributes not only to a better understanding of coaching, one of the significant social roles in our culture, but also to appreciating the crucial role ethics should play in this important area of our sporting life.

Questions for Review and Discussion

1. What significance should be attached to winning in athletic competition? Even if winning isn't everything, what degree of importance should be attached to it?

2. Explain the difference between the Kantian and the virtue contextualist oriented approach (based on *phronesis*) to coaching ethics.

3. What is broad internalism (interpretivism) and how does the author think it applies to coaching ethics? Do you agree that the coach needs a theory of the broad internalist kind to make good ethical decisions? Do others need such a theory in evaluating coaching performance?

4. What is the author's argument that coaches primarily are educators? Is the author's argument sound? Does it apply outside educational institutions—e.g. in youth sports, on one hand, and at the level of elite or professional sports on the other?

Suggestions for Further Reading

Dixon, Nicholas. "On Winning and Athletic Superiority." *Journal of the Philosophy of Sport* 26 (1999): 10–26.

French, Peter. *Ethics and College Sports: Ethics, Sports, and the University*. Lanham, MD: Rowman & Littlefield, 2004.

Fry, Jeffrey. "Coaching a Kingdom of Ends." *Journal of the Philosophy of Sport* 27 (2000): 51–62.

Hardman, Alun R., and Carwyn Jones. "Sports Coaching and Virtue Ethics." In *The Ethics of Sports Coaching*, 72–84. London: Routledge, 2011.

Kretchmar, Scott. "In Defense of Winning." In *Sports Ethics: An Anthology*, 130–135. Edited by Jan Boxill. Malden, MA: Blackwell, 2003.

Russell, J. S. "Are Rules All an Umpire Has to Work With?" *Journal of the Philosophy of Sport* 26 (1999): 27–49.

Simon, Robert L. "Does Athletics Undermine Academics? Examining Some Issues." *Journal of Intercollegiate Sport* 1:1 (2008): 40–58.

———. *Fair Play: The Ethics of Sport*. 3rd ed. Boulder, CO: Westview, 2010. See especially chapters 2–3.

———. "Internalism and the Internal Values of Sport." *Journal of the Philosophy of Sport* 27 (2000): 1–16.

Five

Interpretivism, Conventionalism, and the Ethical Coach*

WILLIAM J. MORGAN

The chapters in Part 2 make a persuasive case that coaches at all levels have significant ethical concerns, responsibilities, and duties. But what ethical resources can they draw on not only to arrive at morally acceptable, or even morally required, judgments, but also to justify the decisions they make? Should coaches act intuitively relying on their practical wisdom and experience, appeal to ethical theories, or just solve problems that crop up on the playing field?

In Chapter 4, Robert Simon forcefully argues that ethical decision making is a central dimension of coaching, and that the theory of sports he dubs "broad internalism" or simply "interpretivism" offers the best account of how ethical coaches should form their ethical judgments and justify them to others. According to interpretivism, coaches should base their ethical decisions on a consideration of the basic purpose(s) and value(s) of sports, on an interpretation that puts the athletic challenges central to competitive sports in

*I want to thank Robert Simon for his incisive comments and helpful revisions on a previous draft of this chapter.

their best light. By interpretively training our eyes on the point of athletic enterprise, Simon claims, we can divine appropriate normative standards of athletic conduct and subject them to critical inquiry. The kind of critical inquiry he has in mind is a rationally based discourse oriented to justification, in which proposed norms are subjected to various challenges and objections by the relevant discourse parties. Only norms that survive such scrutiny and prove their intellectual mettle by defeating all comers meet with our normative approval. Simon has developed this position more fully in several essays cited in later notes, but the main lines of his position are discernible from his discussion in this volume.

In what follows, I will focus on his account of broad internalism (interpretivism) because it is an important approach that has received considerable attention in the philosophy of sports literature. I will question whether coaches faced with important ethical decisions need to rely on a philosophically expansive and ultimately ahistorical account of moral reasoning, as Simon suggests is necessary, and offer an alternative approach, which while culturally and historically based retains critical force nonetheless.

Simon thinks that by focusing on the purpose of competitive sports and by insisting that the normative standards we generate in this interpretive manner pass reflective muster, we will help coaches make ethical decisions that are both relevant to what competitive sports is all about, and rationally justifiable to those who might object to them. Rival ethical takes on sports and coaching, Simon argues, fall short—either because they give short shrift to the proper aim of athletic enterprise or to the justificatory discourse necessary to validate principles of athletic conduct, or to both of these pillars of normative inquiry. An example of the former kind of failure, according to Simon, are Kantian-based ethical theories that bypass the question "What is the purpose of competitive sports?" in favor of universal rules that, for example, enjoin persons qua players to treat each other as ends rather than means, which make their relevance to sports strained at best. Examples of the latter sort of failure are virtue-based ethical theories that bypass the reflective testing of norms in favor of the practical judgments (wisdom) of knowledgeable and experienced coaches in particular situations, which weaken considerably their justificatory force. Simon thus thinks he can avoid both horns of this "dilemma of excessive abstraction from our actual situation, on the one hand, and too uncritical an immersion in it, on the other," by keeping his interpretive eyes fixed on the point of athletic enterprise and his reflective gaze fixed on the intellectual warrant of the normative principles generated in this manner.[1]

There is much to like in Simon's impressively argued account of the ethical coach, and I find myself in substantial agreement with what he has to say. But there is an important part of his argument that I do not find fully persuasive and leads me to believe that he has not solved the above dilemma by steering a middle course between "excessive abstraction" and "uncritical immersion." I am troubled by his strong claim that the intellectual force of the arguments required to justify athletic normative principles must be independent of all social or cultural features of actual athletic practices. In his admirably clear words, the "arguments and reasons" that ground these principles must have "justificatory force independent of particular historical or social contexts."[2] The problem with this claim, as I see it, is that the only principles that could clear this extraordinarily high rational bar would be too abstract, too general, too detached from our present sports practices to do the kind of substantive normative work that Simon claims they alone (or mostly alone) are capable of doing. Insisting, as Simon does, that the intellectual warrant of our normative principles of sports rises or falls on the basis of such reflective generality would not only weaken their capacity to serve as determinative guides as to how coaches and players should ethically comport themselves, but considerably weaken their motivational appeal as well, their ability to inspire the relevant parties to live up to the demands they place on them.

That aiming for principles this far removed from the social and historical contexts of sports comes at the severe cost of making them largely irrelevant to athletic practice in the above two senses is a lesson that the so-called hard cases in sports teach us. For it is these hard cases, which stretch to the breaking point the interpretive judgments and intuitions of coaches and players alike, that Simon himself concedes would likely require that we supplement his favored principles of sports with the practical judgment of wise and experienced coaches and players to determine what is or is not the normatively appropriate way to act. Simon is right that practical judgment is often needed in these tough ethical cases. But I want to argue that what is most needed when our normative predicaments require fine-grained normative judgments and responses from us is not so much the personal counsel of wise individuals but the collective counsel of the battle-tested social conventions of sports that shape, or so I will argue, so much of our understanding and appreciation of the purpose and value of competitive sports, to include the so-called practical judgment of coaches and players. It is because these kinds of conventional principles are embedded in our actual athletic practice, which, as we shall see, does not mean they are immune either from misinterpretation or willful violation, that they are able to speak to us more clearly and more forcefully than any set of abstract principles ever could.

However, it is just such conventional counsel that Simon rules out *tout court*, since on his account social conventions, whatever the kind, always bottom out in some sort of social agreement. They are no substitute, as he sees it, for moral evaluation that is based in theory, that is grounded in general principles that best explain the main features of sports and present them ethically in their best light. Conventions, it is implied, are to be evaluated in terms of such a theory and principles, and have no moral standing of their own. In short, conventions need rational support because they are not self-justifying. So from the fact that they are accepted it does not follow that they warrant our intellectual support.

The main focus of my criticism of Simon will thus take issue with this implication, more explicitly stated in his other publications, that conventions are nothing more than social agreements. I contend that Simon is simply mistaken in thinking that social conventions can be reduced to such agreements, that they simply register whatever the prevailing social consensus happens to regard as the purpose of competitive sports. On the contrary, I will argue that social conventions are what make possible rational discourse about the aim of athletic enterprise and reflective assessments of its value. That is because what counts as a good reason, a compelling intellectual consideration, in favor of conceiving competitive sports in one way rather than another, is itself a conventional matter that requires appeal to the relevant conventions without which we would be clueless as to what is the point of athletic engagement.

Interpretivism and the Ethical Coach

I want to begin, however, by considering why Simon's interpretivist rendering of competitive sports takes the abstract route that it does in seeking to validate its key normative principles. It is useful here to cite philosopher and legal theorist Ronald Dworkin's views on this matter since Simon makes it clear that his own normative approach to sports is indebted to Dworkin's normative approach to law. Dworkin thinks that normative inquiry has to reflectively distance itself from our actual social practices because, as he pithily puts it, the principles it yields are supposed to be "our critic, not our mirror." That is to say, normative principles of conduct are supposed to constrain the ways we may desire to act in law and sports to ensure our actions are indeed ethically justified, that they are in keeping with the central aims and values of these valued endeavors. They can't do this if they merely mirror what we are presently doing, if they simply endorse whatever actions we undertake regardless of their effect on the goods that law and sports trade in and the moral respect owed to the people we interact with in these social circles. As Dworkin sees it, then, normative principles "can make no contribution to how we govern ourselves except by struggling against all the impulses that drag us back into our own culture." This requires, he continues, that we make a rational move "toward generality and [therefore] some reflective basis for deciding which of our traditional distinctions [and justifications] . . . are genuine and which spurious, which contribute to the flourishing of the ideals we want." This reflective nod to generality to vindicate our normative principles, he makes abundantly clear, enjoins that we not let our interpretive judgments be influenced by social "convention[s]," since it is these very features of our cultural situation we need to struggle against with all our rational might.[3]

Simon's approach to normative inquiry differs from Dworkin's in one important respect: it claims to start on an historical note. Simon's concession to history, developed fully in his article on realism and discourse,[4] is a provisional and carefully delimited one that has mainly to do with his claim that rational discourse is a historically and culturally bound argumentative practice. Any claim then that giving and asking for reasons requires we repair to an abstract, entirely neutral vantage point is a nonstarter for Simon. Rather, we can begin the deliberative process, he insists, from where we presently find ourselves, from our current historical and social perspective, and argue our way toward a more coherent rationally defensible perspective from which to normatively assess social practices like sports. But such an historical beginning can only get us to where we need to end up, with universally valid normative principles, if and only if the deliberation that occurs in such an historical context is an impartial one through and through. By impartial deliberation Simon means both that all contributions to the discussion be viewed solely according to their intellectual merits rather than whether they support or undermine our own personal views, and that it be open to all comers. These two features of impartial inquiry go together, since if the only thing that matters in our rational deliberations is "the cogency of the argument or pertinence of the point being made," then who is making the argument is beside the point.[5] That means no one can be excluded from the conversation for any reason other than their contributions are either not cogent, or irrelevant, or, of course, both. The basic point of Simon's discourse approach to normative inquiry, therefore, is that conceptions of the point of athletic enterprise and the normative principles that can be divined from them can be considered universally valid ones if they survive this back and forth reflective testing.

On closer inspection, however, Simon's concession to history turns out not to be much of a concession at all. For the very moment conceptions of the purpose and value of sports and the corresponding reasons for favoring or disfavoring certain principles to ensure that purpose and value is realized are offered up for reflective scrutiny, all parties to the deliberations that follow, Simon holds, are supposed to evaluate them by appealing to standards that are, to reiterate, "independent of particular historical or social contexts." That means we can make quick work of the historical context in which such principles are first proposed and proceed apace to argue ourselves out of our culturally bound interpretations of athletic endeavor simply by making them answer to argumentative norms that transcend these cultural boundaries. The normative force of such back and forth discourse, therefore, rises or falls, Simon avers, on whether "it is based on principles and leads to conclusions that purport to be *something more* than a mere historical consensus."[6]

Simon's rendering of interpretivism suggests, then, that reasons or interpretations that are good and intellectually compelling presuppose some neutral, ahistorical perspective that begins with but ultimately transcends cultural practices in specific historical contexts.

On the view I will develop, however, what counts as a good interpretation of sports and a good argument to conceive and treat it in one way rather than another depends on the cultural context, on the social norms shared by particular communities of inquiry that they use to judge such things at particular times. That means that a justification as to how sports should be conceived and how coaches should ethically comport themselves in the athletic arena that works for one audience may not work, indeed may fall on deaf ears, for another audience.

Let me illustrate what I mean by contrasting two different approaches to the appropriate role of strategy in sports that found favor in two different athletic audiences. The first interpretation originated in England and spread quickly to most of Western Europe as well as the United States roughly from the latter half of the nineteenth century to the first few decades of the twentieth, when it started to lose favor. What has come to be called the gentleman-amateur conception of sports rooted the nobility of athletic competition squarely in trying to win but not too vigorously lest it taint our pursuit of athletic excellence by poisoning our social interactions with our fellow competitors. That meant that coaches of the day were obliged, among other things, to maintain a studied nonchalance toward victory merely for the sake of victory and to exhort their athletic charges to be generous toward their opponents, gallant in defeat, and humble in victory. It also meant, most importantly for our purposes, that coaches were obliged to temper their strategic designs so as not to upset the gentlemanly manner in which, at least on this particular interpretation of the point of competitive sports, it was supposed to be conducted.

This amateur-inspired constraint on the use of strategic means to achieve athletic excellence applied especially to the rules of sports, which coaches were to uphold in both letter and spirit. Coaches were supposed to dissuade players from intentionally breaking the rules and even from strategically bending the rules to gain a competitive edge. The sacrosanct regard for the rules characteristic of this amateur rendering of sports presumed that no self-respecting coach or player would ever deliberately contravene them. And what went for deliberately breaking or tinkering with the rules went as well for protesting how officials interpreted and applied them, which according to the amateur credo was strictly forbidden even if the officials were clearly mistaken in their calls. So the tactic of badgering officials for supposed bad calls in order to get a more favorable call later in the game was ethically taboo for coaches of this era.

The amateur censure of strategic manipulation of the rules extended as well to competitive tactics in the game. So strategies that involved, for example, team members setting the pace for their teammates or boxing in opponents in relay foot races and cycling to aid their fellow players were considered ethically unseemly and were criticized as a kind of "collusion" that no ethical coach rightly so called would, or should, stoop so low to employ. Similarly, efforts to "rattle one's opponents," to put them off their game, were also considered normatively out of bounds, as was exploiting vulnerable opponents even when their vulnerability was due to their own infelicitous actions, for example, running their scull aground in a race or dropping their tennis racket in a match. In such cases, players were supposed to wait for their opponents to recover before the competition resumed full-stop, and coaches were supposed to instruct them to act just so.[7] This scanting of strategy by coaches was not owed to a lack of intelligence or imagination on their part, but rather to an ethical conviction they shared that one and all such tactics were vulgar tricks. And while such tricks might have a legitimate place in the "slick" dealings of the marketplace, it was commonly surmised at the time, they ought to have no place in competitive sports, and no place, of course, in the normative repertoire of coaches.[8]

The second take on the proper role of strategy in sports played to a largely American audience, at first at least, and a very different audience at that thanks, among other things, to its growing concern that capitalism's encouragement of a life of ease and sloth was sapping the vitality of the nation, which depended, it supposed, on an active, strenuous life rather than a passive, comfortable one.[9] Social practices like competitive sports, unsurprisingly, were thought to be the right antidote for such capitalist-induced malaise, but only if pursued with utmost vigor and a committed sense of purpose. In this case, then, the uneasiness capitalist markets induced in the American sporting public regarding their cherished athletic practices, its fear it would turn them into halfhearted, lifeless endeavors, prompted it to reinterpret sports in its own distinctive image, one that directly opposed its amateur predecessors' gentlemanly take, borne of the very different worry that the mercenary motive unleashed by the market would destroy the nobility of sports. So instead of honoring the amateur precept that athletes should hold themselves back in their pursuit of athletic excellence, the devotees of this hybrid, modern conception of sports insisted such excellence should be pursued wholeheartedly, with as much effort, commitment, and passion as they could muster. As a consequence, coaches and players alike were given normative dispensation to spare no effort in their quest for athletic glory. That meant, most importantly again for our present purpose, that the amateur prohibition of strategizing lost whatever normative grip it had on this new American sporting audience, and not long after much of the Western sporting audience as well. Spurred on by this refashioned, modern conception of the aim of competitive sports, coaches began to treat sports as a kind of practical problem, indeed a recurring series of such problems, that are best, in the sense of most efficiently, resolved by exercising whatever strategic acumen they possessed.[10] In relatively short order, therefore, the reliance on strategy to win athletic contests, and the view that coaches are to be judged and compensated, in significant part, by their strategic expertise, went from being a much despised vice and a normatively loathsome way to regard sports to a much admired virtue and normatively respectable way to regard it.

This newfound respect for strenuous engagement in sports thus opened the floodgate for all manner of tactical thinking beginning with the rules themselves. Rules, of course, were not to be summarily violated under this new normative athletic regime, not just because such indiscriminate rule breaking and rule bending is hardly strategic, but because complying with the rules still enjoyed substantial normative support. But the rules were no longer regarded as sacrosanct, as directives to be strictly followed no matter the circumstance. Rather, they became fair game for strategic exploitation at certain points in an athletic contest. The strategic foul in basketball is a case in point, in which the point of breaking the rules, for example, deliberately fouling an opponent who is about to make an easy layup, is to gain a competitive advantage precisely by being penalized, by putting one's opponent at the foul line to attempt to make free throws that are, comparatively speaking, more challenging.

The normative license given strategic fouling on this modern take on sports, of course, was only part of the general normative license extended to other similar tactics in the game. For starters, the old, ethically frowned upon strategy of teammates collaborating with one another to improve their chances of winning by setting the pace in a footrace or thwarting one's opponents from gaining the lead in a cycling competition by boxing them in was no longer considered an example of illicit "collusion." On the contrary, it came to be seen as good athletic form rather than bad sportsmanship, as an example of precisely the sort of rational—in the sense of instrumentally rational that informs all such strategic thinking (divining the most efficient means to achieve predetermined ends)—winning play expected of the contemporary coach and athlete. The same rational compliment was to be paid as well, on this interpretation, to athletes who take tactical advantage of their opponents when they find themselves in vulnerable positions by virtue of their own, however unintentional, maladroit actions (recall my previous example of the sculler who inadvertently runs his scull aground). Being generous to one's competitors in such cases so that they can regain their competitive footing now seemed an offense against, rather than an example of, good athletic play, since such self-inflicted athletic misfortunes were reinterpreted as basic strategic lapses—actions that had the athletes adequately planned for they might well have anticipated and avoided. Letting opponents recover when they fall prey to such strategic gaffs on this new, strategy-friendly conception of sports no longer made any sense, rationally or normatively speaking.

What are we take away from these two strikingly different understandings of the normative status of strategy in sports from these two strikingly different athletic audiences? Well, several things, I think. The first is that there are apparently no super purposes when it comes to cultural practices like sports: there are no fixed purposes of athletic endeavor that remain unchanged across history just waiting to be discovered by those with the fortitude to push rational inquiry to the limit. Rather, as our brief foray into sports history shows, the purpose of competitive sports changes as we human agents ourselves change for many varying and complicated reasons and causes. Although both athletic audiences were motivated by the same desire to prevent sports from being overtaken by the market, because they ascribed markedly different purposes to their respective conceptions of sports, and, therefore, to their accounts of the ethical coach, their worries about the corrosive effects of the market were markedly different as well. The differing ways they construed the aim of competitive sports further changed the way they valued sports, to include, importantly, what specific mix of skills they considered integral to genuine athletic achievement. To say that sports serves a specific purpose is to say that certain ways of engaging in it better serve that purpose than others, and thus warrant our normative seal of approval, and other ways of engaging in it either serve it poorly, or not at all, and thus warrant our normative condemnation. This is, of course, why the amateur athletic community reproached coaches who dared to indulge their strategic fancies, since tactical skills were neither recognized nor valued as bona fide athletic skills, and why the modern athletic community that eventually replaced it lauded these very same coaching strategies, since these tactical skills were now recognized and valued as an important feature of true athletic excellence.

A second important moral to be drawn from these two cases is that changes in the conception of the point of athletic enterprise signal a corresponding change in the relevant community's normative vocabulary, specifically, in the evaluative standards, reasons, and thick moral and nonmoral concepts they employ to justify their normative judgments to one another by arguing for their rational cogency. The argumentative process of giving and asking for reasons presupposes that everyone so engaged is on the same page as to what qualifies as a reason in the first place, that, in other words, all parties to the discourse are of one mind regarding the relevant norms that govern such rational exchanges. It would, of course, be ideal if such a normative accord could be somehow stretched to encompass all past and present communities of inquiry and all future communities to come, but as our two examples show, I think, aiming for such universality in our rational judgments about sports, or anything else for that matter, is wishful thinking at best.[11] The reason why is, as Simon himself noted and I approvingly cited, that rational discourse is a culturally and historically bound affair, which means we can only profitably argue about our normative views of sports if we concur on what makes for a good as opposed to a bad argument. What history tells us is that such concurrence is attainable only within a community of inquiry, only within its operative normative vocabulary, which validates certain rational moves and invalidates others regarding proper coaching and player conduct.

But that rational discourse can do its appointed critical work only if it is moved to the interior of normative vocabularies is no reason to despair. For once this move is made we can argue with one another at length and in the requisite impartial manner regarding our reasons for favoring certain views of sports and disfavoring others. Impartiality of this intramural sort means just what Simon claimed it meant: that all contributions to the discourse be considered exclusively on their intellectual merits rather than whether they accord or not with our own considered views, and that it be open to all comers. But the notions of "intellectual merit" and "all comers" need to be suitably qualified to cover only those who share the social norms of rational inquiry of the particular athletic audience in question. Those who don't share these social norms can hardly expect their contributions to the discourse to achieve their intended rational purpose, since the reasons they put on offer will not be recognized as such by members of the relevant community because they have no place in their normative vocabulary. That is, their contributions will be appropriately dismissed not on the illegitimate grounds of who they are, but on the perfectly legitimate grounds that their contributions are not rationally cogent by present lights. So if we were to imagine a debate between devotees of amateur sports, who stoutly maintain that strategy has no legitimate standing in sports rightly so called because it undermines the kind of gentlemanly social interactions that should obtain there, and members of a modern athletic audience of a different cast of mind, who regard strategy to be pivotal to athletic excellence, what we would witness is not, I think, a fruitful give-and-take of reasons but, at best, rival disputants unprofitably talking past one another rather than profitably to one another.[12] Asking for a rational resolution to encounters of this kind, as I see it, is asking far too much because there doesn't seem to be any inferential path that leads from an amateur conception of sports to the modern one here discussed. That is, there is no apparent way rationally to get from an amateur conception of sports as a gentlemanly, strategic-averse pursuit to a modern, pedal-to-the-metal, strategic-receptive one if the argument begins with premises formulated in the old amateur vocabulary, nor, of course, is there a way to rationally pull this off the other way around. Indeed, the only way a debate of this kind could lead to a rationally persuasive outcome is if all the deliberative parties could repair to a third, neutral normative vocabulary in which to adjudicate their conflicting claims. But, of course, it is just such a leap from what I earlier called intramural impartiality to what I now want to call extramural impartiality, to the infamous view from nowhere, that I believe Simon and perhaps other interpretivists would rightly to my mind dismiss as little more than a rational fantasy.

The third, and for my purposes, last moral to be drawn from these historically contrasting interpretations of the aim of athletic endeavor is, in fact, a corollary of the other two. And that is that the principles that serve as the presuppositions of our normative inquiry into sports, as the basic premises of the arguments we formulate to justify our normative judgments to one another, are social conventions that do their justificatory work in a context-dependent manner as opposed to abstract principles that supposedly do their work in a context-independent manner.

What this means is that the idea that sports is best thought of as a gentlemanly engagement is itself a conventional idea, that is, an interpretation of the purpose of competitive sports that, again for various complicated reasons and causes, originated in and found favor with members of the amateur athletic community, and from which they derived their central normative principles regarding appropriate ethical conduct for coaches and players alike. As we have seen in the case of the ethical coach, that conventional take on sports led to the normative directive that coaches refrain from any tactical attempt to manipulate the rules or their opponents. So the key arguments amateurs of the time mounted to defend their claim that strategizing of this sort was not a legitimate part of the game, that it fell outside the relevant skills that are supposed to be tested in athletic competition, can be traced back directly to their reigning convention that sports warrants our normative approval if, and only if, pursued in moderation. Of course, the contrasting modern idea that sports is best thought of as a strenuous engagement through and through, one that calls for our full commitment and unsparing effort, which as we noted opened the door and gave wide berth to coaches and players alike to exercise their strategic wiles, is also a conventional idea, as are the main arguments its proponents mounted to defend the robust role they thought strategy should play in competitive sports.

The notion that our best interpretations of sports and the normative principles and arguments we formulate on their behalf are conventions is what makes interpretivists like Simon nervous because they view the social agreements that underwrite such conventions as a threat to rational argument itself. If our normative standards amount to nothing more than conventions, then claims such as the cited amateur one that coaches should shun strategizing because it corrupts sports, or its modern successor that coaches should welcome strategizing because it enriches sports, have nothing going for them save that different athletic audiences find them variously attractive or unattractive. What goes importantly missing in such cases is whether or not the claims made are rationally defensible, that is, to paraphrase Simon, whether we agree to them because we find them intellectually meritorious or find them intellectually meritorious because we agree to them. If the former, then our normative principles, to recall Dworkin's point, rightly serve as our "critic"; however, if the latter, then our normative principles wrongly serve as our "mirror." This is no minor point since everything turns on whether or not they maintain their critical edge. For if our normative principles simply rubber-stamp whatever it is we do in the athletic arena, then they have not just served us poorly but have utterly failed us. It is easy to see why because in that event "the status quo [would be] right . . . just [because] it is the status quo, not [because] it is supported by defensible reasons."[13] In other words, it would mean that an athletic audience could never be wrong about its normative judgments as to what is or is not appropriate athletic conduct, because what counts as a correct normative judgment on this conventional rendering is whatever the relevant athletic audience says it is.[14]

Simon's concern that normative inquiry not be coopted by the status quo is a legitimate worry. But his claim that a conventional take on normative inquiry of the kind I am endorsing here cannot but lead to such an uncritical result is, I think, mistaken. For as I have already noted rational discourse is itself a social practice, one that can only do its intellectual bidding if the deliberative parties are of one mind regarding what are the relevant rules of argument. And what I have been arguing is that the sort of social agreements that underlie our conventional interpretations of what is the purpose and value of competitive sports, and that ground the rational standards by which we assess their cogency as applied, for instance, to ethical coaching, are what allow argument and the crucial self-correcting role it plays to do its critical work.[15] So conventions rightly understood are not an excuse for us to take leave of giving and asking for reasons in favor of crudely tallying people's preferences, but what makes possible such giving and asking for reasons in the first place.

Implications for Coaches

If we give up on the idea that we can somehow turn conventional normative principles into unconventional, universal ones by waiving our rational wand, are we not conceding, just as critics of conventionalism like Simon have repeatedly pointed out, that they lack any critical force? For if rational deliberation is powerless to effect such a change in our conventions, then, as noted, whatever an athletic community says is the aim of athletic enterprise must be right, can't be corrected, because all we have to go on, apparently, is its collective word.

Not so, I counter, with one important qualification: while conventionalism, at least the kind I am peddling, doesn't nullify the all-important self-correcting role that rational discourse alone can play, it does nullify what I take to be the more radical and untenable version of this claim that would have us believe that an *entire* athletic audience could be mistaken, and rationally shown to be so, about its conventional understanding of sports. For my conventionalist account does entail, unlike Simon's ahistorical alternative, that we can't meaningfully distinguish between what such a community thinks is the purpose of competitive sports and the ethical conduct that comports with it, and what it *really* is. That might seem like a knock against it, but I think otherwise because the claim that a whole community might be wrong about the point of its athletic enterprises strikes me as implausible on its face given that cultural practices like sports are social rather than natural kinds. That is, the purpose of sports is not something we discover but something we create, and since we, the relevant athletic community, are the creators, it's hard to see how we could be wholly wrong about what we have created. However, we can be, and often are, wrong about what inferences we draw from the premises formulated in our conventional normative vocabulary. For instance, we might come to see by the arguments we trade back and forth with the aid of that vocabulary that the premises of our arguments commit us to conclusions we have not previously drawn, in other words, that we have erred in our inferential judgments and are thereby compelled to accept these new conclusions and drop the old ones. This is quite enough, to my mind, to vouch for the critical credentials of conventionalist accounts like mine, in which the force of the better argument, rather than the sum of the audience members' preferences, serves as the final arbiter of their considered views.

I only have space to offer one example of such an inferential error to buttress my claim that conventional normative principles are not lacking in critical potency. That example has to do with the mix of tactics that fall under the umbrella of so-called gamesmanship, which has been gaining traction of late in certain athletic quarters, and in which its defenders seem to think that its normative legitimacy derives from that accorded to strategizing in general on the modern interpretation of sports. Gamesmanship can take many different forms, but the particular form I want to discuss involves what Howe aptly calls the "artful manipulation of the rules," in which coaches attempt to exploit the technicalities of the rules in order to gain a competitive advantage.[16] Perhaps the most famous (or infamous) case of such gamesmanship was the so-called pine tar incident in which Kansas City Royals baseball player George Brett's winning home run was disallowed because the pine tar on his bat exceeded that allowed by the rules.[17] What distinguished this case from other familiar examples of called rule violations is that Brett's indiscretion would have gone unnoticed, and so uncalled, were it not for the fact that Billy Martin, manager of the opposing New York Yankees, brought it to the head umpire's attention the moment Brett crossed home plate. Now, that Martin acted as he did by informing the chief umpire of the rule violation is, in itself, of no moment, since knowing the rules of baseball inside and out and pointing out when they are broken to game authorities is something we rightly expect of good coaches. What is of moment, however, and what makes this a case of gamesmanship rather than simple managerial acumen, is that Martin had noticed much earlier in the season that Brett's bat had an excess of pine tar on it but decided to wait for the most advantageous opportunity to disclose this information to the umpires. The ruse worked at first, since after being so informed, and after a brief deliberation, the umpires called Brett out for using an illegal bat. But it ultimately failed because when the Royals appealed the ruling to the president of the American League, Lee MacPhail, he overturned the umpires' decision.

MacPhail reasoned that although Brett was technically in violation of the rules, he gained no competitive advantage by his overuse of pine tar, as he clearly would have, for instance, if he had resorted instead to using a corked bat. In other words, MacPhail was saying that strictly applying the rule in this instance interfered with, rather than abetted, the purpose of competitive sports. By implication, he was also saying that Martin's exercise of managerial cunning in choosing at that opportune moment to inform the umpires of Brett's doctored bat also interfered with the aim of sports, because it was that tactical decision that provoked the umpires to rule in the wrong way, and thus to deprive Brett of his rightful athletic accomplishment. MacPhail's reasoning here is crucial to seeing why Martin and his defenders erred in thinking that the normative pass given managerial tactics like the strategic foul on this modern rendering of sports warrants giving the same normative pass to managerial tactics like the artful manipulation of the rules specific to gamesmanship.

That the umpires in the Brett case, in my view, got this wrong and MacPhail got it right, and that other members of the modern athletic community might be similarly divided in their judgments about this and like cases, shows, I argue, that conventional normative principles do indeed have critical force, that they not only make possible but require that we argue about what inferences properly follow from the premises they lay down, that like any other norms they can only do their work if the self-correcting role of rational argument is given its just due.

I'd like to think that if the umpires had the time to reflectively reconsider their initial judgments after the fact, and that if members of the modern athletic audience who were initially inclined to lump Martin's gamesmanship together with tactics like the strategic foul were to do the same, that MacPhail's argument would carry the day.[18] Of course, I may be wrong about this, and, in any event, have no way of knowing what the outcome of such an argument might be without joining in the argument itself—something I have been taking an initial stab at here. But trying to predict how this argument might turn out is beside the point. The moral of this story is that, contrary to critics of conventionalism, like all good normative theories, this theory not only sets us to arguing about what is the appropriate aim of competitive sports but, by spelling out what are the relevant rules of argument in this regard, makes it further possible for us to give a rationally persuasive answer to this all-important question. Thus, one can argue, on the basis of the reflective form of conventionalism that I have defended, that there are important limits to the kind of gamesmanship that coaches can employ that are morally defensible without being ahistorical, and that are rationally supportable without the sort of context-independent philosophical theory required by interpretivism.

Conclusion

To sum up, then, I think Simon is entirely right that ethical decision making is an indispensable dimension of "good" coaching, and that the normative theory he calls interpretivism is, if tweaked in the conventionalist way I suggest here, the best account of how ethical coaches should form their ethical judgments and justify them to others. My only disagreement with Simon, therefore, is his insistence that normative inquiry be carried out until we can certify that the principles that ground coaches' ethical determinations of how they should comport themselves are universally valid ones, which requires, of course, that the conventional starting points of such inquiry be somehow reflectively circumvented. I remain unconvinced that any normative probing of sports or for that matter any other kindred cultural practice can pull off this seemingly magical transition from the historical and contingent to the universal and necessary. That is why I maintain that trying to turn what are essentially conventional athletic normative principles into nonconventional ones is not a surefire way to establish their validity, but rather a surefire way to undermine their critical force and relevance. Coaches, then, should develop their ethical views by critically understanding, probing, and reflecting on the cultural traditions and practices in which they are embedded, which is not an argument for the status quo but for reforming it when such critical examination reveals that the status quo itself violates the conventions that underpin these traditions and practices.

Questions for Review and Discussion

1. Distinguish between Simon's version of broad internalism (interpretivism) and the author's conventionalist version. Now, contrast the author's conventionalist rendering of interpretivism with Kantian and virtue approaches to coaching ethics.

2. Explain why conventionalism of the kind the author develops here still qualifies as a critical theory, that is, as a theory that can be used to criticize dominant views of sports. Do you agree it is a critical theory, or do you think it is far more supportive of the status quo than it intimates?

3. The author distinguishes between intramural and extramural notions of impartiality. Explain the importance of this distinction in justifying coaches' ethical views. Is the distinction valid in your view?

4. Is the author's argument persuasive that the modern view of strategy does not justify tactics like gamesmanship? Or can you think of a way to justify gamesmanship based on the modern understanding of the strategic foul?

5. Is the author correct to argue that proponents of the amateur model of competition and proponents of the contemporary strategic/competitive model must inevitably talk past each other and never engage intellectually because they speak from different cultural and historical contexts? (See note 12 as well as discussion in the text.) Could Simon reply that we can't

know in advance of trying whether they could reach a rationally defensible consensus and cite a sport such as professional golf that blends competitive intensity with courtesy and even generosity toward opponents as an example of a reasonable compromise between both ideals?

Suggestions for Further Reading

Berman, Michael. "On Interpretivism and Formalism in Sports Officiating: From General to Particular Jurisprudence." *Journal of the Philosophy of Sport* 38 (2011).

Dixon, Nicholas. "Canadian Figure Skaters, French Judges, and Realism in Sport." *Journal of the Philosophy of Sport* 8 (2003).

Rader, Benjamin. *American Sports: From the Age of Folk Games to the Age of Televised Sports.* Upper Saddle River, NJ: Prentice-Hall, 2004.

Simon, Robert. "From Ethnocentrism to Realism: Can Discourse Ethics Bridge the Gap?" *Journal of the Philosophy of Sport* 31 (2004): 122–141.

Weatherby, W. J. *Chariots of Fire.* New York: Dell, 1981.

Six

Why the Coach Needs a Philosophy: A Pragmatist's Suggestions

DOUG HOCHSTETLER

You never arrive.
Take care of the little things.

More than twenty years removed from my intercollegiate football playing days, these words continue to resonate. I remember these comments and, more importantly, have attempted to embody these bits of wisdom in my life as I teach, write, and raise a family. These words are connected with a specific location, specific individual, and specific team. I heard them in Orange City, Iowa, as a member of a Northwestern College football team coached by Larry Korver. It is possible that I would have learned these lessons in a different setting (through music, the arts, or some other extracurricular activity), but this experience occurred because of my commitment to *this particular* football team. As a result, and coupled with my own attitude of openness, I grew as an athlete, scholar, and individual. I learned a great deal during this formative time of my life, playing wide receiver—how to explode from the line of scrimmage, run crisp pass patterns, and catch the football with my hands rather than my chest. I also learned lessons that extended past the football field, lessons about preparation, dedication, selflessness, and more. My experience occurred, in part, as a result of an individual philosophy of coaching—the ideas and beliefs embodied in Coach Korver's approach to his profession.

Developing a personalized set of beliefs and values is an important task for coaches, a step acknowledged by those in the sport-related professions.[1] Some recommend formalizing a personal coaching philosophy.[2] David Parsh, for example, outlines "Eight Steps to a Coaching Philosophy," posing questions[3] for coaches that prompt critical thinking and reflection. Helpful as these attempts are, the process of developing a coaching philosophy does not guarantee that the coach will actually live out the identified beliefs in practice. A coach may preach team discipline, for example, while failing personally to live in a disciplined manner. An additional concern, one more central to this chapter, is the tendency for coaches to develop a philosophy with an overly rigid approach—what Dweck terms a fixed mind-set—a belief system that is dogmatic and unyielding to change.[4]

These concerns point toward themes that American philosopher Henry Bugbee examined regarding the idea of certainty.[5] In addition to the technical decision making that coaches face regarding substitution patterns, styles of play, and training methods, coaching involves complex interpersonal relationships. As Hardman and Jones explain, "Coaches work with persons, not machines."[6] Given the difficulty and uncertainty characteristic of coaching, and the tenuous process of developing and living out an examined philosophy, how do coaches know the ideals they have chosen are the right ones, or are effective? Is certainty a state that coaches should necessarily strive for or attain? This certainty extends from the abstract, theoretical commitments to the day-to-day ways coaches live out these ideals as well. For example, to what extent does certainty relate to calling a play, inserting a particular player into the lineup, moving from man defense to zone, switching from primarily long-distance training to training with interval emphasis, and so forth?

In this chapter I will introduce Bugbee's writing and approach to philosophy, examine his notion of certainty, and describe the import for this reframed notion of certainty for coaching philosophies. I have in mind not merely any coaching philosophy and its implementation, but a normative sense of what it means for "good coaches" to develop and implement such a system. Here, following Loland, I am interested in how the good coach combines scientific or technical knowledge with the "practical search for reflective and good choices in the many dilemmas of his or her profession in split decision situations, [which requires] morally sound intuitions and reaction patterns."[7] The capability to negotiate these decisions requires a type of practical wisdom developed through what Standal and Hemmestad describe as the "right experience . . . [through becoming] good by doing good deeds . . . and this in turn is dependent on being in the presence of good role models."[8] Here

Bugbee provides assistance for developing a personal philosophy based on both personal experience and practical wisdom.

Coaching and Philosophy

The relationship between coaching and philosophy may not be readily apparent. Yet, as Walton explains, "To coach is to believe in something: the game, the athlete, the quest for excellence, the process of challenging one's self and striving to overcome."[9] Coaches, like philosophers, intentionally work toward clarifying ideas and beliefs. Although they do not engage in formal philosophical study, coaches deal with theoretical concepts such as justice, equality, and benevolence every day. For example, how might a coach distribute playing time between two athletes, one (a starter with stellar ability) who does not practice during the week because of a chronic hamstring injury and another athlete (one with limited talent) who remains committed to daily practices and workouts? How might a youth sport coach address this situation versus a high school or college coach? Additionally, how might the coach deal with a slumping player? Does the athlete's performance (or lack of it) justify an immediate reduction in playing time? Or does the coach stick with the slumping player in order to demonstrate confidence in a player who has a history of performing well?

When I refer to a coaching philosophy, I mean, borrowing from Lyle, "a comprehensive statement about the beliefs and behaviors that will characterize the coach's practice."[10] This collection of ideals may have philosophical underpinnings, such as a commitment to humanism, equality, fair play, or cooperation. Coaching philosophies have value in that they guide coaching actions and relationships, provide focus and clarity, and enable coaches to communicate their ideas and rationale to athletes, parents, and alumni. In many ways constructing and implementing a coaching philosophy involves the classical notion of *technē*.[11] Individual coaches identify a set of beliefs, guidelines, and practices that they believe will work. They are confident of these methods but not absolutely sure they will be successful. Many coaches copy philosophies from other coaches or modify them to mesh with a particular group of student athletes. At times they are representative of the broader coaching culture, while on other occasions they may be more idiosyncratic.[12]

As an example of specific coaching principles, former college basketball coach and athletic director Harry Sheehy[13] detailed the value he placed on work ethic. More than an abstract notion, this idea guided his approach to coaching basketball and included team selection. Sheehy described a potential team member, a player with limited ability who worked "endlessly" and "had a ball with him all the time." Because of the value Sheehy placed on work ethic, he took a risk and selected the student athlete for his team. This player eventually captained an NCAA Division III Sweet Sixteen team, confirming Sheehy's decision and underscoring the value of work ethic in his coaching philosophy.

All coaches employ a coaching philosophy, even though some may not articulate what ideals drive their decision making. Coaches demonstrate an implicit set of values even if their beliefs are not made explicit. A coach who contends that he does not rely on any general principles—for example, choosing to "wing it"—demonstrates a tendency toward contextualism. This coach makes decisions on a case-by-case basis, which is a particular kind of philosophical approach. Alternatively, deciding to shun the use of general principles may reflect skepticism, another type of philosophical position. The more central concern in these cases is, then, how to evaluate the type of philosophical approaches coaches construct and employ.

Developing this philosophical method—toward the sport, the athletes, and other individuals—requires the approach of a scientist and an artist. Coaches learn about the technical side of coaching in formal settings (through coaching education programs, through apprentice-like positions as assistants), acquiring the wisdom of the coaching community. This might include acquiring coaching education research related to pedagogy, training principles, or athlete coach relationships. Yet coaches must find a way to integrate these conceptual notions as they work with and mold specific teams and individuals This process involves using theoretical knowledge in an applied manner—using pedagogical principles, for example, to teach budding basketball players how to shoot or defend; or leadership concepts to guide team captains toward ideals such as courage or selflessness. Following the development process, the coach must fully implement the philosophy, not simply stating the ideas and beliefs but actually translating these ideals into how one interacts with athletes, other coaches, officials, fans, and the media.

Coaches face tension over telling athletes how to live or letting them learn how to live on their own. Working with eighteen- to twenty-two-year-olds, for example, college coaches arguably should try to prepare athletes to make decisions autonomously, using critical thinking skills to bring this about. The athletes are growing toward adulthood, and the coach will not always be present to hand out praise or punishment. Even at the youth sport level, coaches should allow athletes to help in the decision-making process, guiding them along the way toward a developing personal agency. Part of the creative nature of incorporating a coaching philosophy is determining how to apply the theoretical concepts in practice.

Additionally, the construction of a coaching philosophy is both an individual and a communal process. An individual coach must own the beliefs and has ultimate authority in its authoring, even as the coach may consult other more experienced coaches for ideas, or glean from other coaching philosophies. The coach develops his own belief system, often drawing heavily from personal experience, for good and, at times, for ill. If, as an athlete, the coach played for a disciplinarian, then the younger coach may be more inclined to implement a similar coaching style. Likewise, a coach who spent time as a benchwarmer may develop ways to help all team members feel empowered and valued.

While coaches construct their philosophical ideals individually, this process often occurs against a communal backdrop such as an athletic department, institution, and athletic conference. For example, institutions may hire coaches with philosophical ideals consistent with an overall athletic department belief system. The coach develops these beliefs within the context of a particular sport ethos and practice. A youth soccer coach may construct a philosophy different from a collegiate soccer coach whose philosophy may be different yet from one constructed by a Premier League coach. Yet all three philosophies may contain common threads, given the nature of soccer and the wisdom found in literature of the coaching profession.

Coaches are not interested in merely theoretical ideas. They may love to discuss the intricacies of the triangle offense or particular motivational strategies, but they are much more concerned with how these ideas work. Division I coaches, for example, do not receive contract extensions based on their philosophical ideals but on how their teams perform, meaning how many wins or championships they attain; or, more recently, how many student athletes graduate from their programs. Coaches generally only philosophize in terms of the cash value. They want to see results and effectiveness, regardless of how this is quantified or valued.

Coaches strive for certainty and being absolutely confident in team selection, play calling, practice planning, and goal creation. Yes, there may be times of doubt or regret, times when they wish they had made different decisions. But when the moment of decision making appears, any hint of indecision appears, generally speaking, as weakness. Proceeding with certainty provides direction and projects confidence. Athletes do not want to follow or listen to coaches who project uncertainty. Granted, there may be occasions when a coach's uncertainty is viewed with respect, for example, in regard to situational play-calling. The coach may solicit input and place the ultimate decision-making responsibility with the athletes, in other words placing certainty in soliciting player input. Former Los Angeles Lakers coach Phil Jackson was especially noted for allowing his players to make decisions in particular situations. While this may have worked for Jackson, on occasion, it, like so many coaching decisions, depends on the relationship between coach and athletes. In these situations the coach becomes vulnerable and has to trust the players.

What kind of balance should coaches seek with regard to certainty? How does a conviction to act impact coaches, their philosophies, and ultimately how they interact with their athletes? Part of this depends on what we mean by certainty and how this concept is applied. Bugbee wrote at length about certainty, the import of which impacts sport and coaching in meaningful ways.

Bugbee and Certainty

Henry Bugbee (1915–1999) is an important part of the American philosophical tradition, following on the heels of Ralph Waldo Emerson, Henry David Thoreau, William James, and John Dewey. Bugbee's work is not intentionally instrumental and yet his writings contain themes at the heart of this philosophical creation process for coaches. To understand Bugbee, it is important to examine the philosophical conversation to which he belongs. As an American pragmatist, Bugbee reacted to themes found in earlier theories of knowledge known as rationalism and pragmatism. Rationalist philosophers such as René Descartes argued that knowledge grew out of foundational beliefs that were certain, impossible to doubt, and grounded in reason. Empiricists such as John Locke and David Hume argued instead that knowledge was founded on the senses, but viewed basic sense experience as foundational and certain. Rationalists and empiricists alike, then, maintained that knowledge was established on a foundation and regarded proof based on the foundation as the source of knowledge. Some later foundationalists relinquished the requirement of certainty but still maintained that knowledge rests on base beliefs that are fundamental compared to those derived from them.

Pragmatists developed an alternative approach that rejects foundationalism but also attempts to avoid skepticism and relativism. What they hoped to move toward instead is warranted assertibility, evidential support that is less than certain. In other words, the pragmatists emphasized that a specific position is or at least should be regarded as correct and true until something better is found. Closely related to pragmatism, writers such as Thoreau and Emerson represented transcendentalism, which advocated for a sense of self-reliance and self-awakening. These writers believed that some form of the "good life" (including knowledge) was available to those who remained alert to both self and nature.

Bugbee drew heavily from both pragmatists and transcendentalists, but refused to be defined by either philosophical tradition. He describes his mode of inquiry as "experiential," carving out a position for philosophical discovery that is not "a disclosure of the nature of objects."[14] Rather, Bugbee places more emphasis on the transactional relationships between humans and their environments. For example, both Bugbee and John Dewey emphasize the importance of aesthetic experiences—moments when our senses become heightened and are etched in memory. While Bugbee advocates for this meaning-seeking kind of life, he did not believe Dewey's scientific method or technical explanations generated this meaning by itself. The meaningful life, Bugbee argues, is not derived at entirely through scientific deduction or method, but also through direct contact with things and built on relationships. Bugbee advocates for a "felt clarity" rather than a strict reliance on "analytical clarity."[15] In this sense Bugbee runs alongside the transcendentalism of Thoreau with a premium placed on attentiveness.

Bugbee's approach toward philosophy related directly to personal experience, sifting through streams of consciousness as they appeared to him beside the Schuylkill River or Canadian Rockies. He advocates for attention to these wilderness experiences, especially noting their aesthetic qualities. His experiential approach began not with formal hypotheses or rigid formulas, nor did it necessarily entail any logical schema. Rather, Bugbee's method involves the very situation at hand and the themes that develop through the course of his immersion experiences. He then develops these ideas through the course of his journals and other academic writing.

Certainty became a prominent topic for Bugbee and runs throughout his writings. Rather than seeking a foundational version of ultimate certainty, however, Bugbee aimed to reclaim the concept in another manner. He writes that "certainty lies at the root of action that makes sense . . . a basis for action rather than arrival at a terminus of endeavor."[16] Certainty, for Bugbee, is the starting point, a place to begin, a place that acknowledges an aspect of fallibilism yet proceeds with hope. In this sense the theme of certainty aligned with a pragmatic notion of warranted assertability. Anderson describes Bugbee's certainty as a "working certainty" rather than a final and closed version.[17] Again, Bugbee writes that "certainty is profoundly resolute, but I would mark it out in diametrical contrast with complacency or being of a closed mind."[18] This notion of certainty helps inform our understanding of coaching and decision making, especially the point about open-mindedness.

In the same way, a coach's philosophy does not need to be dogmatic and may be written in pencil, so to speak. The coach must start somewhere, a particular point in time and space with a particular experience as a backdrop. With this working certainty the coach takes into consideration past experience and the present circumstances in order to reach the felt clarity. To do so the coach must listen to "things [or in our case, players] saying themselves" as Bugbee notes.[19] Coaches, then, are certain to the extent that this mind-set enables them to make decisions, identify beliefs, plan practices, recognize recruits, discern plays, and so forth. This type of certainty does not restrict reflection or dialogue. At times coaches may realize they have made a poor decision but use this as an opportunity for growth. In this way certainty becomes a continual testing ground, placing the felt clarity alongside personal experience to see what works in the real world. Bugbee continually verified his experiential intimations, and good coaching requires a similar confirmation of sport-related intuition.

Finally, this working certainty does not entail any "having" or "possessing." Bugbee writes, "I seriously doubt if the notion of 'certainty of,' or 'certainty that' will take us accurately to the heart of the matter. It seems to me that certainty is at least very much akin to hope and faith."[20] In this way, Bugbee reframes the concept in a surprising way, aligning certainty with the seemingly uncertain concepts of hope and faith. His point is that in order to act—for the philosopher, theologian, or coach—one must have a starting point and belief that the actions are pointing somewhere and make a difference. Bugbee continues that certainty is "not a matter of knowledge we can be said to *possess*" and instead is "a mode of being rather than of having."[21] He places great emphasis on relationships and the interchanges between people, between individuals and nature. As coaches relate to and with their athletes, for example, they learn about themselves, lessons of patience, dedication, love, and sacrifice through their commitment to the coaching profession.

Bugbee, Knowledge, and Truth

Bugbee's theory of knowledge and truth draws from both transcendental and pragmatic veins of thought. He argues for attention to both self and others, an alertness to intimations through reflection and commitment. Bugbee also recognizes that these intimations potentially lead toward growth: "That which illuminates our labors, in reflection as in other channels of endeavor, that which decisively empowers us in the deed, comes as an unanticipated precipitation of meaning."[22] By acting in concert with nature we acquire meaning and understanding in ways that we would not be able to fully predict, rationalize, or explain. Yet Bugbee wants us to trust these intimations, even as we test them out in the course of our lives. Arriving at meaning or knowledge does not mean avoiding rational thought but is rather an extension, enhancing how we interpret nature and understand our place in the world.

The attentive coach develops an awareness that provides knowledge and guidance in many ways. This awareness enables coaches to develop a feel for how their athletes are performing, which can inform substitution patterns and tactical methods. In terms of decision making, this alertness enables the coach to call a particular play as it comes to mind, one that fits the particulars of the situation, or mindfulness that impacts how one deals with disciplinary or relational issues. In addition, an attentiveness to team dynamics provides the coach with necessary information to develop team rules of conduct. At times the coach may decide to take more leadership in determining these guidelines, while on other occasions he may solicit more team input. For example, a team with seasoned veterans could benefit from this athlete wisdom, while a younger team, with unproven leadership, may benefit from the coach providing more of the input.

Bugbee goes on to write that philosophy is not "set up like the solution of a puzzle, worked out with all the pieces lying there before the eye. It will be more like the clarification of what we know in our bones."[23] Constructing a belief system, in other words, is not a predetermined, totally logical method of attaining certainty but rather an ongoing confirmation through experience. In this sense, experience impacts knowledge. From experiences interacting with others, coaches know, if they are attentive, how people act and react. Coaches understand how individual athletes respond to discipline, to encouragement, to direction—and that each athlete may respond in different ways throughout their respective career. In addition, coaches also recognize their own particular style, forming judgments about the methods and goals that seem to fit. Hopefully, coaches have the individual athletes' and team's best interests in mind, although at times the coach's ego may get in the way.[24]

The knowledge Bugbee has in mind, while challenging to describe, is not ineffable. Bugbee hopes to describe the everyday places and experiences that give rise to this kind of meaning. In this sense Bugbee is democratic in his appreciation for human experience to shape knowledge. He uses narratives as a method to understand the process of acquiring knowledge and meaning, detailing his experiences swamping, building a dam, and rowing. In the same way, we need to recognize and acknowledge the ordinary experiences that coaches undergo, experiences that have a bearing on the way these individuals develop, interpret, change, and understand their coaching philosophies. As an example of the import for coaches, Bugbee writes of his time spent rowing under the tutelage of Coach John Schultz. In Bugbee's words, Schultz was "interested in rowing wherever it was being done. . . . There was never any doubt about John's absorption in any rowing."[25] Bugbee's experience rowing for Schultz impacted Bugbee in terms of knowledge—not only in a physiological manner but also as a means to grow in his writing and philosophical thinking.

Bugbee is not renouncing deductive logic, critical thinking, or the scientific method. Trained as a philosopher, he realizes the value of the philosophic method and the analytical approach. His point is that the analytical approach is not the only method at our disposal, nor is it necessarily the best one. Bugbee points toward other means: "I want the truth, marrow-bone truth, and I find the intimations of it whenever I am alive to things, even the most familiar and commonplace things, for the wilderness I take them to comprise."[26] Knowledge, then, requires getting close to, or immersed in, our everyday milieu as opposed to merely observing our surroundings from some theoretical and detached point of view. For coaches this means through attentiveness to practice and game settings, with athletes, colleagues, parents, and alumni, an immersion and commitment to the coaching profession.

Anderson, writing of Bugbee's sense of knowledge, says we "live in wilderness with things, and their residual wildness both demands our respect and attention and resists any complete 'knowing' on our part."[27] In a similar way coaches live in and with their athletes, their assistants, and the public. To coach well demands an attentiveness to and respect for these various groups and individuals. However, the coach cannot, now matter how much she tries, know her athletes in totality regardless of this attentiveness. As Bugbee clarifies, "Things exist in their own right; it is a lesson that escapes us except as they hold us in awe."[28] In other words, coaches can accept athletes for who they are, acknowledging that through a sustained commitment to the practice community, both coach and athlete will grow.

A coaching philosophy begins with various commitments (e.g., to humanistic coaching, to treating athletes as individuals, man-to-man defense, nationwide recruiting), and yet the coach may find that some, or all, of these judgments need to change over time—with a different team, against a different schedule, in a certain economic situation. Experience breeds confidence with decision making and developing this quality of certainty. Novice coaches make decisions that provide information for future decisions. This process helps develop a sense of certainty, fostering clarity of focus and direction. Throughout the course of his professional life, the coach with this working certainty remains firm in day-to-day decisions, yet open to ongoing interactions with the world and others. Despite the tension that exists between firm commitments and openness to change, the coach must move forward. On this note, Anderson writes that "it is precisely because of the precariousness of our situation that we require faith and working certainties to act, to live."[29] We need at least a working certainty in order to live out our humanity. We may never have a final sense of certainty, may never know *for sure* of our athletes' devotion to the team, or our own job security, but we need at least a modicum of these qualities in order to act and live. This working certainty develops through promises and trust, between individuals who interact with each other over time.

Implications for Coaches

If Bugbee is right about this working certainty, what does it mean for coaches with regard to their philosophies and the way this impacts their coaching? In this final section I want to briefly suggest three aspects crucial to these tasks—risk, humility, and alertness—and the extent to which they relate to both coaching philosophies and also their application to ethical issues. First, Bugbee's working certainty involves a degree of risk, a willingness to commit and become immersed in projects without absolute clarity. By its very nature, coaching necessitates taking calculated risks, developing and living out beliefs and ideals. Attempting to construct or even modify one's coaching philosophy is a daunting task and often is scrutinized by a public audience. Should the coach emphasize trust or integrity or excellence or perhaps another theoretical ideal?

In an ethical sense, our human projects and relationships inevitably contain both complexity and risk. Perhaps the safest route is to forgo coaching altogether—whether this is on a volunteer basis or as a profession. Some individuals actually come to this conclusion, determining that overinvolved parents, spoiled athletes, or unreasonable administrators and alumni create too much stress. In many ways highly pressurized sport settings are not about learning and growing through risk. Rather, coaches often seek to control as much as possible, from pregame meal selection to curfew hours to warm-up drills and more.[30] Yet the decisions coaches make require risk on a daily basis—which athletes to recruit, which drills to employ, or which motivational strategies to use and to what degree.

However, the very uncertainty and degree of risk in sport can be viewed through an appreciative lens. Anderson contends that our human achievements occur because of our individual and corporate exertion. He writes that these efforts "require that both we and those who have a stake in our performances take a gamble. They require a risk, and we are all too often afraid."[31] Some coaches realize the inexact nature of their position and yet are willing to invest in their athletes. Bugbee's crew coach, John Schultz, provides an example in this respect. Because of his love for rowing and for people, he entered the coaching ranks and remained committed to his craft. Furthermore, the decisions Schultz made impacted Bugbee and other athletes as well—his choices (and risks) made a difference. Simply put, coaching philosophies matter a great deal. These beliefs impact how coaches interact with others, how they handle disappointment and success. Coaches stake themselves to their beliefs and, in the right situation, coaching philosophies lived out by men and women impact the lives of their players, some of whom become coaches as well.

This aspect of risk also comes into play with regard to how coaches treat their athletes. This means considering these individuals as ends in themselves rather than as means to another end, not placing the athletes in situations where the likelihood of harm may occur. For example, the coach should understand that pushing an athlete to return to the playing field too soon after a concussion, even with a championship on the line, may create long-term health hazards. Other areas of note may include measuring the risk inherent in training programs, practice drills, and techniques, in addition to the overall emotional climate of team activities. As a friend of mine, a highly successful college basketball coach, once noted, he tries to use his program to build up athletes, rather than using athletes to build up his program.

In addition to involving risk, Bugbee's work necessitates humility, a theme that permeates Bugbee's work and fittingly serves as his final entry in *The Inward Morning*: "I am not content with what I have worked out; but I have worked out enough, perhaps, to be content to consider more carefully as I move along, and to welcome all manner of thinking other than my own."[32] Similarly, as coaches make decisions they need to work out their philosophical ideals, moving forward as though they are correct—while accepting the fact that they could be mistaken or that these beliefs could change. Heie describes humility in a similar manner: "I will seek to express my *commitment* to certain 'truths' with clarity. At the same time, I must be characterized by *openness* to the possibility that I am all wrongheaded about some of my present beliefs and need correction."[33] Coaches find themselves living with this tension of commitment on the one hand and openness on the other. This quality of humility impacts the way they interact with other people and conduct their responsibilities.

While many coaches demonstrate humility, other coaches become chained to their beliefs with very little flexibility and may exhibit hubris rather than humility. These individuals may be reluctant to even consider other approaches because they have been successful with their methods and beliefs thus far. They may be successful in spite of these ideals, however, rather than because of them. For example, many point to accolades heaped on former college basketball coach Bobby Knight. His motivational strategies included harsh and even arguably abusive tactics. One could certainly ask whether he might have attained similar objective measures of success (i.e., wins and championships) with a style of coaching representative of humility and openness.

The coach who demonstrates humility remains open to growth and change. This openness involves listening, being considerate, pondering the benefits of various philosophical ideas, interacting with players and assistant coaches from a variety of backgrounds, entertaining notions of different regimens, and considering both criticism and praise. The coach does not remain receptive by keeping the office door closed, shunning other coaches in the department, or refusing to relate with parents or alumni. Despite the openness that this quality of humility entails, the coach still remains confident, and in this sense humility should not be confused with meekness or any aspect of timidity.[34]

Coaches need to deliberate about their individual philosophy, choosing the path by which they intend to coach, working out their beliefs in the process. This ongoing course of discernment and decision making is a crucial aspect of successful coaching. It provides the needed structure for program goal-setting and individual growth. Further, coaches need to carefully explain these beliefs and ideas to others so as to be understood and not misunderstood. Yet coaches cannot draft these documents in a narrow way that restricts growth, nor in any final, solidified version for eternity.

This aspect of humility deeply impacts how coaches treat others, and a lack of humility often results in unethical consequences. The recent case of Bobby Petrino, former football coach at the University of Arkansas, serves as an example. Despite his stellar record, Arkansas administrators fired Petrino in the spring of 2012 for a series of embarrassing unethical acts.[35] In this situation, Petrino failed to recognize Bugbee's sense of humility related to nature and one's surroundings. As Bugbee wrote of his singular place within the larger natural surroundings, exemplary coaches recognize their own place as one part of the coaching system or one member of the athletic department (or university). These individuals maintain a healthy sense of self-regard without allowing hubris to gain a foothold.

Finally, Bugbee's notion of certainty requires on ongoing attitude of alertness. I want to turn again to Bugbee's narrative of his rowing coach, John Schultz. Once Bugbee was riding with Schultz in a Model-A Ford, following the crew team along the Schuylkill River. Bugbee writes:

> At the half mile the boats were even. John shoved the gas clear to the floor, and as we began to move ahead of the procession, jerking past a scattering of cars, I just heard him over the violence of the engine: 'When they come out from under the bridge. . . . That's where they need me!'[36]

Bugbee uses this story to demonstrate the type of attentiveness or attitude he has in mind. Coach Schultz knew, by virtue of countless hours spent with his athletes, from his watchful presence, the precise instant when his athletes need his guidance. Schultz sensed this occasion, one that he "felt in his bones." Similarly, reading this passage prompts us to remember our own awakening moments and those individuals or places where we felt such interactions. Bugbee tries to prod others toward analogous frames of mind, providing encouragement to seek out relationships and locations where we become open to self and others as we seek clarity and ultimately our own working certainty.

Through human commitments, entered into with this spirit of attentiveness, coaches discover, identify, and reformulate their philosophical beliefs. Bugbee wants us to approach interactions with others, however, not solely "in terms of goal-oriented endeavor, nor in terms of acquisition or achievement, nor in terms of the fulfillment of explicit moral standard, nor in terms of the realization or satisfaction of the ego."[37] Yes, coaches form commitments, in large part, to work toward common goals. However, Bugbee desires that we also recognize and appreciate the experience itself and the relationships we form in the process.

This quality of alertness impacts the ethical attitudes and behaviors of coaches, the way they interact with others, especially their athletes. The attentive coach strives to understand the athletes, to gain a sense of their perspective. By taking this approach, the coach demonstrates a willingness to appreciate the team members not only as athletes but as unique people. These kinds of coaches carve out deliberate moments to interact with their athletes, seeking to understand the athletes' broader lives when it comes to school, relationships, athletic performance, and so forth.

Let me conclude with several specific issues related to coaching philosophies with respect to ethics. Too often coaches either wholly embrace the philosophy of a mentor coach, or rely on a template drawn up in coaching education programs. These approaches are helpful to a degree but can be problematic. In this vein, Anderson observes that "we try—mostly ineffectively—to *produce* teaching and learning. But these are not the sorts of things one produces—teaching [coaching too] and learning are found in life's transitions, in the agency of a fundamental alertness, awareness, and attentiveness."[38] Coaches too seek to address problems (e.g., how to win, how to recruit, how to manage, how to discipline, how to relate to parents) through finding technical solutions. They go to clinics, trying the next best idea on motivation or team building, training programs, or off-season workouts. But in their haste they may cease being alert to the needs of their athletes, to the overall principles of their university, or to the mission of their own family. Bugbee reminds us, through narrative and through his own careful reflection, of the importance of attention as we relate with others and develop coaching philosophies.

To further clarify this point, consider the following example from a team sport. A college basketball coach may, through experience and observation, believe in an unstructured offense (dribble-drive) that relies heavily on the athleticism of his players. However, since his school is no longer able to attract top athletes and he is unwilling to adapt his style to these fundamentally sound yet less athletic players, the coach and team struggle. A new coach comes in and does well with these same players using a structured offense that relies more on intelligent shot selection than athleticism. The first coach did not revise his theory of basketball offense in light of experience and hence was dogmatically rather than pragmatically certain.[39]

It may appear that Bugbee's acceptance of and confidence in experience as a valid philosophic approach potentially suffers from a lack of critical justification. As compared with Dewey's scientific method, Bugbee's transcendental claims seem speculative or even solipsistic. In reality, Bugbee realizes that his claims, and the backdrop from which they arose, still need to be validated. Like other American philosophers, he believes philosophical ideals need to hold a cash value—they need to solve real problems. So, while Bugbee does not oppose the rigor of the scientific method, neither did he want this approach to totally dominate our approach to doing philosophy, especially at the expense of experience and the discoveries this mode of thinking and writing holds.

At this point I want to address the potential tension between Bugbee's philosophical ideas and the demands of highly competitive big-time NCAA Division I sports. As presently structured, the incentives in Division I run counter to a coach developing a philosophy emphasizing the virtues of sport (e.g., developing player skills, respecting players, teaching the game) due to the pressures for instant success, achieving conference and national championships, and above all bringing in revenue streams. Given these conditions, to what extent is it possible for the qualities Bugbee emphasizes to fit with the elite sport culture? It may be difficult to conceptualize elite level coaching in the manner Bugbee's themes suggest. Popular opinion does not view elite coaches as individuals who embody humility or risk. Yet I would argue that these qualities are even more important for elite-level coaches because of the pressures involved.

Focusing on the concepts Bugbee mentions, when formulating and living out a coaching philosophy, does not guarantee additional wins or a more lucrative contract. Bugbee's concerns are clearly not instrumental in this sense. Rather, this kind of attention could encourage a greater appreciation for the craft of coaching and for sports in general. Furthermore, the sense of working certainty and the openness this concept involves could help encourage coaches at all levels to continue toward growth and development—positive character traits that are useful for youth sport coaches and those at the elite and hypercompetitive levels. Finally, the notion of a normative approach to coaching philosophies is a crucial aspect of coaching. As Standal and

Hemmestad rightly contend, "Top-level sport is not a domain where 'anything goes'. There are already ethical guidelines for sports, such as fair play principles. . . . Thus, ethical judgments are always being made . . . [and] the coach with [practical wisdom]is better suited to deal with such dilemmas in a good way."[40] With increased television exposure and lucrative contracts, elite coaches are tempted to skirt ethical responsibilities to reap financial rewards. Their unethical, selfish behavior ultimately has a bearing on their team, department, and university. Conversely, coaches such as Tony Dungy, Dean Smith, or Vivian Stringer provide examples that it is indeed possible to coach in ways representative of Bugbee's ideals, with manners that respect both the player and the game.

When I was playing football at Northwestern, Coach Korver exemplified the risk, humility, and alertness characteristic of the working certainty Bugbee describes. Through my time and commitment, I developed as a football player and individual. My own distinctive life experiences and self-identity provided the ground from which I responded to Korver's coaching philosophy. In Davis's words, Korver "lit up" his coaching philosophy in a way that captured my attention and prompted me toward growth.[41] Not only did Korver's attitudes influence me, but his ideals also impacted many others including two players who later would succeed him when he retired. To be fair, not every player embraced Korver's philosophy. Some continued playing but did not wholly agree with his ideals. A few left the team for other pursuits. This was a risk Korver accepted, however, as he realized that while he could not impact everyone on the team in a way that he would have liked, he could impact many—including me.

Questions for Review and Discussion

1. To what extent have your coaches and their philosophies impacted your view of sport?

2. To what extent did the coaches and their philosophies impact your experience as an athlete?

3. How do coaches develop a coaching philosophy and how should they do so?

4. What did Bugbee mean by "certainty" and how does this relate to a coaching philosophy?

5. To what extent is it possible for coaches to approach their task in a manner consistent with Bugbee's themes?

6. How would you evaluate the pragmatic approach to the philosophy and ethics of coaching developed in this chapter as compared to either Simon's version of broad internalism (interpretivism) or Morgan's more context-specific modification of it? Is pragmatism of the kind suggested compatible with either Simon's or Morgan's views? If not, which approach do you think is intellectually more satisfactory? Which might be more useful to coaches?

Suggestions for Further Reading

Anderson, Douglas. *Philosophy Americana: Making Philosophy at Home in American Culture.* New York: Fordham University Press, 2006.

Bugbee, Henry. *The Inward Morning: A Philosophical Exploration in Journal Form.* Athens: University of Georgia Press, 1999.

Davis, Paul. "Objectivity and Subjectivity in Coaching." In *The Ethics of Sports Coaching,* 56–71. Edited by A. Hardman and C. Jones. London: Routledge, 2011.

Descartes, René. *Meditations on First Philosophy.* Cambridge: Cambridge University Press, 1986.

Dweck, Carol. *Mindset: The New Psychology of Success.* New York: Random House, 2006.

Fry, Jeff. "On Playing with Emotion." *Journal of the Philosophy of Sport* 30:1 (2003): 26–36.

Hardman, Alun, and Carwyn Jones, eds. *The Ethics of Sports Coaching.* London: Routledge, 2011.

Heie, Harold. *Learning to Listen, Ready to Talk: A Pilgrimage Toward Peacemaking.* Lincoln, NE: iUniverse, 2007.

Kretchmar, R. Scott. *Practical Philosophy of Sport.* Champaign, IL: Human Kinetics, 2005.

Loland, Sigmund. "The Normative Aims of Coaching: The Good Coach as an Enlightened Generalist." In *The Ethics of Sports Coaching,* 15–22. Edited by A. Hardman and C. Jones. London: Routledge, 2011.

Lyle, John. "Coaching Philosophy and Coaching Behavior." In *The Coaching Process: Principles and Practice for Sport,* 25–46. Edited by N. Cross and J. Lyle. Oxford: Butterworth & Heinemann, 1999.

Sheehy, Harry. *Raising a Team Player: Teaching Kids Lasting Values on the Field, on the Court, and on the Bench.* North Adams, MA: Story, 2002.

Standal, Oyvind, and Liv Hemmestad. "Becoming a Good Coach: Coaching and *Phronesis*." In *The Ethics of Sports Coaching*, 45–55. Edited by A. Hardman and C. Jones. London: Routledge, 2011.

Walton, Gary. *Beyond Winning: The Timeless Wisdom of Great Philosopher Coaches.* Champaign, IL: Leisure, 1992.

Warren, William. *Coaching and Control: Controlling Your Team, Your Program, and Your Opponents.* Upper Saddle River, NJ: Prentice-Hall, 1997.

PART 3

Coaching and the Ethics of Competition

ROBERT L. SIMON

It is the next-to-last inning of a high school softball game—the semifinal game of a sectional championship—with the visiting team down by one run. The team has a runner in scoring position and a solid senior player is coming to bat. She has been injured a good part of her senior year and has worked hard to come back. In fact, she has dreamed about helping her team in just such a situation. It was her dream that motivated her to work so hard at rehabilitation; without it she might have worked less or even fallen into depression or given up. If the team loses, it will be the last game of her high school career.

Her coach is aware of all this and wants to let her bat. However, the coach also knows that a sophomore substitute on the bench who has filled in for the senior while she was out has hit well against this particular pitcher in the past and is probably a better hitter overall than the senior. Should the coach send the sophomore in to pinch-hit for the senior, ending the senior player's dream and possibly her career, or let the senior bat even though it may not be best for the team?

Although I'm sure you would like to know my answer, any response is debatable. In my view, this is a hard case where there may be reasonable arguments on both sides. But coaches face such situations all the time. If winning is everything, the coach will send in the pinch hitter. Moreover, the coach needs to consider the other players on the team who all want to win and advance in the play-offs, possibly to sectional play and a state championship. On the other hand, this at-bat is especially significant to a senior player who has helped the team for many seasons. What about loyalty to her in light of her work ethic, courage, and past contribution? Even if such considerations are outweighed by other factors and the coach decides to pinch-hit, I would argue that the reasons on the other side need to be considered and given due weight. Indeed, the chapters in Part 2 made a cumulative argument that coaching involves constant evaluation and moral decision making.

In Part 3, contributors turn to the activity of coaching itself. As the above example illustrates, coaches constantly face ethical issues in games and practices: decisions about who to play, who to schedule, how to react to unfavorable calls by officials, when and how to discipline players who misbehave, and a host of other kinds of cases every season. The chapters in Part 3 explore a number of such key decisions and the ethical issues raised by them.

Three of the chapters question a set of widely held assumptions that are not usually challenged. For example, many athletes, coaches, and fans would acknowledge that bad calls by officials often influence the outcome of contests but deny that the coaches who benefit from such calls and know the calls are incorrect have an obligation to do anything about it. Bad calls by officials are just "part of the game" and there is no moral duty on the part of the beneficiary to attempt to rectify the unearned advantage. As a former student once said when I asked her in class what she would do if a basketball referee made an outrageously bad call in her favor, she replied, "Refs have made so many bad calls against me, I would just figure he owed me one!"

However, in Chapter 7, J. S. Russell argues for a different perspective; namely, that coaches have an obligation to help officials get the call right and where appropriate to rectify bad calls, even bad calls in favor of the coach's own team. Russell considers objections to his view (e.g., that bad calls eventually "even out") and concludes these replies do not withstand critical scrutiny.

Similarly, in Chapter 8, Scott Kretchmar explores the coach's obligations to bench players, team members who see little playing time in actual contests except when the score is so lopsided that the outcome is settled, and concludes the case for their participation in meaningful moments of competitive games, even at higher levels of competitive athletics, is much stronger than often appreciated. In Chapter 11, Cesar Torres and Peter Hager call into question the widely held view that children's and youth sports should be noncompetitive. These authors explain that competition, when properly directed, can have benefits even for children and present principles, based on an explicitly broad internalist conception of sport, to guide coaches in this area.

Chapters 9 and 10 explore the ethics of the coach's relation to players, the dangers of abuse of that relationship, and the benefits that might develop when the relationship is an ethically appropriate one. In particular, Mark Hamilton, while recognizing that coaches often need to be tough and demanding, distinguishes intimidation and bullying from appropriate ways coaches might relate to their athletes. He explains the harms a bullying coach can cause and argues that bullying and related forms of intimidation have no legitimate place in coaching ethics.

In Chapter 10, Jeffrey Fry draws on recent findings in neuroscience to suggest that coaching behavior can affect the developing brain of young athletes and thus perhaps have deeper effects than previously thought. If so, positive behavior by coaches can have an even more significant effect than previously believed, and the kind of bullying described by Hamilton might have even more dire consequences than many have believed.

It is worth noting that the chapters in Part 2 of this book and those in Part 3 have a number of interconnections. In particular, the models of coaching and of ethical justification outlined in Chapters 1 through 4 may provide a framework for evaluating those in Part 2, while the latter may provide concrete examples of the implications of some of the ideas developed in Part 1. For example, Torres and Hager, as noted above, explicitly appeal to a broad internalist conception of sports while Russell and Kretchmar implicitly rely (or so I would suggest) on a broad theory of what is important about participation in sports. Hamilton and Fry, on the other hand, explore the virtues and vices that coaches may exhibit and what means may be properly employed as they pursue the goals of competitive athletics.

I hope these chapters encourage thoughtful discussion of the issues raised and illustrate why Douglas Hochstetler's thesis that the coach needs a philosophy is not just a theoretical point but clearly applies to the practice of coaching itself.

Seven

Coaching and Undeserved Competitive Success

J. S. RUSSELL

I suspect that the central moral problem facing all coaches is the problem of distributive justice, or how to allocate scarce goods or resources fairly. At all levels of sports, key goods such as playing time, access to training, and instruction are almost always in short supply. Norms for distributing those resources fairly are therefore required. Since coaches generally control allocation decisions, they have special duties to ensure fairness. Coaches from the recreational level to elite athletic development programs will recognize this as a constant moral demand (encapsulated in the idea of "being fair" to their players). It is a problem even at elite levels of sports, including professional sports. Coaches at these levels also need to develop talent and have obligations to give competitors opportunities that are due them. Yet these demands will inevitably conflict with the legitimate demands of other competitors and the priority that is placed on competitive success. At the highest levels of competition, then, these problems of distributive justice may only be heightened.

However, problems of distributive justice run more deeply in sports than these familiar examples. Although they are worthy of systematic treatment, I will not address them here. Rather, I want to focus on an issue in sports that is barely recognized as a problem of distributive justice although it is at least as profound a problem as the ones just mentioned. This is the problem of accepting undeserved advantages in competition. The undeserved advantages I shall focus on are erroneous judgments made by umpires. I shall argue that there should be a greater role for coaches in rectifying these injustices. This is bound to have an air of paradox about it. Unlike the idea that playing time, training, and instruction should be allocated fairly, which is unlikely to be gainsaid by anyone, being the recipient of undeserved advantages may not readily appear to be a problem of distributive justice. And of course even if we recognize that it is, it does not follow that coaches should act to mitigate the injustice or that, under certain circumstances, they have a moral obligation to do so. There is some work to do here, then.

Are Umpiring Errors Matters of Distributive Justice?

Consider the following scenarios:

1. An umpire blows a call at first base, calling a player out who was clearly safe. The out is the final out in the bottom of the ninth inning of a one-run game with the tying run on third and winning run on second. If the proper call were made, the batter-runner would have been safe, the runner at third would have scored (thus assuring that the game would at least go to extra innings), and perhaps the runner at second would also have scored, meaning that the game had been won by the home team. The coach of the fielding (visiting) team turns to one of his co-coaches and, shaking his hand over a successful win, says "we got one there." His colleague nods. The pitcher and his teammates leave the field inwardly (or perhaps even outwardly) acknowledging their great good luck.

2. An umpire awards three bases to a runner who started the play at first base when an infielder, on the initial play after the ball is hit, throws the ball out of play. This adds the winning run to the contest. However, the umpire has misapplied the rule, which states that only two bases shall be awarded from the base the runner occupies at the beginning of the play. The coach who is the recipient of this benefit knows this is an error and says nothing when the other coach formally protests the call.

These two scenarios illustrate the range of errors an umpire can make in the course of competition. One is an error making a call, the other is an error applying the rules. To put this in legal terms, we have "errors in fact" and "errors in law." This identifies the two sorts of mistaken judgements that umpires, or judicial officials generally, can make.

What makes these sorts of umpiring errors undeserved advantages and issues of distributive justice?

The first thing to notice is that competitive athletic successes can properly be described as *necessarily* or *inherently* scarce goods. This is evident from the nature of competitive sports. The competitors each strive to win, but only one can do so. Athletic success in this sense is a scarce good, in a way that many goods or resources are not. Gold, for example, is contingently scarce. There might be a vast store of it in some unknown but easily accessible place on earth so that all could have as much of it as they wanted. There would then be no scarcity of gold, and no problem of distributive justice regarding it. Winning is different. It is not contingently scarce but necessarily scarce. It is what economists and theorists of justice refer to as a "positional" or "relational" good. Classic instances of positional goods are awards and honors, because one person's possession of them excludes others who may also desire them. Competitive sporting success reflects this type of scarcity—all the competitors strive to win or be the best among their peers, but only one can win a game or a championship. The possibility of ties extends the idea of scarcity, since each competitor would prefer to win outright rather than tie an opponent.

Seen in this light, competitive successes appear to pose special problems of distributive justice. However, the fact that they are necessarily scarce does not mean that the problem of distributive justice takes priority over settling other claims of distributive justice. That depends on the importance or value of the good or resource that is scarce. But it does mean that our options for responding to the scarcity are limited. In normal circumstances, we might address problems of distributive justice by attempting to add resources, say, more seats at universities, more jobs to the economy, or increased food production, and so on. These sorts of avenues are not open to us in competitive sports. We cannot try to address (or, in many cases, sidestep) the problems of distributive justice by reducing scarcity, because we do not have the option of adding resources to address the problem. We cannot make everyone a winner in a competitive contest because that would contradict the very idea of a competitive contest. Our options are limited. Indeed, we have only one further option in the examples just given, and that is to correct the mistaken call.[1]

An obvious response at this point is to say that, contrary to appearance, the advantages or successes that come from umpiring errors do not pose problems of distributive justice, nor are the advantages and successes undeserved. The argument might go that it is not a problem of distributive justice because these sorts of errors tend to even out, and this evening out is sufficient to address any problem of distributive justice. Call this the "evening out argument." Second, they are not undeserved because the recipients of the advantage did nothing wrong to obtain the advantage. Call this the "innocent advantage argument." There are other objections that could be given against the arguments just presented, but these are, I suspect, the two main lines of objection, and I will consider them first. They are each easily answered.

Conventional sporting wisdom notwithstanding, we have no reason to believe that umpiring errors always, or even commonly, even out. This is just a hopeful claim that we comfort ourselves with. Over an entire season, it is always possible that one team or competitor will be the victim of more bad calls than other teams, or ones at crucial times, and that this will disproportionately affect their competitive success. A team might well lose a regular season championship because of a small number of "extra" or "especially consequential" umpiring errors made to its disadvantage perhaps in combination with errors that redounded to the advantage of the "winner." In fact, from an empirical perspective, we simply do not know how many season-long league championships (or play-off spots, etc.) are won or lost under these circumstances. My guess is that it is not an exceptional occurrence. If we are talking about a championship game or series, then the period of competition will normally be too short for any evening out to occur. In this context, umpiring errors may well determine an outcome. (Suppose the error at first described above occurs in the ninth inning of the seventh game of the World Series.)

Furthermore, we should not measure competitive athletic success simply as a matter of winning and losing, for there are other necessarily scarce competitive athletic goods that need to be allocated fairly. Athletes are often competing for individual awards or records (in baseball, for example, gold gloves for defense, or batting or pitching titles, or MVP awards, etc.) or team records (most wins in a season, longest winning streak, etc.) or for personal bests, and so on. Suppose that in the first scenario described above the runner had rightly been called safe, and as a result the fielder who threw the ball to first was charged with an error because it was a routine ground ball that he bobbled before throwing it. Suppose further that the failure to charge him with an error meant that he won a gold glove that someone else should have won. And suppose that the earned run that was not charged against the pitcher's record meant he finished the season with the lowest earned run average among pitchers, rather than finishing second. These are also examples of necessarily scarce competitive goods that are affected by umpiring errors. Evening out arguments can be applied in this context too, but once more we do not know whether the evening out occurs. This is particularly true where the margins of superiority over rivals are small and can be affected by a difference of one or two mistaken calls for or against an individual. For example, a batting title may be won by a few thousandths of a point, which might result from one "extra" scorer's decision to award a hit on what should have been a defensive error and no hit.

Moreover, there are situations where the evening out argument does not apply and a competitor is denied a scarce and highly prized good. Take an example from the recent history of baseball. In the 2010 baseball season, veteran umpire Jim Joyce wrecked a perfect game for Detroit Tiger pitcher Armando Galarraga by mistakenly calling a Cleveland Indian runner safe who would otherwise have been the final out of the game. By all accounts, the call was an obvious error. Replays showed a clear error even without benefit of slow motion. Slow motion replay showed the call to be an exceptional lapse of umpiring judgment. In this case, however, the call cannot be evened out with another blown call that evens things up. Galarraga already no longer had a perfect game because of the blown call. And there is no plausible opportunity for any evening out to occur in another game. We can confidently assert that Galarraga will never be in a position where an umpire's blown call will produce a perfect game for him. (As of May 2012 there were only twenty-one perfect games in major league history.) And who would want to be recognized and remembered for such a "perfect" game? The only other option in this case, as in the scenarios described earlier, is to overturn the mistaken decision. These are all good reasons to want to reduce the number of umpiring errors and to try to find creative ways to do so that are consistent with the good conduct of competitive contests.

A further response to the above argument might be that the advantages or successes given to opposing teams or competitors from these errors are not undeserved, since those who benefit from the errors did nothing wrong. They did nothing to seek or (let us say) encourage the error. They just happened to benefit from being in the right place at the right time. But this is not convincing. Let us put the example in a different context involving distributive justice. Suppose through a mistake at my bank someone else's money is transferred into my account. This is an innocent advantage in that I did not seek it but happened to be in the right place at the right time. The argument that I am entitled to this money and have no duty to disclose the error will not work. I am morally required to report this and to try to return it. If I knowingly take advantage of the windfall and spend it, I will be legally liable to repay it (and may be criminally charged).[2] If this reasoning is correct, it suggests by analogy that a similar thing is true of advantages conferred from recognized umpiring errors on teams or competitors who did not seek those advantages. If this is true in the bank error case, it creates a similar presumption about disclosure and repayment in the competitive case. That presumption can be overturned with an argument that demonstrates some important disanalogy between these cases, but the arguments that I can think of do not seem convincing.

Perhaps it will be argued that what distinguishes the banking from the competitive example is that these sorts of umpiring errors represent adversities that teams should be prepared to work through as part of competition. This is another bad argument, for changing a blown call just replaces one type of adversity for another—the adversity of having to deal with a changed blown call that was wrongly to one's advantage. As well, it will never be possible to eliminate all umpiring errors, and so teams will have to test themselves against this more familiar type of adversity in any event. Thus, since there is no evident loss of sporting adversity to test oneself against, the way remains clear to eliminate umpiring errors wherever reasonable on the grounds that what is at stake are scarce, much sought-after goods. More important, there is good reason to regard such adversities as irrelevant to sporting competition per se. If we think that competitive sports is something like a "mutually acceptable quest for excellence through challenge,"[3] as Robert Simon has argued, then competitors have an implicit fundamental commitment to each other to distribute the scarce goods of athletic competition in a way that is determined by the skills that are displayed in competition and not by mistakes that corrupt this process. If so, we now have arguments grounded both in distributive justice and in the agreement of competitors to do what can reasonably be done to minimize these sorts of errors. As in other areas of life, we will never get perfect justice, but we should do our best to strive toward it and to obtain the fairest results possible. The results may remain imperfect, but hopefully they will at least tend to be better measures of competitive athletic success. Moreover, if we do what is reasonably possible to allocate fairly the scarce goods of competition, the results will be ones that everyone should be prepared to accept as the most just outcome that could be achieved (more on this later).

I imagine one other response. Call this the "it's only a game" argument. It claims that while there may be an undeserved advantage from umpires' errors, it does not matter because games are basically trivial or gratuitous affairs. But this seems to be false. Games are not merely trivial or gratuitous to anyone who is serious enough to want to compete against others. People also invest great time and effort into developing and exercising game skills. They will not associate trivial value to their skills or sporting outcomes. But even if games are trivial or gratuitous in some sense, the fact that the goods that are sought through them are scarce and highly prized is sufficient to demand that distributive justice be taken seriously and reasonable efforts be made to minimize errors in distributing those goods. Compare how standards of distributive and corrective justice are carefully applied to many things that are at least as trivial. Think of allocation of rare gemstones and baseball cards, for example. There is no reason, then, to fail to regard distribution of athletic advantages and success as a serious issue of distributive justice just because what is at stake is arguably trivial.

Should Coaches Help Umpires?

So far I have argued that certain sought-after competitive athletic goods are scarce and that we should take reasonable measures that are at our disposal to ensure that they are fairly distributed. This should not be controversial. What is likely to be controversial is my claim that coaches should be enlisted, at least from time to time, to assist umpires to correct errors. In these cases, game players might also be consulted, but I have special reasons for wanting to focus on coaches which will become apparent in the following discussion.

This is bound to seem like a provocative idea. However, we have seen evidence by analogy and grounded in ideas of distributive justice and competitive sports that coaches, or participants should accept this obligation. There are other arguments that can be given as well. To begin with, there are important precedents in sports that suggest we should be open-minded about this proposal. For there are sports like curling, golf, and ultimate that are essentially self-officiated. Each has a role for officials, but participants are expected "to call their own game." Each of these games works pretty well, so that should encourage us to take seriously the practicality of a proposal to enlist coaches to assist umpires from time to time.

Why coaches, though? Why not go straight to the players, who arguably are in the best position besides the umpires, to make the calls? My reasons for this require some extended discussion. To begin with, sometimes players are not in the best position to see what happened, and coaches can be in a better position. Although I think that players should be consulted by their coaches in cases where there is a reasonable concern that an error has been made, there are certain advantages, particularly in team sports, to making the decision to assist umpires a team or "corporate" one. The competitors are teams, and so it is a team responsibility to address the issue, not specifically a matter for an individual player. This takes a burden off the individual player. A player may understandably feel that his or her honesty is being pitted against the interests of the team. Thus, a player may worry about recriminations from fellow players. Other players may disagree with a teammate's perception but not be in as good a position to say what happened. Some players called on to assist umpires may be concerned about the accuracy of their own assessment but will be understandably concerned about how this will be perceived by the umpires and others. Coaches can assist players to be comfortable reporting their views honestly. These are some good reasons to make the decision a corporate one, involving coaches and players offering advice to umpires when requested to do so. The burden for everyone is mitigated if the decision is made, in effect, by the team through the coach.

There will also be a useful symmetry to enlisting coaches in this way. Since the review of a call is most likely to be initiated by an opposing coach's complaint to an umpire, the umpire could then ask the other coach if he believes his team has just received an undeserved advantage and/or whether he wishes to confer with any of his players or coaches about this. This will mean that the leaders on the field, the coaches and the umpires, will be seen to work together to ensure that the competition produces a just outcome. There is an important symbolism here that shows that those participants who have direct responsibility for overseeing the good conduct of games and ensuring that standards of fairness and sportsmanship are applied will work together to achieve these goals and not be pitted against each other on these issues, and indeed against these goals, as is often the case.

There are related moral advantages to having coaches participate in these decisions and speak for the team. For one thing, it imposes on coaches a responsibility of moral leadership that is consistent with their managerial and supervisory role. For another, it is a way of responding, at least partially, to the morally flawed aspects of sports. Most critiques of sports argue that the problems that we see in sports—the win-at-all costs attitude, in particular—are the product of corrupting elements from outside sports, in particular, the desire for recognition or money.[4] These would, I think, be combated to a substantial degree if the proposal outlined here were accepted. For if coaches either led the effort, or were required to take steps from time to time, to ensure that the scarce competitive goods were fairly allocated, this would do much to put competition in sports on a higher moral ground. A win-at-all-costs approach is, of course, prepared to accept undeserved advantages to the extent it facilitates winning. But it does this at the expense of corrupting the idea of sports as a mutually agreed upon quest for excellence, and it ignores the demand that we allocate the scarce goods of competition fairly.

I have argued elsewhere that the moral flaws of sports extend beyond the common criticism that sports is corrupted by the culture outside it. While I am sure there is truth to these latter arguments, I argued that sports, despite its actual and potential moral virtues, is also internally flawed like many, and perhaps all, human institutions.[5] The arguments advanced here also would help to address these flaws, even if they would not completely eliminate them. My arguments about the morally flawed nature of sports are twofold. First, competitive sports is not simply a mutual quest for excellence in the sense that Simon describes. It is also a ritualized form of conflict.[6]

More specifically, I claim that competitive sports is better described as a mutually acceptable quest for excellence through ritualized conflict. As a result, it naturally (if not necessarily) engages suspect human motivations, like desires to dominate others or to seek retribution or revenge or to have feelings of hatred, to sharpen competitive desires and promote the pursuit of excellence. Such emotions are familiar features of the psychology of competitive sportspersons at all levels and in all sports. Thus we have baseball manager and hall of famer Leo Durocher stating that he wanted "scratching, diving, hungry ball players who come to kill you" playing for him, and Tiger Woods asserting that for him competition in anything from cards to golf is always about "wanting to kick your [opponent's] butt."[7] I argued that competition marked by friendly behavior and good sportsmanship may not always, or perhaps even often, be conducive to the highest level of athletic achievements, and that certain morally suspect motivations may be necessary for many athletes to excel at the highest level. These motivations plausibly exist in part because of their ability to focus the mind and assist us to succeed in human conflicts. A second, deeper argument claimed that sports contains a morally flawed conception of value. The pursuit of winning is a pursuit of relative value as an end, not perfection for its own sake. The relative value of winning is superiority over others. Thus competitive sports conceptually requires us to see success in part as dominance over others rather than pursuing something that is valuable for its own sake, like human perfection. There is a tension in sports then between the pursuit of perfection (the mutual quest for excellence) and the desire to win or come out on top of others as an intrinsic end of competition. Here I was following an argument from Kant[8] that aiming to be better than others as an end is a corrupt form of value that will encourage us to fail to recognize the value of pursuing perfection for its own sake and, implicitly, the absolute value of all persons. Thus it will encourage exactly the sorts of suspect motivations just mentioned. Kant's views are perceptive and in fact predict the sort of behavior that we find commonly in sports and that are reflected in the remarks of sportspersons like Durocher and Woods.

It should be clear now how enlisting coaches in helping to ensure that scarce competitive goods are allocated fairly can also help to respond to morally problematic features that are internal to competitive sports. The simple fact is that having coaches take responsibility for assisting umpires in their roles will deemphasize winning as the ultimate goal of competition and bring the focus more closely on ensuring that the excellences that the contests are designed to test are duly recognized and the scarce competitive resources are fairly distributed. If a coach acknowledges that an umpire made an error that wrongly awarded his team a win, that has the obvious effect of downplaying the idea that winning is everything in favor of recognizing that successful execution of individual skills should determine competitive results. To put this in Kantian terms, we downplay (although we do not eliminate) the focus on relative value and redirect it toward things that are properly valued intrinsically, such as human perfection. And while competitive contests may remain imperfect in their distribution of scarce competitive goods, the results will be ones that all should be better prepared to accept, since the participants will themselves share responsibility for ensuring that they are shared fairly. All should be able to acknowledge, then, that this is the best that can be done to ensure that competitive successes are fairly distributed. This is an advance from the perspective of distributive justice and from the perspective of competition. More generally, I can think of no other proposal that would go so far to ameliorate many of the most troubling moral problems that have come to pervade contemporary competitive sports. Although it is needed at all levels of sports, it should be accepted most readily at recreational and amateur levels where there is a greater need to use sports as a tool for moral education and where practices need to be adopted that will allow these levels of sports to separate themselves from the example that is often set by professional sports and its embrace of the competitive flaws described earlier.

Can Justice Be Done in Sports?

"This is fine in theory, but it won't work in practice." This challenge deserves to be taken seriously. Answering the question, What is justice? is fundamental but of little consequence without also answering the question, How shall justice be done? There is always a burden, then, to show how justice can be practically implemented.

Let me start, however, by pointing out a limitation about practical objections. Admittedly, the position that is being defended has the weight of culture going against it. But this is not a good reason not to adopt it, and it is a very bad reason for saying that it cannot be done. Moral progress typically depends on responding to injustices that are entrenched culturally. We have often seen practical moral revolutions occur in response to seemingly insuperable cultural obstacles (e.g., securing the abolition of slavery, rights for women, religious freedom, and democratic government, to name a few). The obstacles in the current context do not appear so insuperable, since much less is at stake. We have also already seen that certain successful sports are self-officiated. Given that self-officiated sports appear to reflect better examples of sportsmanship and civility and produce fewer complaints about results, we can reasonably hope that adding a measure of self-officiating to competitive sports wherever this is possible would have similar results. This gives us some reason for optimism that involving participants in umpiring decisions can be practical. Also, if we look at the history of sports, there are precedents that should encourage us. For example, it used to be common in tennis for players to concede umpiring errors. This all but disappeared long before the institution of electronic aids to officiating. Similar sorts of examples of corrective justice appear to have been more common in the past in many sports. This shows that there is no reason that competitors cannot make decisions or take actions to rectify injustices. Moreover, it is interesting that these sorts of examples occurred under circumstances where there were no rules requiring the competitors to rectify umpires' errors. It was done out of a sense of fairness and honor between competitors that seems to have disappeared in recent times. The arguments I have presented indicate that we should seek to recover and try to formally institutionalize those lost virtues.

A more interesting objection is a problem that is familiar from implementing recognized standards of distributive justice. Suppose the above arguments are accepted and rules for implementing them are adopted. The proposal will only work if coaches can reasonably expect other coaches to participate honestly in this process. If coaches expect other coaches to violate standards of distributive justice to their advantage, say, by lying about what they believe were the right decisions when consulted by umpires, the process will break down and the rules will not achieve their goals. Even coaches who would like to participate in these practices will, then, have no reason to participate honestly in this process. They might even plausibly argue that they have duties to be dishonest.

This is a familiar problem of rationing scarce resources under conditions that are fair but nevertheless permit "free riders" to take advantage of other persons' compliance with the rules and obtain unjust advantages. If the problem of free riders goes unaddressed, there is no reason to be confident that a system of distributive justice will work at all.[9] Since we can never assure perfect compliance, the problem is to reduce the number of free riders so that it is rational for coaches to comply because they expect other coaches will reciprocate. The typical, albeit imperfect solution is to codify punishments and enforce them against individuals who fail to comply with their duties. Such punishments, for example, fines and suspensions, could and probably should be adopted, say, for failing to participate in good faith regarding a review of a call. Admittedly, they will be difficult to prosecute. A coach can always say he was not sure enough about a call to make a decision, and it will be difficult to prove that he is lying. However, there are bound to be some cases where it is evident enough that a coach has lied and that a prosecution is successful. That may be sufficient to encourage enough compliance that the process would be workable.

I doubt, however, that problems prosecuting the enforcement of rules should lead us to be pessimistic about addressing the problem of free riders. What is helpful about sporting competition is that the events under scrutiny are *public*, so any free riding takes place directly under the scrutiny of others. Free riding tends to be a more serious problem in contexts where the free riders can hide their cheating behavior out of public sight (e.g., claiming a tax write-off for a business lunch when the meal was purely for personal reasons, etc.). However, even in these cases we often get reasonable compliance so the system does not break down. For example, doctors could lie about or exaggerate a patient's medical symptoms to push him to the front of the line for a special test, but it is not clear that this is a systemic problem. So even where there is a low probability of detection for free riding, we often get reasonable compliance with stated norms of distributive justice. The case of competitive sports should be less conducive to free riding than these sorts of examples. First, requests to assist umpires will probably be limited to a narrow range of important calls to ensure that games are not bogged down by stoppages. And it would be important that the umpire have some reasonable belief that he or she has made an error. So these are likely to be a small number of cases, and they are likely to concern cases where the errors are pretty clear to everyone else, except perhaps the umpire, who may nevertheless strongly suspect he has made an error. Second, as already noted it will be difficult in these sorts of cases for participants to hide their free riding. For example, an umpire who was unable to see whether a ball was hit over a fence or bounced over a fence because he was blinded by the sun, but wrongly believed it bounced over and calls a ground rule double on what was a home run, will have many reliable reports to draw on. Indeed, probably all other players will know exactly what happened. (In a two-umpire system, the base umpire would be watching the base runners while the plate umpire is watching the ball, so there would be no other umpire in a position to correct the call.) A coach who denies that he knows what happened in that case is pretty obviously lying, and it is reasonable to consider that his reputation will suffer, and that he may suffer further social consequences from lying. There is no way to eliminate all free riders, of course, but it will become well known soon who the free riders are, and they will be regarded by their peers and others as "cheaters" and rightly so. Whether or not such a coach was prosecuted, these considerations may be a sufficient deterrent for most coaches to ride free.

Perhaps the opposite problem will now seem pressing, namely, that individuals will be falsely accused of free riding and suffer social and other consequences as a result. This is possible, and can undoubtedly occur from time to time. However, it is unlikely if the coach has a record of honesty and he consults with his players and umpires in good faith (who can then report how a decision was arrived at). To protect the reputation of individuals, we might have a standard that the coach be certain beyond a reasonable doubt, or on a preponderance of evidence, that the call was an error (rather than simply on the balance of probabilities). In any event, we can only speculate at this point about the potential for casualties. It is encouraging, however, that self-officiated sports seem to proceed without victimizing the innocent. That empirical fact and the arguments given here are sufficient grounds to implement and test the ideas being proposed.

As an aside, it is worth noting that the problem of free riders helps to explain why the practice being proposed has not arisen naturally. Unless there are accepted norms of cooperation that there is some reason to think will be enforced either with legal or social punishment, it is not rational for a coach to offer to assist an umpire to correct a call or to answer such a request in good faith, because he has no reason to believe such an offer will ever be reciprocated. The corrupt conception of value that is part of sports adds further resistance. Participants have the goal of winning over others, after all. As well, the arguments about the connection between competitive success and distributive justice are not well understood. Perhaps if all these issues were understood better by sports participants and umpires, a practice of umpires consulting coaches could emerge naturally at some point. But it is undoubtedly too hopeful to expect education to solve this problem in any broad and systematic way, particularly in the current climate in which sports operates, and given reasonable concerns about free riding. Rules that clearly define and enforce expectations will be needed.

It is reasonable to ask how this would work in a formal sense. What sorts of rules should be adopted? This will be partly a matter of experimentation and experience, but some suggestions can be made. Sports leagues should explicitly recognize in their rules that umpires may consult with coaches about official decisions and that coaches have duties to comply honestly and in good faith with those requests. The rules should also state that a coach may consult with his or her players as part of responding to such a request. To ensure the efficient conduct of games, umpires could be directed to use this discretion on what appear to be key plays, like the ones described in the scenarios outlined at the beginning of the paper. However, I am not sure this is necessary. Baseball has a rule that permits umpires to overturn their own calls. It states that "the first requisite is to get decisions correctly. If in doubt don't hesitate to consult your associate" (Rule 9.05, *Official Baseball Rules*, 2011). This rule is not often invoked, but when it is, it is reasonable to think that umpires would be assisted if they could also consult coaches. But, as in law, there is a virtue, even if it is not overriding, in making a decision and letting the parties get on with the rest of the game (or their lives). In this respect, the *Official Rules of Baseball* set an instructive precedent in advising that umpires should not allow themselves to be "stampeded" by appeals to consult "the other man." It is fair to say baseball umpires have not fallen victim to this. It also remains to be seen how often coaches will request that umpires seek help from other coaches. They will probably learn quickly that they cannot put other coaches on the spot for "bang bang" plays because an opposing coach can reasonably claim uncertainty about the correct call. It is even possible that an ethos might emerge that only clear errors that are unaddressed by the umpires themselves will be pursued. The suggestion that the standard of proof for changing calls be a preponderance of evidence or no reasonable doubt standard should limit both coaches' requests for changes and umpires' willingness to pursue those requests. Taken together, these considerations show that there is good reason to believe that umpires can manage this area of discretion without jeopardizing the good conduct of games. Having said this, giving general direction to umpires that they may consult with coaches on judgments in an effort to ensure that the right calls are made is something that can also be experimented with in a variety of ways. For example, proposals can be applied initially in preseason games or in certain leagues in order to generate evidence for putting this practice into effect. We may learn from these and other efforts what works and what does not, including whether appeals of decisions should be limited in certain ways. Proper education of coaches, sports officials, and players on these matters should also be vigorously pursued.

The application of this proposal is bound to be different for different sports. For example, fast-moving sports with continuous play may sometimes make it difficult to review calls, since the play may advance despite the error. But it is still possible at a break in play to go back and consult coaches and their players as to, say, whether a goal was scored or some other key event occurred. For example, Frank Lampard's unrecognized goal in the 2010 World Cup semifinal, which would have pulled England into a 2–2 tie with Germany, would have been allowed, since the German goaltender Manuel Neuer acknowledged that Lampard's kick landed a foot inside the goal line, as replays confirmed. The German side won 4–1, but the outcome might have been different if that crucial play had been acknowledged. The basic point is that umpires in all sports will miss key events from time to time. If coaches, speaking on behalf of their teams, can agree that those errors should not be allowed to contribute to the outcome of a game, the goals as well as the morality of competitive sports will be advanced.

The proposals I have been making would appear to be less relevant in professional sports now that video replay is becoming a common aid to umpiring. But most professional sports below the highest levels will probably never use video replay, and virtually all amateur sports will never have video replay. So the proposal has practical relevance to nearly all sports. Even where video replay is available, it would nevertheless be useful and instructive to players and fans to permit umpires to consult opposing coaches from time to time about disputed decisions. If these could be resolved without recourse to video replay, or perhaps while it was going on, it would help to address the moral problems found in sports that were mentioned earlier.[10]

Conclusion

For some, my proposal will sound too radical to be taken seriously. But it is not clear that it is radical in any way that counts against the proposal. The conclusion of the argument that has been presented is perhaps surprising. But that is just a feature of any original argument. Moreover, in this case, the argument just traces out the implications of some compelling, and for the most part, familiar ideas about the nature of sports and justice. It also responds to plausible objections. There is nothing about the arguments, then, that makes them particularly radical. The proposal may be radical in the sense that it asks us to overturn some well-entrenched cultural practices. But this is often what philosophy, particularly moral philosophy, does. John Locke's rejection of the divine right of kings to govern and his idea that all humans, regardless of social rank, are entitled to the same inalienable rights was once such a radical idea that its author could claim authorship only after he died for fear that he would be executed. Mary Wollstonecraft's eighteenth-century defense of the rights of women presented a similarly radical challenge to cultural practices. The current proposal cannot be compared to these in either the originality of the arguments or its radical rejection of cultural orthodoxy. These historical examples, and many others besides, show us that we should be prepared to follow the arguments where they give us solid grounds for improving our cultural practices. The culture of competitive sports is no exception. We should insist that sports, like any other human institution, live up to reasonable moral standards. This becomes more important as sports become a more central part of human culture, as they are bound to do as basic human needs are met for more people and they have more opportunities for recreation and leisure. As competitive sports become a focus of more and more people's lives, the claims of justice will become more pressing, as will the importance of using sports as an example for other areas of human activity. Since coaches will be at the center of the sort of changes being proposed, they should be prepared to take these arguments seriously and assume a leading role in their implementation.[11]

Questions for Review and Discussion

1. Why does Russell think that umpiring errors reflect failures of distributive justice?

2. What arguments does Russell think will be used to show that coaches whose teams have benefited from an umpiring error should not be expected to assist umpires overturn that error? How does he respond to those arguments?

3. In addition to an argument based on distributive justice, Russell uses an argument from Robert L. Simon's work to show the importance of doing what is reasonable to ensure that umpires make the right decisions. What is that argument? Is one argument more fundamental than the other?

4. Is Russell right that the culturally entrenched practice of not having umpires consult with coaches is not a good ground in itself for rejecting his proposal?

5. Would Russell's proposal undermine the authority of umpires and kill the flow of many fast-paced sports such as basketball?

Suggestions for Further Reading

Aristotle. "The Varieties of Justice." In *Justice: Alternative Political Perspectives.* Edited by James Sterba. Belmont, CA: Wadsworth, 1980.

Berman, Mitchell N. "Replay." *California Law Review* 99 (2011): 1683–1743.

Browne, Alister. "Violating Rules of Rationing." *Canadian Journal of General Internal Medicine* 3:3 (2008): 127–128.

Chun, Janean. "Bank Deposit Error in Your Favor? Give It Back." *Daily Finance,* December 9, 2009.

Collins, Harry. "The Philosophy of Umpiring and the Introduction of Decision-Aid Technology." *Journal of the Philosophy of Sport* 37:2 (2010): 135–146.

Jailler, Ben. "Can You Keep Money Accidentally Paid into Your Bank Account?" www.money.co.uk/article/1005023-can-you-keep-money-accidentally-paid-into-your-bank-account.htm.

Major League Baseball. *Official Baseball Rules.* http://mlb.mlb.com/mlb/downloads/y2011/Official_Baseball_Rules.pdf.

Midgley, Mary. "The Game Game." In *The Ethics of Sports: A Reader.* Edited by Mike McNamee. London: Routledge, 2010.

Morgan, William J. *Why Sports Morally Matter.* New York: Routledge, 2006.

Rawls, John. *A Theory of Justice*. Cambridge: Harvard University Press, 1971.

Royce, Richard. "Refereeing and Technology: Reflections on Collins' Proposals." *Journal of the Philosophy of Sport* 39:1 (2012).

Russell, J. S. "Are Rules All an Umpire Has to Work With?" *Journal of the Philosophy of Sport* 26 (1999): 27–49.

———. "Competitive Sport, Moral Development, and Peace: Skeptical Reflections." In *A Companion to Sport Philosophy*. Edited by Cesar Torres. Forthcoming.

———. "The Concept of a Call in Baseball." *Journal of the Philosophy of Sport* 24 (1997): 21–37.

———"The Moral Ambiguity of Coaching Youth Sport." In *The Ethics of Sports Coaching*. Edited by Alun R. Hardman and Carwyn Jones. London: Routledge, 2011.

"Scarcity." Wikipedia: The Free Encyclopedia. http://en.wikipedia.org/wiki/Scarcity.

Simon, Robert L. *Fair Play: The Ethics of Sport*. 2nd ed. Boulder, CO: Westview, 2010.

Eight

Bench Players: Do Coaches Have a Moral Obligation to Play Benchwarmers?

SCOTT KRETCHMAR

Anyone who has ever played on a team or coached one knows the high stakes involved in grouping athletes into starters and reserves. Undoubtedly the public nature of organized sport contributes to these dynamics. After all, it is in front of fans, friends, parents, and sometimes national television audiences that athletes play lead roles, secondary roles, or no role at all.

I know there is safety on the bench. I have spent time there. Athletes who do not get into the game will never make the mistake that turns a certain victory into an improbable defeat. Those who live at the end of the bench will not face the sometimes extreme pressure and so-called trait anxieties encountered by those who play regularly (Smith et al. 1995). But there is potential harm there too. Every athlete, from the fabled Rudy of Notre Dame to the youngster on the local sandlot team, wants to get into the game.[1] While simply belonging to a team has its rewards, that is usually not enough.

In this chapter, I do not present knock-down arguments in favor of more equitable methods for distributing playing time. Rather, I argue that concerns over winning and excellence should be toned down in favor of better meeting the rights and interests of the players to get on the court or field. My theoretical framework is informed by deontological sentiments. I believe that context matters in deciding appropriate amounts of playing time. Thus I generally favor act over rule approaches to this problem. The deontological side of my thinking privileges the rights of players over arguments for utility. I will not be arguing that spreading out playing time maximizes pleasure or any other benefit. Rather, I argue that it is the right thing to do for the players involved.

Others take different positions on this issue and have good reasons for doing so. Isn't it sufficient, they would ask, to be identified as a talented performer by virtue of one's team membership, to wear the jersey, to work under the watchful eye of a coach, to practice and improve, to go on team trips, to experience the friendships that grow between members of close-knit groups? Shouldn't players be able to gain satisfaction by helping the squad in ways other than making plays on the court or field? Furthermore, if coaches are forthright about playing time, if they tell athletes and parents up front that they will be making decisions based on maximizing chances for competitive success, where is the harm? Sport is egalitarian, but it is also a meritocracy. Nobody is guaranteed playing time. It must be earned.

These considerations are persuasive but not decisive. I say this because the issue of rights to playing time is complicated. First, it depends, at least in part, on context. Moral qualms about a lack of playing time are typically greater in youth sports than, say, Division I NCAA college athletics, and even less so in professional sports. In other words, from the fact that it is morally appropriate to keep a reserve on the bench at one level of sports, it does not necessarily follow that it is equally appropriate at other levels or in other athletic contexts. Many youth leagues have rules that require minimum levels of participation. Such rules, however, would be inappropriate or even laughable if applied to the Boston Celtics or New York Yankees.

The second complicating factor is related to the goods that are said to accrue to benchwarmers. They may or may not be sufficient. We cannot assume that reserve players are "getting a good deal" merely by being members of the team. Much would seem to hinge on how these individuals were treated and on such contingent issues as whether or not the athletes were on scholarship or were being paid. And much would depend on how we adjudicate individual rights against corporate goals and how much weight we give to such stakeholders as fans and those with business interests.

Third, while a coach's honesty about playing time is laudable and helpful, it is not sufficient. Telling players up front that they may be treated, in effect, more as means than ends does not necessarily mitigate or excuse harms befalling athletes from subsequent manipulations. Of course athletes, so informed, could choose not to play. But in sporting situations where many players achieve elite status on the foundation of large financial and psychological investments, the choice not to participate or to participate only under unfavorable terms places them in a very difficult situation, to say the least.

These kinds of considerations suggest that the rights, goods, and harms associated with access to playing time will not be easily determined. Before launching into this matter, however, I will clarify precisely what the issue is.

Benchwarmers are athletes who rarely play in actual games or play only for short periods when the game outcome has been decided. Typically, these are the younger, less seasoned, and less skilled individuals. These are the players who sit at the proverbial end of the bench. I am not as concerned about reserves who play significant minutes, who come off the bench regularly as role players, or who otherwise get into many contests when outcomes are still up for grabs. While some arguments presented here apply to them as well, their status as game contributors significantly reduces ethical concerns related to playing time.

In addition, playing time does not necessarily mean equal playing time. "Meaningful playing time," as I call it, has to do with when an athlete plays as much as how long that individual is on the court or field. Allowing subs in high school basketball to play the last twenty-two seconds of a blowout victory would not count as meaningful playing time to my way of thinking.

My analysis works better for team sports like basketball, football, soccer, and baseball, for example, than individual sports like tennis, golf, swimming, and track and field. Some of the sting of not getting to play seems less severe in these activities if only because many of them do not typically take place in front of large crowds. Yet even in these sports, there are individuals who get into the game and others who do not. The question of the ethics of playing reserves is still relevant, even if at a lesser level.[2]

Finally, it is important to distinguish between ethical and prudential reasons for playing reserves. Coaches may have strategic reasons to use their entire bench, but these motives and decisions do not speak directly to moral duties or responsibilities. To be sure, moral and prudential reasons can coincide, and when they do so, we count it as fortunate. But this need not be the case. Thus I will not be focusing on strategic reasons for playing benchwarmers, such as the following:

1. The importance of keeping starters fresh and ready for late-game surges

2. The importance of having starters get out of the game to watch and reflect, get instructions, improve their mind-set, or spend time on the bench for other reasons

3. The significance of preparing for injuries to starters, of having well-seasoned reserves ready to step in

4. The possibility that reserves may mature into better players than some current starters

5. The likelihood that disgruntled reserves will quit the team or, at the college level, transfer to another institution

6. The fact that team morale may be improved, that practices may go better if everyone can look forward to playing time

7. The importance of providing stability to a program, of protecting it from the ups and downs due to graduation or departures for other reasons

Clearly coaches have strategically sound reasons for playing reserves. Consequently it is both ethical *and* smart for coaches to give meaningful playing time to all or most of their bench players. But once again, for purposes of this analysis, I will focus on the ethical requirements for such a decision.

First Experiences: Playing Time, Learning, and Fun

Moral hackles about lack of playing time seem to be raised most often when young children do not get onto the field or court. If my seven-year-old were to remain on the bench because some coach is nervous about losing a game, I might justifiably conclude that things are not right. Youth sport, it is commonly thought, should afford participation opportunities for the talented and untalented alike. Winning, if it is to have any influence on coaching decisions, should be a secondary consideration at most.

Even Little League, an organization that has been criticized for placing financial objectives over educational values, has a mandatory play rule.[3] Rule 8.3 reads as follows:

> In all divisions except Senior and Big League, every player on the team roster must have at least one plate appearance and play three consecutive outs on defense in each game. The penalty for a manager violating the rule is a two-game suspension. This rule is waived if the game is completed prior to the usual duration of the game (six innings in Little League and below, seven innings in Junior League). http://en.wikipedia.org/wiki/Little_League_Baseball#Mandatory_Play_Rule

Virtually all youth sports coaching books include similar recommendations, and most town leagues around the country have mandatory play rules. A virtual consensus exists that all team members in what might be called early or first-experience sporting contexts should get to play in all the games.

This insight seems to rest on what Simon (2010) and others have identified as rights to basic benefits. In a nutshell, the argument runs as follows: in youth sport, the focus should be on learning the game, on developing personal skills, and on enjoying the activity. Every kid, it would seem, has a right to learn and improve. Every child has a right to play in a physically and psychologically safe environment. Because of this, playing time should be well distributed. Performance anxiety should be kept to a minimum. This is a time for development and fun.

The developmental or educational side of the argument is a powerful one. It relies on old physical education principles related to preparation for life. Everyone, physical educators would say, should have skills that allow them to engage in healthful and enjoyable recreational activities across the life span. With a so-called obesity epidemic facing American youth, it is important for kids to get away from their computer screens, develop some skills for negotiating outdoor activities successfully, and enjoy themselves.

The idea of playing time as a basic benefit and an educational experience also points to the future well-being of young athletes. It is very difficult to tell who will excel in different domains of learning. Some mature slowly but pick up the pace later. Particularly in anatomically and physiologically intensive activities like sports, it is sometimes difficult to predict later performance capabilities. Thus in a liberal democratic society like our own, we should err on the side of opportunity. We should provide a basic education to everyone and keep these doors of empowerment open as long as possible so that late bloomers, as well as those who face socioeconomic, racial, ethnic, or biological developmental barriers, will have a chance. In most youth sports settings, this means that children should have access to the full sporting experience . . . both the practicing and the playing.

Furthermore, positive affect is crucial to the educational agenda. Those who enjoy the sporting experience are more likely to persist. Those who persist will continue their activities into adulthood and even old age. Those who have the lifelong companionship of a favorite sport or outdoor activity will lead healthier, happier, and longer lives. Positive affect, on this line of thinking, is tethered to participation. And, all things being equal, it is far more fun for a seven-year-old to play than to watch.

Empirical studies support these speculations. In a landmark survey of 20,000 American youth, researchers found that the number one reason given by athletes for participation was "fun" (Seefeld et al. 1992). Fun was followed by "doing something I am good at," while "staying fit and healthy" ranked third. Winning did not even crack the top 10. Children want to play, and they enjoy doing things that show some degree of competence.

Nationally recognized youth coaches like Bob Bigelow take positions that are consistent with this research. He argues that "meaningful playing time for every player is job one." He goes on to suggest that if playing reserves "ends up costing the game, and if that hurts [coaches] too much, they should get out of coaching youth athletics and do something else" (Bigelow 2011, 1).

Youth Sports: Playing Time in a Period of Transition

The language of rights and benefits works well with young children, but it loses force at higher levels of competition. As already noted, it does not carry much weight in professional sports where athletes are elite performers, where imperatives of winning and market logic hold sway, and where even bench-warmers command handsome salaries. But what about college . . . high school . . . or even junior high? Where do the right to playing time and the commitment to education and play disappear or at least carry less weight?

Many years ago I learned that the cut-off point could be found at the middle school level. Our family had just moved from upstate New York to rural Pennsylvania. My daughter had successfully tried out for the seventh and eighth grade girl's basketball team. Prior to the start of the season, the coach called a meeting for the parents and players. We were told to sit on the bleachers in the gym.

The coach was all business. With a serious expression on his face he informed us that the team would be focused on winning and preparing select players for future membership on the JV and varsity teams! Regular practices would be demanding, voluntary practices were not really voluntary, and playing time would be limited or nonexistent for "those who are not ready." Before sending us off, he reminded us that he, and he alone, would decide who, when, and how much anyone played.

I have some sympathy for the message delivered by the coach. I can appreciate problems presented by basketball parents who expect the coach, as the old joke puts it, "to start their child and the next four best players." Furthermore, this coach's businesslike, competitive approach is probably not unusual, even at the middle school level. These kids are in the pipeline, as it were, for future athletic experiences where winning and losing will matter more and the public will take greater interest in game results.

However, it still makes sense to ask if this approach is appropriate, particularly for middle school athletes. After all, we do not usually cut students out of any significant learning opportunities at this level of education. We don't say to those who are less capable in math or English that "they do not get to play anymore." Should we not, therefore, keep the educational door open and the play spirit alive a little longer in the athletic domain? A heavy focus on winning and excellence can come later. The earnestness against which Johan Huizinga (1950) railed—that overly sober and serious attitude that replaces the play spirit—can come later too.

These concerns are not shared by everyone. Some might cite the fact that schools place gifted academic students into accelerated curriculums by the seventh grade. Less talented students simply "do not make the team" and are channeled into less demanding courses of study. Also, some schools participate in competitions sponsored by Knowledge Masters, National History Day, Mathcounts, spelling bees, or science fairs—events that are designed to pit the best intellects from one school against those from another. Critics might point out that nobody is guaranteed "playing time" in these activities either.

While this is true, and while playing time for athletes might be dealt with more judiciously in middle school than in children's sports settings, this argument does not settle the case. To be sure, caution about playing time for a low-end reserve is warranted both for the sake of the team and the potential embarrassment for that individual. On educational grounds alone, we would not want to put a youngster in a situation where high cost and publicly visible failure is likely. Similarly, we would probably not want a coach to sacrifice all team goals for any hard and fast commitments to equal playing time.

On the other hand, we have to remember that we are dealing with eleven-, twelve-, thirteen-, and fourteen-year-olds in this situation. And we have to remember that controversy often surrounds educational stratifications and the limitations they place on those who are deemed "unqualified." Many educational policies are based on the premise that individuals need time to develop . . . sometimes even through their college years and beyond.[4] For reasons that are often outside their control—reasons that range from biological and economic to cultural—some students arrive at desirable destinations earlier than others. While the promotion of excellence is culturally important and while the rights of the gifted are as important as the rights of others, some balance would seem to be in order, particularly at these earlier levels of education. Because of this need for balance, some weight should still be given to the basic benefits argument. How much weight is merited is, of course, open to question.

I don't see any slam-dunk answers to this question. Conclusions have to do with judgment, with how values are prioritized. Middle school athletes are, as my daughter's coach reminded us, preparing for varsity experiences several years hence. Such preparation places a priority on excellence, winning, individual rights, and ultimately on public or fan interests and so-called front porch values of athletics for a school or school system. These can be important considerations.

The basic benefits argument, on the other hand, prioritizes competence and learning rather than excellence, group rights and participation, personal educational benefit over fan interest, and sports as an educational laboratory more than a high-visibility vehicle for educational or noneducational ends. These too are, or can be, important values.[5]

My own judgment is that the junior high school level of sporting experience should privilege basic benefits over scarce benefits, educational values over public entertainment benefits and related emphases on winning. Perhaps the ratio should be something like 70:30 or 60:40. This would suggest that coaches still have an important moral obligation to play all their athletes. The moral obligation is tethered to the fact that middle school is still a time for development, fun, and protection from overspecialization and high doses of performance anxiety. While the winnowing process has begun, while victories take on increased importance, and while all individuals cannot expect or get equal playing time, the logic of education and play should still provide the dominant themes for the experience. The coach should still be far more the inclusive, duty-bound educator than the exclusive coaching technician or instrumentalist.[6]

High School Athletics: Playing Time and Reciprocity

If my argument is on track, it stands to reason that high school coaches are less obligated to give playing time to benchwarmers. In this setting the group works more exclusively toward common ends—a victory, a winning season, a championship. Sacrificing individual interests for corporate goals is expected. Coaches can lose their jobs if win-loss records are not favorable. Hardly anybody in this kind of competitive environment is guaranteed playing time. This is where a commitment to excellence makes sense—both individual and team excellence. And arguably, team excellence cannot be achieved when coaches have to worry about playing time for low-end reserves, individuals whose play will likely endanger team objectives.

Furthermore, reserves at the high school level enjoy any number of benefits, even if playing time is not one of them. Several of these goods or benefits appear at the beginning of the chapter. Given these realities and under these circumstances, shouldn't lesser players be happy with their lot . . . or at least appreciate the reasons for their spot on the bench? I am not sure that they should.

First, although the educational, basic benefits argument is less weighty in high school and high school age settings,[7] it does not follow that it should disappear altogether. After all, high school sports take place in an educational context. Extracurricular activities like varsity sports are compatible with core educational values and purposes espoused by school systems and contribute to those ends. If playing, in addition to watching and practicing, carries educational benefit, and if rights to educational benefit apply to all members of a team, then coaches have a prima facie obligation to allow kids to play. Coaches, in other words, have a moral obligation *as educators* to give lesser players meaningful playing time.

I say that there is a prima facie obligation because I admit that the *actual* obligation, as noted previously, is undoubtedly less than the ideal of equal playing time. Rights to educational benefit do not trump all other values or considerations. Equal respect accorded to starters and reserves, for instance, may well provide a rationale for meaningful but unequal playing time.

Second, the ethics of fair play in the form of reciprocity could be used to forge a more equitable arrangement between coach and bench player. Coaches need the services of reserves, even individuals who are not required for game contributions. Much team success can be attributed to how well reserves practice, how well they serve as "scout team" members, how much spirit and enthusiasm they show, and so on.

But reserves want to play. They hope against hope that they will improve enough to become starters. If not that, they picture themselves getting into a game when the outcome is still undecided, perhaps even doing something heroic. But for that story to have any chance of becoming reality, the coach needs to put the athlete in the game.

Ethics enters this scene of mutual need and potential benefit, as Singer (1995) noted, on the foundation of two virtues—trust and fidelity. The athlete has to trust the coach because the player has to meet his part of the bargain first. A coach could defect and not put the player into the game in spite of the player's previous goodwill actions. Thus the coach must show the second virtue—fidelity—in order to make good on his promise to the player.

Kohlberg (1981) argues that this kind of "I'll scratch your back if you scratch mine" ethic involves a relatively low level of moral thinking.[8] It would be better if the issue could be settled on principles of justice—on the idea that fairness requires the coach to provide at least a taste of what the benchwarmer really wants in light of that individual's hard work and contribution to the team. But in the absence of high-minded ethics, trust, fidelity, and reciprocity might provide a degree of protection for athletes who want to get into the game but find themselves blocked by coaches who have the final say.

Critics might insist that the reciprocity argument does not work. First, reserves may be expendable. To that extent, coaches have no incentive to enter into such agreements. In addition, some might point out, this is not a relationship among equals. The coach is in charge. Compliance on the part of the player can be required. Coercion can serve as a substitute for ethics by agreement. The coach does not need to promise playing time because the coach does not need to offer it in order to get what he wants.

I do not find these arguments persuasive because they seem more descriptive than normative. The unequal status of the coach and the players fuels many of the ethical dilemmas that occur in sports. While the coach may be able to replace a reserve who is audacious enough to bargain for playing time, and while the coach has most of the power, the coach is still mentor and educator. As an individual who should have concern for all athletes on the team, the logic of reciprocity should appear attractive both ethically and motivationally. The coach should be sympathetic to the fact that the hardworking reserve has at least some call on a benefit that all players desire—getting on the court or field in a real game when it still matters . . . and for more than a couple of seconds.

It stands to reason, then, that prima facie educational obligations and the ethics of reciprocity (if not principles of justice or loyalty) would suggest that high school coaches do have a moral obligation to find meaningful playing time for all reserves . . . at least those who are dedicated, hardworking, and committed to team success.

Collegiate Level: Playing Time and Competitive Excellence

It's not unreasonable to hold that basic benefits arguments, educational obligations, the ethics of reciprocity, and even principles of loyalty and justice continue to be operative at the collegiate level. This is still an educational setting. A reasonable presumption is that sports in this environment should privilege players and their interests over business-related, front porch–driven, win-at-all-costs philosophies. Thus college athletes who sit at the far end of the bench should get a chance to play too.[9]

A number of utilitarian economic arguments might be offered in opposition to this perspective. Particularly at the NCAA Division I level, and most notably in football and basketball, it could be argued that economic imperatives do (and should) trump educational objectives. Winning is essential. The use of low-end reserves flies in the face of this reality. Even coaches who would like to play reserves regularly will not do so. Unilateral disarmament, in big-time sports, is a nonstarter.

But there is another, less controversial argument against using reserves in games: college sports require the prioritization of excellence over mediocrity.

College athletes are elite performers. They should focus on team and individual excellence. They should aim at perfection . . . even if they never achieve it.

Here is where the ethical rub comes in. Arguably, team excellence is promoted most efficiently and effectively by catering to the best players on the team or those with the greatest potential. Time and energy investments make more sense there than elsewhere. On this line of reasoning, reserves in general, and end-of-the-bench reserves in particular, should serve facilitating roles—not to foster each other's performance but to maximize better players and thus the team. For any low-end reserves, this facilitating role will perpetuate their lesser status. After all, time used to facilitate teammates' growth is, at least in part, time lost for one's own performance needs.

This claim could be verified empirically. How do reserves spend their time in practice? How many reps do they get? How often does a coach give them individual attention, especially in contrast to the starters? How often are they required to learn the next opponent's offense in order to facilitate the starting team's defensive preparations? How infrequently are the starters asked to return the favor and facilitate the reserves' readiness to play against the next opponent?

Answers to these questions, for anyone who has participated in or observed college practices, are clear. Lower-end reserves are asked to sacrifice their own quest for excellence for the sake of the team. To be sure, this can still be a gratifying experience, and college athletes enter into such agreements with their eyes wide open. But it still needs to be made clear that the quest for excellence (and the winning that goes with it) carries risks for those who show less promise of achieving high levels of expertise and whose services are needed to facilitate the excellence of others.

Many reserves who are used as means to team ends but are not compensated with opportunities for playing time still approach practice with determination and hope. Like Rudy, they may put forth twice the effort of some starters. Because they are part of the team, they have a chance to get on the court or field . . . even if the cards are stacked against them.

And the cards usually are stacked against them. They begin their team journey with lesser skills and less game experience. Without equal attention at practice, and without learning opportunities provided by playing time, the gap between the starters and reserves tends to increase. In corresponding fashion, the odds of the reserve earning much playing time before graduation grow longer.

However, excellence is a powerful value and worthy objective. Sacrifices by teammates in its pursuit may be warranted, particularly at elite college levels. Nevertheless, when the value of excellence is combined with the logic of instrumentalism, individual rights may be put at risk and a more balanced view of sporting values may be lost.

These are precisely the concerns raised by the NCAA Committee on Women's Athletics (CWA) in 2007 when it argued that male practice players should be barred from women's intercollegiate programs. They claimed that the use of men violated the spirit, if not also the letter, of Title IX legislation and cited two reasons. First, the availability of males for practice allowed coaches to carry fewer women on their rosters. This reduced opportunity. In addition, with males on the court or field at practice, women reserves were standing on the sidelines and thus receiving less practice time.

No less personages than Tennessee's Pat Summit and Rutgers's Vivian Stringer supported the use of male practice players, and their primary argument rested on an appeal to excellence. Stringer said, "It is the male practice players that allow us to get better. . . . Male practice players are the most important element to the continued growth of women's basketball players" (*USA Today* 2007).

Jim Foster, the Ohio State women's basketball coach, took an opposing view. When told of all the good the male practice players brought to the sport he replied, "I'd like to hear the stories of the [women] who didn't get to practice and had to stand and watch." He continued, "To take even more time and more reps from a segment of players almost dooms them to mediocrity" (*USA Today*, 2007).

Most women coaches and administrators sided with Summit and Stringer. They agreed that male practice players can expedite the development of good female players and women's teams in the direction of excellence. At this level excellence should trump opportunity. There should be no turning back on the commitment to enhancing the quality of play. If males proved more efficient and effective in producing excellence in women's basketball, they should stay.

Predictably, the legislation proposed by the CWA went nowhere. Thus in Division III, male practice players are still permitted with certain restrictions.[10] In Divisions I and II, males can serve as "practice guys" with few limitations.[11]

This nexus between excellence and instrumentalism has obvious and important implications for the rights of benchwarmers and for any moral obligations of coaches to let them play. If those last few seats on the game bench can be left vacant—for purposes of promoting excellence—any and all moral obligations about playing those individuals disappear. No one needs to worry about the rights and interests of players who no longer exist.

Some might argue that the last few positions on the bench, at least at the college level, are not playing positions anyhow. Normal rotations in football, basketball, soccer, and the like do not require the full complement of athletes carried on a team. The use of male practice players, therefore, merely formalizes a relationship that existed before their use. End of the bench positions are de facto practice positions, not playing positions. Whether they are males or females makes no difference. They are facilitators. If men function better than women as practice facilitators, why not use them? Either way, no *playing* positions are lost.

But this begs the very question at issue. Should end of the bench positions be strictly practice positions? And should individual and team excellence stand as sufficient warrant for the sacrifices required of those who would facilitate such excellence? Could the logic of excellence and facilitation be extended to male teams too?

Why not reduce men's collegiate basketball teams to ten or eleven players, just as many women's teams have done? Perhaps new NCAA legislation could be passed to allow recently retired NBA players or semipros who are not even students to serve as practice guys for the men's teams—all for purposes of promoting excellence.

Michael Sandel (2007) confronted similar logical possibilities when he examined issues of technology and interests in achieving perfection. He worried that an unbridled quest for perfection can rob us of crucial elements of our humanity—humility, responsibility, and solidarity.

The most relevant of these for current purposes is probably solidarity. Teams, it seems to me, pool both their resources and their risks. Because individuals cannot control all sporting variables, they join hands in hopes of flourishing on the back of combined talents but also in recognition that protection is needed from unforeseen problems. Not all will play starring roles, but all could play important roles. Humility and mutual dependency lead to strong feelings of community, of "us."

According to Sandel, Promethean hopes for total control work against an ethic of solidarity. Social and psychological engineering replaces the magical "chemistry of a team" that often surprises us and fills us with gratitude. Maximal developmental strategies, controlled environments, and ideally prepared practice players replace the nonlinear and unpredictable drama of learning. Efficiency substitutes for the uncertain dynamics of the benchwarmer who lives with hope of playing time while sacrificing for the good of a larger cause. These trade-offs move us to a place where we no longer depend, wonder, and support.

Sandel would prefer the messier situation in which individuals willingly and humbly choose to pool their assets in order to minimize their liabilities. This is a world in which choice is tempered with chance.

The coach should be part of this pooling of risks and resources. A team is a family of stronger and weaker members, of individuals who serve different roles but have common aspirations. The coach and superior team members should be rooting for the lesser players to improve and succeed—to get into a game and do something well.

Conclusion

Benchwarmers occupy the real estate for a variety of reasons. Some individuals deserve to be there . . . and perhaps some even deserve to *stay* there. There is no absolute right to playing time at the upper levels of sports. Correspondingly, coaches have no absolute moral obligations to play reserves.

However, I have argued that a prima facie obligation does exist. It is stronger at introductory and youth levels of sports and lesser at higher levels. In youth sports settings, education, development, opportunity, healthful exercise, and play are basic benefits that should trump any concerns over winning, excellence, financial gain, and the like. Everybody should play, and everybody should play for significant portions of the game.

I derided the overly serious attitudes of middle school coaches for quickly abandoning these values. Late bloomers deserve a chance. All kids are still learning the basics. The spirit of play should be kept alive. All players should be given a reasonable chance to get on the court or field.

I suggest that educational values should play a role in high school sports. The ethics of reciprocity might serve to mitigate potential harms of the unequal power relationship between coach and benchwarmer. A coach might feel that justice requires at least a degree of compensation (in the form of playing time) for the hardworking low-end reserve. I agree, however, that both for the sake of the lesser player and the team, decisions about how much playing time is provided need to be judicious.

At the college level, commitments to excellence provide arguments that justify the parsimonious use of low-end reserves or even their elimination . . . if and when practice functions can be assumed more efficiently and effectively by others. In such an instrumental sporting world, a coach would be blamed not so much for abusing reserves but for having them on the team in the first place.

I prefer to err on the side of opportunity. I like the moral ties that exist in large families where one person in encouraged to look out for the other. I think it is a sign of strength, not weakness, when a coach worries about providing meaningful playing time for the last person on the bench. It is when those concerns disappear, and even more so when the players who should be the objects of such concerns disappear, that I worry about the health of the entire sporting enterprise.

Questions for Review and Discussion

1. Why does Kretchmar argue that context is so important in deciding on the ethics of playing time? Can you identify ten contextual issues that might affect an athlete's right to play . . . and a coach's moral obligation to put him on the court or field?

2. How important is it for a coach to be honest with players and parents up front about playing time? Do you agree with Kretchmar that such "truth in advertising" does not remove moral obligations for playing benchwarmers?

3. Was it useful to organize the article chronologically—from youth sports through intercollegiate athletics? Can you imagine other ways in which this argument could have been formatted?

4. Kretchmar places great emphasis on education in order to support his arguments for more equitable playing time. If one removed this issue, what other kinds of arguments remain?

5. Where do you stand on the issue of promoting excellence? What kinds of trade-offs are justifiable in a society that honors fine performances? Can you rally an argument to the effect that excellence should trump learning and athlete's rights to playing time at elite levels?

Suggestions for Further Reading

Bigelow, B. Youth Coaches: Meaningful Playing Time for Every Player Is Job One. 2011. www.monsteam.com.

Huizinga, J. *Homo Ludens: A Study of the Play Element in Culture*. Boston: Beacon, 1950.

Kohlberg, L. *The Philosophy of Moral Development*. San Francisco: Harper & Row, 1981.

MacIntyre, A. *After Virtue: A Study in Moral Theory*. 2nd ed. Notre Dame, IN: Notre Dame Press, 1984.

NCAA Division III Manual: Constitution, Operating Bylaws, Administrative Bylaws. Indianapolis: NCAA, 2011.

Patrick, Dick. "Women Practicing versus Men: Yea or Nay?" *USA Today*, January 16, 2007.

Sandel, M. *The Case Against Perfection: Ethics in the Age of Genetic Engineering*. Cambridge: Harvard University Press, 2007.

Seefeldt, V., M. Ewing, and S. Walk. *Overview of Youth Sports Programs in the United States.* Washington, DC: Carnegie Council on Adolescent Development, 1992.

Simon, R. *Fair Play: The Ethics of Sport.* Boulder, CO: Westview, 2010.

Singer, P. *How Are We to Live? Ethics in an Age of Self-Interest.* Amherst, NY: Prometheus, 1995.

Smith, R., F. Smoll, and N. Barnett. "Reduction of Children's Sport Performance Anxiety Through Social Support and Stress-Reduction Training for Coaches." *Journal of Applied Developmental Psychology* 16 (1995.): 125–142.

Nine

Coaching, Gamesmanship, and Intimidation

MARK HAMILTON

Having lived in Ohio all my life and being an avid Ohio sports fan, I know about coaches who use intimidation. I grew up watching Woody Hayes coach Ohio State; Bobby Knight is a local hero who grew up less than an hour away (my high school basketball coach was one of his college teammates). Throughout junior and senior high school I watched basketball games coached by Bill Musselman at Ashland College. Known for creating intimidating, energy-charged pregame warm-up drills and for later coaching the University of Minnesota in college basketball's best known on-the-court fight against Ohio State in 1972, Musselman is quoted as saying, "Losing is worse than death because you have to live with defeat." The list of intimidating coaches from Ohio is extensive—coaches who know how to threaten officials, players, and reporters, who bully anyone else who gets in their way on or off the playing field. And they are praised as coaches who know how to motivate players and win games. This used to be an accepted practice among coaches. While it has waned, it is still overlooked in a coach who wins. Any serious evaluation or moral critique of coaching ethics must include a close inspection of intimidation and bullying by coaches as a means of gamesmanship.

Gamesmanship

Gamesmanship is a method used by coaches or athletes to gain an upper hand in a contest. The concept originates from Stephen Potter's 1947 book, *The Theory and Practice of Gamesmanship*. In this well-known satirical work Potter calls it "'The Art of Winning Games Without Actually Cheating'—that is my personal 'working definition.'"[1] Leslie Howe characterized it "as an attempt to win one game by playing another . . . [it] is a deliberate strategy of competition . . . designed for winning regardless of athletic excellence."[2] It is using numerous strategic tactics to better one's position in the game or using dubious methods to secure an unfair victory while remaining within the constitutive rules of the game.[3] Although some consider all gamesmanship cheating, it is not cheating narrowly understood as intentionally violating the constitutive rules of a contest. Gamesmanship ruthlessly pursues victory by all means short of apparent rule breaking. Most consider it a legal but not necessarily moral approach to playing games. Howe continues, "Violation of the rules is already [necessarily] prohibited by the rules; attempting to violate the rules is cheating [which nullifies the game], and gamesmanship [I am supposing] is not identical with cheating, though it might have much the same end, namely, winning with less strictly athletic effort."[4] So while it may not technically violate the written rules of the contest, gamesmanship uses maneuvers that threaten the spirit of the game and attains victory through skullduggery.

There are numerous species in the genus of gamesmanship. These include attempting to gain competitive advantage by (1) manipulating but not actually violating the rules,[5] (2) withholding information, (3) practicing outright deception, or (4) using intimidation in its various forms.[6] This chapter will focus on the use of intimidation as it intensifies into bullying, which includes nonphysical ploys primarily expressed as verbal intimidation and threats or actual physical violence.

Potter describes the lesser forms of intimidation as attempts to disrupt the opponent's play or "break the flow." This encompasses getting "inside one's opponent's head" by such things as intentionally disrupting an opponent's play, distracting him, getting him to "over think" his moves, or disrupting his concentration.[7] Potter provides an example of disrupting a rival's concentration by falsely and intentionally accusing him of cheating.[8] Using trick plays, stealing signs, or bantering with opponents are acceptable forms of psychological subterfuge. Other measures include growing a shadow beard to create a "menacing" appearance or wearing ominous-looking uniforms. These are amusing more than intimidating, though they are motivated by a desire to apply psychological intimidation. More serious intimidation attempts include calling timeouts to "ice" a shooter or kicker, taunting, throwing inside in baseball, or firing slap shots at a goalie's head or stacking the ice with thugs in hockey.[9] But if these practices do not actually violate the rules of the game, can they possibly be justified?

Intimidation is always negative and should never be used, but at advanced levels is disputably a part of the regulative nature of the game.[10] Howe argues that "the good of competitive sport is that it is a test of the whole athlete—not just his or her physical skills."[11] It is a misconception to think that advanced sports involve only physical participation, when in fact there are strong intellectual dimensions and players participate as whole beings. This is the justification, says Howe, for using intimidating methods: "The opponent who directs a strategy of gamesmanship against a competitor constructs an opportunity for the other to fail, but the decisive move, the failure, belongs to the target. If the gamer's behavior is within the rules, it cannot be unfair, and the competitive failure of the target is not the result of unfair advantage. It is because the target did not pass one of the fundamental aspects of competition: the test of psychological strength and preparedness."[12] This can only be defensible at higher echelons of competition. Can the receiver running a pattern over the middle who is legally popped by a linebacker mentally recover from the linebacker's intimidating hit to repeat the pattern? Does the field goal kicker waiting to attempt the game-winning kick on the last play of the game withstand the pressure of the defensive team calling a time-out to ice him? Can the visiting college free throw shooter weather the intimidating pressure of the screaming hometown crowd? These mental tests are part of the challenge, and to remove this form of gamesmanship could radically alter the contemporary challenges of these sports.

Howe also makes a moral distinction between different forms of gamesmanship and argues that some forms are necessary while others are impermissible: "We have to make a distinction between 'weak' and 'strong' forms of gamesmanship, the former designating the forms of gamesmanship that are compatible with an ideal of sport as a 'mutual challenge to achieve excellence' and the latter marking out those that are not. Actions such as throwing inside, the fast break, hard tens, and withholding line-up and injury information would fall into the weak category; deception with regard to line calls and fouls ('simulation'), gross acts of intimidation such as physical abuse (especially where this is above the norm expected in that sport), mobbing officials, and disrupting players' preparations would count in the strong category. The criterion we need to apply, then, in attempting to distinguish between appropriate and inappropriate forms of gamesmanship is whether the practice improves both participants or not."[13] Or whether it contributes to the merit of the challenge. Some forms of gamesmanship are valuable and possibly necessary to games if they do not degrade the participants and they contribute to the success of the challenge. Others are morally suspect, asserts Howe, since they are athletically self-defeating.[14]

However, even weak forms of intimidation are unacceptable in recreational games or where the participants are young. These additional mental challenges are a legitimate part of the game only among those who have a sophisticated level of understanding of the sport and are playing at a reasonably competitive level.[15] Forms of weak intimidation are acceptable in higher levels of sports that include psychological testing as part of the regulative aspect of the game. Bullying is always immoral.

Intimidation and Bullying as Gamesmanship

Intimidation is intended to elicit fear, to browbeat or to frighten someone into submission by inducing distress or a sense of inferiority.[16] Consequently intimidation excludes the mild or weak forms of intimidation. Coaches use intimidation as a form of gamesmanship to gain an advantage over their opponents by breaking the will of the officials, the opponents, or their own players so they can improve their positioning in sporting contests. When understood this way, intimidation is nearly synonymous to bullying.

Bullying is "a conscious, willful, deliberate and repeated hostile activity marked by an imbalance of power, intent to harm, and/or a threat to aggression. Severe bullying can lead to a feeling of terror on the part of the person being bullied."[17] Bullying employs deliberate and repeated antagonistic activity that includes swearing and uncontrollable screaming as its most common manifestation, lurid, offensive comments hurled at an athlete including insults and put-downs. There is constant negativity and criticism that is derogatory in nature and includes publicly ridiculing and humiliating players. "The bully-coach's repertoire includes shouting, cursing, personal denigration, and humiliation. So intimidating is the bully-coach that few young people dare to summon the courage to approach him, let alone challenge his technique or pronouncements."[18] Bobby Knight exemplifies this behavior. As one observer reports, Knight had been seen to "get in kids' faces, grab them by the arms, and spray his spit onto cheeks as he ranted at them. We had seen him show disrespect to referees. He used his body, his eyes, facial gestures, and words to intimidate in the hope of affecting performance or decisions. . . . But his public bullying not only damaged his players, it also set a public example that amateur coaches inevitably mimicked."[19] The most dreadful forms of sports bullying include acts of violence, threats of physical violence, or blaming athletes for failure. Knight once said to player Steve Risley, "The reason we lost the game was you, it was your fault."[20]

However, Knight is not a rarity. Consider the following example of bullying as public humiliation in a seventh grade gym class by a junior high school football coach, probably similar to what has gone on in gyms or on playing fields everywhere. "We would play some sort of group game where the winners could return to the locker room one by one, leaving the loser for the end. This last would be called the 'Green Weenie' and his name would be placed on a chalkboard for everyone to see. I remember how hard I would try to avoid being last. On one particular day, I tried as hard as I could and actually came in second to last. I wasn't last!!! The coach just looked at me and said, 'You are always the greenie weenie' and wrote my name on the board as he laughed."[21] Some coaches are just mean. They pump themselves up to feel good and self-important by acting this way. Former NFL star defensive lineman Joe Ehrmann says, "Bullies act tough in order to hide feelings of insecurity and self-loathing. Coach Bully has an incomprehensible need to dominate his players."[22] Despotic coaches find pleasure in breaking people down. They make players feel inferior and in the process make themselves feel superior. This coach could be reliving his own glory, whether real or imagined, by destroying others. This has to be stopped, yet we inexcusably look past the indiscretions of these coaches if they generate enough wins.

Clarifications on Bullying

Bullying, first, is an overused term describing anyone who is demanding or expects competence and results. Unfortunately, any negative corrective is now interpreted as bullying. A boss who expects workers to complete a task or a parent who disciplines a child appropriate to the misbehavior is not a bully. We should be careful not to include every authoritarian coach who believes in a vigorous sense of personal discipline and carries this over to the competitive arena as being a bully. Bullying is a very specific type of strong intimidation that is aggressive and antagonistic and uses humiliation from a position of authority. It is selfish and does not consider the ends of the victim, though the bully can deceive himself into thinking it is for the victim's benefit.

Second, we should distinguish intimidation from toughness. Modern sports are complex, arduous, and demanding. They require toughness as part of preparation and performance. Practices for these sports are hard and should be if they are to create excellence. Coaches can be demanding and need to teach both physical and mental toughness without turning to strong forms of intimidation and bullying. Teaching toughness is not equivalent to bullying.

Third, intimidation should not be confused with intensity. A coach can be intense without being a bully. Intensity involves strong depth of feeling and great coaches have exceptional concentration levels. Some coaching personalities are naturally forceful and competition can be intense. A vehement, intense coach may not intend to create fear, but fearful feelings may result and an athlete may feel threatened by this coach's personality. Not all intimidating actions are bullying or necessarily immoral, however. Intense coaches must be acutely self-conscious and aware of how they come across to their athletes, especially young ones. Intensity may be perceived as intimidating, though the intent to intimidate is absent. Coaches like John Wooden, Tom Landry, Tony Dungy, Pat Summit, Larry Brown, and Phil Jackson are intense, but they never threaten the personhood of their players and are never bullies. A coach must teach that the actions and performances of athletes have consequences but without attacking the person or without being a raving lunatic. I had a high school basketball coach who was intense and very competitive. He had a steely stare and stood 6 foot 5. If he seemed imposing to a 5 foot 7 point guard, it was certainly not his intent to be threatening. We knew he cared about us personally and that his corrective instruction, while it may have seemed harsh at times, was not understood as personal. On the other hand my ninth grade football coach and college JV basketball coach were intimidating and did not seem to care about me. I believe they acted this way because they thought they were supposed to (one had played for Woody Hayes at Ohio State) and felt insecure. Many erroneously believe that creating this atmosphere earns them respect. I did not respect either coach. They both confused fear with respect. Intimidation may elicit fear but never earns respect.

Targets of the Bully Coach

The bully coach uses intimidation to coerce officials not to make calls against his or her team, to remove or diminish the opponent's ability to be an athletic threat, [23] or to motivate and challenge his or her players. Some coaches browbeat officials to gain advantage by causing the official to hesitate when making a marginal call against their team. This coach virtually terrorizes officials through violent bursts of indignation accompanied by yelling, arm waving, and menacing glares. Coaches will even feign anger in order to exert pressure or "work"[24] the official to get the next call. Some coaches cultivate a reputation as putting fear in the hearts of adjudicators. Major League Baseball has a long history of managers like Billy Martin, Earl Weaver, Lou Piniella, and Bobby Cox who have excelled in this practice. They wanted officials to ask themselves, Why inconvenience myself to make this call and take this abuse? I won't call it because I don't need him screaming in my face again. Although coaches are not necessarily in a dominant power relationship with officials, some use intimidation as a strong form of gamesmanship for which there is no moral justification. Some coaches teach their athletes to be intimidators and may offer a bounty to harm an opposing player.[25] Weak forms include directing a pitcher to throw inside or emphasizing hard contact in full contact sports. Others might call an opponent a name not worth repeating to rile him up or use excessively aggressive players to intimidate opponents or even take out an opponent's best player by causing a malicious intentional injury. Joe Ehrmann tells the following story:

> I was 11 years old. It was during a youth league basketball game, and I was in-bounding the ball from under the basket. But the opposing player was all over me and I could not get the ball in. The coach called 2 consecutive timeouts to avoid a 5-second call that would have cost us possession of the ball. The jumping-bean kid guarding the in-bounds pass was too close to me and the he wasn't giving me room. Coach pulled me aside after the 2nd time-out, gripped my arm, and would not let go as the referee's whistle summoned us back on the court. He put his face very close to mine so no one would hear and looked me straight in the eyes without blinking. "Bring the ball back over your head with both hands and smash it into his face," he said. He put his right hand on my left shoulder and squeezed it so tightly that it hurt. "Smash the ball as hard as you can in his face. You will teach him a lesson about who he is playing against." I remember walking to the space below the basket and looking at the kid whose nose I was about to break. I remember knowing I was going to do it even though most of me didn't want to. . . . I looked at my coach as the ref blew the whistle and handed me the ball. The coach kept staring at me without blinking. I gripped the ball, slammed it into my hands as my teammates broke in zigzags, lifted it above my head, and brought it down with all my force right into the kid's face. Blood shot everywhere and the kid's mother came rushing from the stands screaming at me as her son lay crying on the court. The whole gym stared at me. . . . Coach praised me in the locker room, upholding that play as something positive, and "the way the game was to be played!" Shame engulfed me.[26]

Here is a youth team coach forcing a young boy to direct violence at an athletic adversary. Attempting to win through gamesmanship can include bullying as a means to enhance and motivate performance by using fear rather than pursuing excellence to perform at a higher level. This behavior is rationalized as a way to toughen up young athletes in order to advance their performance and prepare them for real life. People like Hayes, Knight, and Musselman used these strong types of intimidation and became clichés. Their actions have been self-perpetuating. A multitude of coaches model these harmful methods. Coaches emulate one another, and "bully-coaches in youth and interscholastic sports have plenty of institutionally accepted role models whose fame condones such behavior."[27] They are all around us at every level of sports. Recently I became acquainted with a female college coach who bullied her athletes by depriving them of meals, harshly berating them, and treating them as nonentities.

Bullying is wrong for a variety of reasons. A coach who tries to intimidate officials, team members, and opposing players is attempting to win in ways other than exhibiting the abilities the game was designed to test. The bullying coach, then, is undermining the challenge of the game. Bullying coaches who treat their own players in objectionable ways are violating their moral duty to care for the welfare, health, and safety of their players and to treat them with respect and dignity. (On this point, see Mitten's discussion of the legal duties of coaches with respect to the health and safety of their athletes in Chapter 13.)

Creating Fear

Bullying creates fear in its victims. There are different kinds of fear and some have utilitarian value. Fear can alert one to real danger or cause one to focus energy and attention where it is needed. A proper fear response can save a life. And there can be appropriate forms of fear in sports coaching. A tough coach may justifiably use a tempered realistic fear of losing, fear of failure, or fear of a loss of playing time in order to get a player's attention or to inspire a player who is underachieving or lazy. But this should be done while affirming the athlete's personhood so that the athlete knows the coach is appropriately evaluating her performance and not dismissing her personhood. Coaches who cared about me caused me to be appropriately afraid of losing playing time. This kind of fear is closer to disappointment than to terror and does not threaten the athlete's personhood or identity. It is not the same as the fear elicited by a bully. Coaches who cannot control their tempers, punish athletes by overpracticing, withholding rewards, screaming in their faces, grabbing them, and throwing objects may deteriorate to the point of irrationality and actually lash out physically.

Bullying generates different responses: outright fear and fearful anxiety; both include fear of humiliation. The philosopher Martin Heidegger sharply distinguishes fear from anxiety. "Fear is always fear of something, and for the sake of something, for example one fears for one's life, or one fears about some possibility."[28] Anxiety, on the other hand is more subtle. "Anxiety is precisely anxiety over nothing,"[29] because it is not due to a singular event but an atmosphere or mood of despair that is just there.

Outright fear includes an expectation of physical injury. It is a pragmatic response to a frightening entity or experience. An aggressive coach poses a direct threat. The coach may use threatening language expressed in an angry tone, possibly expressing uncontrolled anger where the recipient may even perceive physical danger. Many coaches erroneously equate athletics with the military and with manhood and prowess. Some team-training camps and practices have been modeled on military boot camps emphasizing toughness, discipline, and a rigid chain of command.[30] These bullying coaches often make bold analogies between sports, war, and manhood. Like marine drill sergeants, these autocratic coaches find pleasure in breaking people down. I remember a college coach once coming out to a local basketball court where I was playing with some high school friends and bringing with him several large men who enjoyed pounding on younger, smaller high school guys. We had several pickup games with them, and when we finished we were physically beaten and emotionally broken. These were not impressive basketball players but thugs who bullied us into submission on the court that night.

At their most extreme, these coaches use threats of violence to induce a kind of terror. Players then have a choice: fight or flight. Those who fight become more aggressive and may challenge the coach or direct their aggression toward the opponent. They may achieve a higher level of athletic performance, but at what cost? Longtime NFL star defensive lineman Joe Ehrmann, who has coached high school for many years, says, "I realized that anger had driven much of my athletic success. Coaches leveraged it—they fired me up and charged me up by angering me."[31] This can become a way of creating cult-like devotion in athletes who would mindlessly run through a wall for the coach. The end, however, cannot justify such degrading means.

The other common response is flight. Many parents refuse to allow their children to quit teams because they fear quitting will become a pattern that carries over into all the difficult challenges in life. But there are behaviors more detrimental than quitting a team. Sometimes it is better to quit than endure abuse. The young athlete flees the sport, realizing that a game is not worth the pain or abuse.

We homeschooled our daughter Tess through eighth grade. Along the way she participated in lots of soccer, softball, and dance. She was ready to enter high school and participate in softball but wanted to take a look at other sports, especially basketball. She spent much of the summer before ninth grade becoming a respectable shooter. We met the new coach of a weak program that most of the good athletes were avoiding. The coach invited Tess to an open gym. When I picked her up, she was uncharacteristically quiet and only said, "Dad, I'm never going back there." The next day she picked up a tennis racket, and by her junior year she was a starter on varsity tennis, later playing college tennis. She was so upset by one day of basketball that she never went back. Years later she described the verbal mistreatment she experienced from a female coach who intimidated her. Tess fled to maintain her dignity.

The second type of fear is anxiety. It is more covert but possibly more damaging. Here a perpetually negative coach creates a destructive mood. It usually includes critical, degrading remarks but could also include punishing the team through abusive workouts or withholding privilege such as meal money. The coach is self-deceived into thinking he or she knows how to inspire athletic performance when in reality it creates a crushing feeling of anxiety and self-annihilation.

When a coach targets an individual, the intimidation begins slowly and the athlete may be oblivious to the effect it is having on her. The coach may speak derisively or make false insinuations, such as "you look like you're gaining weight." "You are not putting forth the effort." "You don't care." This coach knows how to humiliate the athlete and create a sense of anxiety. The athlete feels anguish but may not know precisely why. Her life is not being threatened, but she feels like a nonentity. She feels ashamed but does not know the reason. Athletes in this state will lower their eyes, retreat to solitude, and experience a sense of dejection. But they likely will blame themselves and may be deceived into thinking if they stick with it they will eventually succeed or become better persons.

These menacing coaches thrive on creating an atmosphere of anxiety; their coaching identity is tied to their ability to vex or trouble the athlete. It is part of an unbounded vanity. Bullies get enjoyment from intimidating others. The bully coach calls male athletes "girls," pansies, or worse if they don't measure up and pushes them by demeaning them. Coaches devoid of moral courage become defensive and attack anyone who questions their methods or motives.

Bully coaches create feelings of worry, unease, and dread, like the main character in Dostoevsky's novel *Notes from Underground*, who is overlooked and abused by everyone and feels like "an object of contempt," "like an insect on the wall" and states of his experience, "I sat ignored by everyone, crushed and annihilated."[32] Young athletes are particularly vulnerable to anger experiences and the resulting anxiety. The athlete bullied this way is more liable to stick it out, become depressed, and blame herself. A sense of failure too early in life can create a fear of failing, and immature athletes do not know how to cope with this. They retreat into solitude to survive. "Anxiety leads us to drop the mask of our everyday familiarity with the world. Anxiety makes everything of such little significance that even our own sense of self is lost. Anxiety is the recognition of a certain nothingness, the groundlessness in our existence."[33] The athlete experiences a sense of personal betrayal and alienation though she may not know why. "Anxiety reveals to us a certain homelessness—we are not at home in the world, the world faces us as something weird or 'uncanny.'"[34] Bullied athletes feel estranged, no longer at home in the game they love. (Indeed as Jeffrey Fry points out Chapter 10, recent research in neuroscience strongly suggests that the behavior of influential individuals can change the brains of young athletes, for the better in the case of good coaches but for the worse in the case of bullying ones.) Coaches unfortunately rationalize these actions by a naive pragmatic argument that it works, but it is destructive and dehumanizing. In the past, some allowed coaches to berate, humiliate, and physically and emotionally punish athletes in order to shape and inspire them, but no longer.

Players never forget their coaches. One coach has stated, "I have coached hundreds of players by now and I am certain of this: 100 percent of them will remember my name, the words I spoke to them, and the emotions generated by our conversations and interactions. Forever! This is part of the awesome power and responsibility of coaching. You give your players memories, for better or for worse that stay with them until the day they die."[35] How true this is. Coaches who bully and intimidate seldom understand the ongoing effects they have on young athletes. These coaches naively and irresponsibly think they are helping their players prepare for life when in reality their misbehavior can create a long-lasting fear in the athlete and damage a person more seriously than we imagine. Sports can beat up people and break them down so that they barely recover as adults.[36] And coaches seldom realize that they will be remembered for it. "Would these coaches behave differently if they comprehended the long-term effect of their behavior?"[37] I wonder what my ninth grade football coach and junior varsity college basketball coach would say if they knew how I remember them. Authority is not intimidation; bullying should not be confused with an intense personality or with teaching toughness. Bullying does not inspire respect, and coaches should bear in mind that they will be remembered long after an athlete's sporting days have ended.

Conclusion

Coaches who use intimidation as a means of gamesmanship have been given a pass for far too long. Of course, many coaches, I hope most, avoid bullying tactics and are important role models for their athletes. Unfortunately the bullying style has been viewed as normal in some coaching circles, and some coaches credit their aggressive bullying approach as the source of their success. In these cases the means are justified by the results, and few ask whether there is something intrinsically wrong with treating persons as less than persons. If humans do not have intrinsic significance as persons, then it is perfectly fine to treat them as objects to be degraded and abused. But then sports will have no real value and will become nihilistic endeavors of futility. Coaches are never justified in resorting to berating, humiliating, or bullying their athletes. It is wrong regardless of the spin. "While coaches . . . once routinely yelled, cursed, embarrassed, humiliated, and even physically grabbed [their] players, the reality is that those techniques simply do not work if you want to motivate players and help them reach their full athletic potential. Unfortunately, a few loose cannons . . . have fooled fans into thinking that an authoritarian, dictatorship leadership style is a winning style."[38] This is a myth of the past.

There is no doubt that "the 'strong' sort of gamesmanship certainly can bring one profit, in terms of victories scored, but it closes off the participant to the other benefits of sport, specifically, those that concern personal growth and development, and conceivably athletic development, as well."[39] Though these coaching practices have a long and often successful history in terms of winning success, gamesmanship through strong intimidation has no valuable, useful, or moral role in our contemporary sporting practices, and tolerance for this type of practice among coaches should be eliminated.

First, it fails as a strategy because it disrespects sporting contests and alters the nature of the game's challenge. Instead of asking whether one is a better coach, player, or team it asks who the best intimidator is. The game becomes secondary to the skill of intimidating.

Second, it fails because many successful coaches, like Tony Dungy and Phil Jackson, have proven that it is not needed.

Third, it is absurd to believe that bullying is required to motivate. How strange it would look for a college professor or music instructor to scream in a student's face, grab a student by the shirt collar, or curse a student for not performing adequately. Yet many condone the coach who uses these methods. Good teachers and motivators do not need to be bullies to succeed. As one student asked in class when covering this issue, "Is intimidation covering for their shortcomings as coaches?"[40]

Finally, the inherent worth of humans should have a great effect on coaching philosophy. Sports should be a humanizing activity whereas gamesmanship through intimidation and bullying is dehumanizing. Many coaches use athletes as a means to an end. Sporting contests should be arenas of integrity, and the intimidating, bullying approach to coaching eliminates honor from what should be an honorable profession. People deserve to be treated with dignity and respect because they have intrinsic value. Good coaches evaluate performances, not persons.

The coaching profession has been in need of redemption, and redemptive coaching must include discussion of the humanizing elements of sport and the dehumanizing elements of gamesmanship. Coaches can implement the teaching of virtue as one of their goals, but it must be planned and modeled.[41]

Questions for Review and Discussion

1. How does the author analyze the relationship between gamesmanship and bullying? Explain in some detail.

2. Are there forms of intimidation that are not bullying? If so, when does intimidation cross the line into bullying? Is there an age-appropriate level at which intimidation should never be part of our games? At what age if any should it be acceptable?

3. Do you agree that there are acceptable forms of intimidation at higher levels of our sporting contests which are a part of the moral regulative psychological challenge of the game? Why or why not?

4. How does the use of intimidation and bullying alter the goal of allowing the game to be decided by the participants and their skills?

5. Have you ever been bullied by a coach? Which type of fear did you experience and how did you respond?

Suggestions for Further Reading

Ehrmann, Joe. *InSideOut Coaching.* New York: Simon & Schuster, 2011.

Fry, Jeffrey. "Coaching a Kingdom of Ends." *Journal of the Philosophy of Sport* 27 (2000): 51–62.

Howe, Leslie. "Gamesmanship." *Journal of the Philosophy of Sport* 31 (2004).

Potter, Stephen. *The Theory and Practice of Gamesmanship.* New York: Bantam, 1947.

Stankovich, Chris. "Coach-Player Intimidation, Humiliation, and Physical Aggression Is Never Warranted." http://blog.drstankovich.com/blog/2011/02/coaching/coach-coercion-intimidation-and–humiliation.

Ten

The Neuroethics of Coaching

JEFFREY P. FRY

According to neurologist V. S. Ramachandran, we stand at the threshold of another scientific revolution. As recounted by Ramachandran, prior scientific revolutions challenged received views of our standing in the universe. Copernicus removed the earth from the center of the cosmos.[1] Darwin situated humans squarely within the animal world. Freud raised significant questions about the degree to which we consciously control our actions.[2] But Ramachandran claims that we are now "poised for the greatest revolution of all—understanding the human brain." This revolution, he says, is "about ourselves, about the very organ that made those earlier revolutions possible."[3]

Given the widespread implications of this neurorevolution, what ramifications could it hold for the world of sports? The recent past witnessed reluctance among some individuals to confront the issue of how the brain might be affected by sports participation.[4] Now there is a dawning realization of the extent to which engaging in sports can change the athlete's brain, particularly in the case of brain trauma. This raises urgent ethical questions about the roles and responsibilities of those who render decisions about who participates in sports under what conditions.

Consider the case of American football. Clearly the problem of concussions and other head injuries in American football, as well as in soccer, boxing, and other sports, warrants preventative measures, therapeutic intervention, and ethical reflection. In this chapter, however, I want to focus on ways that the choices and actions of coaches may over time be *subtly* changing their players' brains. Do coaches in their everyday interactions with athletes influence the functioning of their brains in ways that could be considered either harmful or beneficial to the athletes? If so, what are the ethical implications of these practices?

The issue of concussions in American football and other sports has been obscured in part by the long shadow cast by the profit motive. But inattention to subtler changes to the brain that potentially result from participation in sports is likely due to a widespread assumption of mind-body dualism, famously articulated by René Descartes (1596–1650). It is the view that the mind is immaterial or spiritual in nature, as opposed to the material body. This view is pervasive in Western thought.

Against this background I want to argue that we should take the brain more seriously in the context of sports, particularly in the context of coaching and being coached. In their introduction to *The Ethics of Sports Coaching*, Alun R. Hardman and Carwyn Jones claim: "Most, if not all, coaching exchanges have a moral dimension to them."[5] I suggest that this claim is supported by consideration of what I will call *the neuroethics of coaching.*[6]

Our brains are *responsive* to our interactions with individuals—coaches and others alike. But if, as the neuroplasticity thesis suggests, our brains are *malleable*, might it be the case that when one changes one's coach, one also changes one's brain in significant, perhaps lasting ways? If so, what kinds of change would be desirable? Furthermore, if coaches do exert this kind of influence, should they adopt a paternalistic stance to their role as game changers who are also brain changers? Or should coaches merely seek to do no harm? These and numerous other questions might be relevant in an account of the neuroethics of coaching.

To sum up, in this chapter I consider how neuroscience may help illuminate how sports, and coaches in particular, help or hinder us in our quest for "the enlargement of life."[7] This chapter is about sports, neuroscience, and the good life.

This chapter has three main sections. In the first section, I look at recent exciting, but sobering, findings from neuroscience on the plasticity of the brain and the ethical significance of mirror neurons. In the following section, I examine the implications of the themes outlined in the first section for the neuroethics of coaching. Finally, in the third section, I reply briefly to some reservations about the significance of the revolution in neuroscience.

In response to criticisms examined in the third section, I will argue that the brain is not the whole story of the good life. Nevertheless, it is a significant part of this story. By drawing attention to this critical three-pound, jello-like organ, I bring into sharper relief the vulnerability of the coached athlete. In turn, this may help enlarge our understanding of "the fragility of goodness," in the words of Martha Nussbaum, and thereby create greater empathy for the athlete.[8]

The Plastic Brain

There is a joke that goes like this. How many psychoanalysts does it take to change a lightbulb? The answer: one, but the lightbulb must really want to change. Although this joke reflects an assumption that engrained habits of thought and action are difficult to change, it allows that change is possible. But what if changes in one's thoughts, feelings, and behavior are paralleled by, and even intimately connected with, subtle and not so subtle changes in one's brain? In the recent past, the received view was that the brain's malleability is lost early in a human being's development. This view has now been spectacularly challenged.

One of the exciting discoveries by neuroscience in recent years has been the extent to which the brain exhibits plasticity, or the capacity to change, adapt, and rewire. As you read these words, your dynamic brain is in flux. Neurons are firing. Chemicals are being secreted. Neural circuits are being activated. Among the looming important questions regarding the plastic brain are the following: What is causing these changes in the brain? How much and what kind of change is occurring? How durable are these changes? And what are the implications of the brain's plasticity for conscious experience? In order to begin to respond to these issues it will be helpful to engage in some neurophilosophical reflection.

The Mind-Brain Problem

What connections exist between our brains and our experiences? There is a correlation between reported experiences and brain states. For example, neuroimaging technology reveals that when various experiences are reported, activity occurs in certain areas of our brains. Correlation is a relatively weak form of connection, however, since correlation in and of itself does not establish a causal relationship, let alone an identity relation. If condition A and condition B occur in correlation with one another, A may be the cause of B, B may be the cause of A, both A and B may be caused by some third factor, or by unrelated factors, and in some cases, it might turn out that A and B are identical.[9]

A stronger logical connection between brain states and putative mental states is posited by the identity thesis, a version of materialism which holds that mental states just are states of the brain and nervous system. On some variants of this view, there are no subjective mental qualities like sensations of pain or color, but rather only physical states of the brain.[10]

The jury is still out on the nature of the relationship between brain states and mental states. In this chapter, I assume an intimate connection between brain states and experiences, without resolving the issue of whether or not mental states are material brain states. In particular, I look at possible implications that follow from the hypothesized view that brain states and putative mental states are causally connected in bidirectional fashion.[11] I will leave aside the question of the identity thesis. But if it, or some other reductionist account of mental states, turns out to be the correct view, then this would strengthen my argument for the relevance of a neuroethics of coaching. I will also look at how our social interactions influence our brains and conscious states. But first we will look at the surprising extent of the brain's plasticity.

The Gospel (and the Sobering News) of Neuroplasticity

Norman Doidge is a psychiatrist, psychoanalyst, and researcher who has served on the faculties of the Columbia University Center for Psychoanalytic Training and the University of Toronto's department of psychiatry. In his book *The Brain That Changes Itself: Stories of Personal Triumph from the Frontiers of Brain Science*, Doidge examines the phenomenon of neuroplasticity.[12] Doidge's book is filled with inspiring and hopeful stories of the rehabilitation of damaged, but still plastic, brains. Sometimes this capacity is shown in response to traumatic injury to the brain itself, such as damage caused by a stroke. The brains of stroke victims sometimes adapt in remarkable ways that lead to a significant recovery of abilities.[13]

Nevertheless, Doidge acknowledges that the phenomenon of neuroplasticity is double-edged:

> Neuroplasticity isn't all good news; it renders our brains not only more resourceful but also more vulnerable to outside influences. Neuroplasticity has the power to produce more flexible but also more rigid behaviors—a phenomenon I call the "plastic paradox." Ironically, some of our most stubborn habits and disorders are products of plasticity. Once a particular plastic change occurs in the brain and becomes well established, it can prevent other changes from occurring. It is by understanding both the positive and the negative effects of plasticity that we can truly understand the extent of human possibilities.[14]

Doidge claims that our brains can both change and solidify in certain respects. Both of these abilities are potentially connected to our everyday interactions with one another.

V. S. Ramachandran has also written about the plasticity of the brain as evidenced in its remarkable adaptability. Ramachandran specializes in the study of anomalous neurological conditions, for example, phantom limb syndrome, which is experienced after the loss of a limb.[15] In treating a patient who had his left arm amputated above the elbow, Ramachandran encountered something truly noteworthy. When he touched the patient's left cheek, the patient reported that he experienced the sensation of being touched on the thumb of his amputated left arm. Ramachandran's explanation for this phenomenon is that there is a representation of the body (the so-called Penfield homunculus) mapped onto a strip of the cerebral cortex known as the postcentral gyrus. On this strip the representation of the face is next to that of the hand. After the patient's left arm had been amputated, no signals went to the part of the cortex representing the left hand. But that part of the brain became, as Ramachandran puts it, "hungry for sensory input."[16] Ramachandran writes that "the sensory input from the facial skin now invades the adjacent territory corresponding to the missing hand. Signals from the face are then misinterpreted by higher centers in the brain as arising from the missing hand."[17] The claim is that the brain has undergone "remapping" or "rewiring"—a capacity in the adult brain not recognized by earlier neurological orthodoxy.[18]

The theme of neuroplasticity is highlighted in a burgeoning area of neuroscience known as social neuroscience. It suggests that brain plasticity is manifested not merely in responding to sudden traumatic injuries, whether in the brain or elsewhere in the body. Instead, our brains are highly social and are constantly responding to our social interactions. Psychologist Daniel Goleman writes:

> Neuroscience has discovered that our brain's very design makes it *sociable*, inexorably drawn into an intimate brain-to-brain linkup whenever we engage with another person. That neural bridge lets us affect the brain—and so the body—of everyone we interact with, just as they do us.[19]

According to Goleman, even routine encounters affect our brains and emotions. Especially significant are connections with people we spend time with and care about. Our interactions with one another are, says Goleman, "like interpersonal thermostats." By means of our interactions "we create one another," even at a biological level.[20]

Goleman asserts:

> Repeated experiences sculpt the shape, size, and number of neurons and their synaptic connections. By repeatedly driving our brain into a given register, our key relationships can gradually mold certain neural circuitry. In effect, being chronically hurt and angered, or being emotionally nourished, by someone we spend time with daily over the course of years can refashion your brain.
>
> These new discoveries reveal that our relationships have subtle, yet powerful, lifetime impacts on us.[21]

Consider the insight of behavioral psychologist Donald O. Hebb regarding what is referred to as "Hebbian learning." Hebb's insight is encapsulated by neuroscientist Carla Shatz in the words "neurons that fire together, wire together."[22]

When we view neuroplasticity in the context of human relationships we once again see the importance of what Doidge calls the "paradox of plasticity." Plasticity allows for both change and lasting effects. This fact takes on added significance when we consider that, as Goleman points out, the brain is responsive to both nurturing and toxic environments. Goleman claims that these findings suggest an aspect of a "life well lived"—we live in a way that will benefit others at this subtle level of neural circuitry.[23]

All this suggests that our encounters with others are shaping not just one another's experiences, but also one another's brains. This entails ethical responsibility on our part. In particular, it casts a spotlight on responsibility in the sense pointed out by H. Richard Niebuhr. How we respond to one another in given situations takes on an added ethical dimension.[24]

The Role of Mirror Neurons

Another important development in neuroscience that bears on our understanding of our plastic brains has been the discovery of mirror neurons by neuroscientists in Parma, Italy.[25] They are thought to help us internalize the emotions of others and may provide a foundation for empathy.[26] As Goleman writes, "By mimicking what another person does or feels, mirror neurons create a shared sensibility, bringing the outside into us: to understand another, we become like the other—at least a bit."[27] Again, as he puts it, "mirror neurons bridge brains."[28]

UCLA neurologist and neuroscientist Marco Icaboni ties mirror neurons to watching sports. According to Icaboni, due to mirror neurons, when the cameras pan the crowds at televised sporting events and capture the emotion of the fans, this creates "emotional contagion" in the viewers watching the game at home. When we see a player catch a ball during a game, some of the same mirror neurons are activated as when we catch a ball ourselves.[29] In fact we are moved in a variety of ways at a prereflective level when we observe sports.[30]

Perhaps coaches, teammates, and others we encounter through sports can leave lasting impressions on our neural circuitry. In light of the sheer number of hours coaches and athletes spend together, as well as the emotional impact of sports, this becomes important. As we know, sports often create lasting memories, possibly because they are laden with emotion, and experiences with intense emotional salience can create memories with great staying power. Perhaps perceiving oneself as the "goat" of an important game or as a loser, and having such perceptions buttressed with continuous negative reinforcement from a coach or teammate, have a lasting impact on a young athlete's brain.

Even as the outline of a rationale for a neuroethics of everyday life comes into focus, it is important to note that the philosopher Thomas Metzinger argues that neuroethics is not enough. Metzinger proposes that in addition to neuroethics we need to develop consciousness ethics, which would focus on "acts whose primary goal is the alteration of one's experiential states or those of other persons."[31] According to Metzinger, "a desirable state of consciousness" should meet three criteria:

> It should minimize suffering, in humans and all other beings capable of suffering; it should ideally possess an epistemic potential (that is, it should have a component of insight and expanding knowledge); and it should have behavioral consequences that increase the probability of occurrence of future valuable types of experience.[32]

As I am employing the term "neuroethics," it fits hand in glove with Metzinger's "consciousness ethics." Indeed, Metzinger writes:

> In the new era of neuropedagogy, now that we know more about the critical formative phases of the brain, shouldn't we make use of this knowledge to maximize the autonomy of future adults? In particular, shouldn't we introduce our children to those states of consciousness we believe to be valuable and teach them how to access and cultivate them at an early age.[33]

Whether in a particular situation the cultivation of states of consciousness deemed valuable by adults meshes with the promotion of autonomy is debatable, as we will see. Nevertheless, I think that what Metzinger is getting at in highlighting autonomy is that we should promote states of consciousness that will help individuals realize aspects of what I referred to earlier as the enlargement of life.

Critical Periods of Brain Development

Coaches who are aware of developmental psychology, at least intuitively, may have some understanding and empathy when young athletes seemingly on cue exhibit familiar patterns of behavior at various age levels. But how many coaches and administrators consider that the brains of young athletes are undergoing development, and that they may go through critical stages in the course of this development? Some awareness of brain development may help coaches exhibit patience in dealing with athletes during the sometimes turbulent period of adolescence. For example, when a teenager is not up to a learning task or exhibits risky behavior, this may not simply be merely willful obtuseness, but rather an indication of the developmental stage reached by the individual's brain.[34] It behooves us, then, to consider the findings of what science writer Barbara Strauch refers to as "a brand-new discipline of adolescent neuroscience."[35]

Strauch cites research which supports the view that "the adolescent brain undergoes a massive remodeling of its basic structure, in areas that affect everything from logic and language to impulses and intuition."[36] According to John Mazziotta of UCLA, it is with babies and teenagers that one finds the "greatest change in the brain's structure and function."[37] Research by Jay Giedd of the NIH supports the claim that during puberty and early adolescence the gray matter of the brain thickens, marking a period of exuberance, followed by a pruning process. Furthermore, Giedd has found evidence that the frontal lobes, the so-called chief executive of the brain, may be among the last areas of the brain to reach stability and maturity.[38] Again, to quote Strauch: "The teenage brain is not only incredibly interesting but appears to be still wildly exuberant and receptive."[39] But again, this plasticity of the brain does not entail good news only. Strauch writes: "In fact, as the teenage brain is reconfigured, it remains more exposed, more easily wounded, perhaps more susceptible to long-lasting damage than most parents and educators had thought."[40]

We have considered neuroplasticity, mirror neurons, neurocircuitry, and their possible effects on the quality of our conscious experiences, particularly in critical periods of the brain's development. As I have already indicated, there is evidence for plasticity in the adult brain as well.[41] The issue is not whether we affect each other's brains as adults, since this seems to be going on all the time, but rather the extent and durability of the effects of those interactions. How might these and other insights drawn from neuroscience inform a neuroethical analysis of sport and of coaching in particular?

Your Brain on Sports

Participation in physical activity may have various kinds of salutary affects on our brains. In his book *Spark: The Revolutionary New Science of Exercise and the Brain*, John Ratey of Harvard Medical School makes a case for a number of these effects, including contributions to learning and to subjective states of well-being.[42] But what happens when physical activity is linked with coaching?

Change Your Coach, Change Your Brain?

The prospect of the plasticity of the brain, coupled with its mirror neuron systems, presents us with some intriguing possibilities in connection with sports, especially the idea of critical periods of development. If we accept the notion of plasticity of the brain, and the claim from social neuroscience that our social interactions can, over time, shape our neural circuitry, then the case of the parent-coach who oversees a child's athletic development over a period of years is of particular relevance and import.

Consider what may have been taking place in the brain of a young tennis prodigy by the name of Andre Agassi. In his book *Open: An Autobiography*, Agassi recounts how he hated tennis in his youth.[43] He felt unrelenting pressure from his father to practice and improve. Agassi recounts his anguish after losing a match at a tennis tournament while participating in a ten-year-old and under bracket:

> After years of hearing my father rant at my flaws, one loss has caused me to take up his rant. I've internalized my father—his impatience, his perfectionism, his rage—until his voice doesn't just feel like my own, it is my own. I no longer need my father to torture me. From this day on, I can do it all by myself.[44]

Having mirrored his father's emotional life for so long, the neural pathways had become well established in his brain. Once again, neurons that fire together, wire together.

There is no easy formula for a life well lived. We cannot always predict the long-term effects of adversity. Adversity may arguably play a role in the good life. But clearly there were aspects of Agassi's experience with tennis that did not represent for him the enlargement of his life. On the contrary, at times he experienced his life in tennis as a prison from which he longed to escape. This interpretation is buttressed by an epigraph to Agassi's book from a letter that painter Vincent van Gogh wrote to his brother in July 1880:

> One cannot always tell what it is that keeps us shut in, confines us, seems to bury us, but still one feels certain barriers, certain gates, certain walls. Is all this imagination, fantasy? I do not think so. And then one asks: My God! Is it for long, is it forever, is it for eternity? Do you know what frees one from this captivity? It is very deep affection. Being friends, being brothers, love, that is what opens the prison by supreme power, by some magic force.[45]

What is it that confines us? What barriers, gates, and walls are there? We can respond to these questions at various levels of description.[46] Icaboni suggests that our social interactions can set limits on our autonomy by implicating our imitative mirror neurons.[47]

Brain Change and Game Change: Neuroethical Coaching

In keeping with neuroplasticity and social neuroscience, author and educator Robert Leamnson writes in his book *Thinking About Teaching and Learning: Developing Habits of Learning with First Year College and University Students:* "Learning as brain-change, rather than brain use, is an idea that can make people uneasy."[48] This idea is not new. As William James once noted: "Things which we are quite unable definitely to recall have nevertheless impressed themselves, in some way, upon the structure of our mind. *We are different for having learned them*. The resistance in our systems of brain-paths are altered."[49]

The idea that teaching and learning involve brain change has particular relevance in sport. Coaches at the university level in the United States frequently tout the notion that they are teachers. Surely this is true in some sense. If coaches are effective teachers, learning must be going on. If learning is occurring, then according to Leamnson and James, the brain is changing. This warrants paying serious attention to what coaches are teaching.

This consideration takes on further relevance when we consider the fact that coaches often work with young athletes who have developing brains. Coaches need to understand, and to exhibit patience in light of, the biologically based limitations of children with their immature, developing brains. In addition, recognition of the plasticity of the brains of children and young people suggests a special responsibility for coaches. If what affective and social neuroscience suggest is correct, and the plastic brains of young people are developing in connection with the interactions that young people have with significant people in their lives, coaches may be contributing in important ways to how that development proceeds.

This potentiality takes on further significance when coaches spend a significant amount of time with athletes, in some cases years. Coaches and athletes often develop strong affective bonds, with coaches becoming something like surrogate parents. Coaches often place athletes under stress and demand heightened concentration in situations where athletes care deeply about their sport.

Even with more mature athletes, coaches may help shape the underlying neural circuitry for what psychologist Carolyn Dweck calls mind-sets. Dweck identifies two mind-sets: the fixed mind-set and the growth mind-set. According to Dweck, the fixed mind-set and growth mind-set were exemplified by Bob Knight and John Wooden, respectively.[50] Both were highly successful collegiate basketball coaches. Dweck believes Knight exemplified the fixed mind-set—losing defines someone as a loser. This perspective highlights rigidity over plasticity. Dweck writes: "A loss made him a failure, obliterated his identity. So when he was your coach—when your wins and losses measured him—he was mercilessly judgmental."[51] Again, in Dweck's words:

> It's not that Knight had a fixed mindset about his players' ability. He firmly believed in their capacity to develop. But he had a fixed mindset about himself and his coaching ability. The team was his product, and they had to prove his ability every time out. They were not allowed to lose games, make mistakes, or question him in any way, because that would reflect on his competence.[52]

On the other hand, Dweck views John Wooden as someone who exhibited the growth mind-set. Wooden highlighted improvement over time, an emphasis that is in keeping with the notion of a plastic brain—one that can change—but not immediately. Wooden asked for effort, but he did not demand victory.[53] For our purposes, it is important to note that both Knight and Wooden may have been helping to create the supporting neural frameworks for mind-sets in the athletes they coached.

Consider this possibility in light of mirror neurons, which, among other things, lead us to mimic those with whom we interact. Goleman writes:

> Mirror neurons create a shared sensibility, bringing the outside into us: to understand another, we become like the other—at least a bit. That

> virtual sense of what someone else experiences fits with an emerging notion in the philosophy of mind: that we understand others by translating their actions into the neural language that prepares us for the same actions and lets us experience alike.[54]

This raises a sobering question. *Whose* experiences do you wish to share?

Then there is Phil Jackson, former National Basketball Association coach, who at times has had athletes meditate. Jackson himself practiced meditation in the hope of becoming less dictatorial as a coach. He also utilized a psychologist and Zen practitioner to guide his NBA players through meditation with the goal of relieving stress and promoting relaxation.[55] These conditions have correlations in our brains. Imagine transitioning from the volatile coaching style of someone like Bob Knight to the Zen-like approach of Phil Jackson. Change your coach, change your cortisol level, change your brain!

With this is mind, how should we respond then to a book coauthored by Craig Clifford and Randolph Feezell, *Coaching for Character*?[56] Perhaps coaches are always coaching for character of some sort or another. But suppose that coaching for character entails shaping neural circuitry in the brains of youths. How should we feel about the role that coaches play in establishing neural dispositions that may have correlations with character? Further, how should we assess this potentiality given the fact that some people view sport as a realm unto itself, with its own special morality?[57] Are coaches qualified to coach "for character?"

To this point we have considered a few reasons to think about the applications of neuroplasticity and social neuroscience to sport, and specifically to a neuroethics of coaching. While some of this is conjectural, I think that there is sufficient cause to warrant interest and concern about one's brain on coaching.

The Neurorevolution: Reservations and Responses

Finally, I want to respond to three reservations about the looming neurorevolution and the applications of neuroscience, including applications to sport. One concern is that it may be premature to think that we know enough to make such applications. As touched on above, one might argue that my attempts to apply neuroscience to sports are speculative. Yet even if some of the issues raised in this chapter are speculative, it seems reasonable to consider what *could* be the case, given the significance of what is potentially at stake.[58]

A second concern is linked to the work of philosopher Peter Hacker and his collaborator, neuroscientist Michael Bennett. The two have together investigated and challenged presuppositions of neuroscience and neurophilosophy. Hacker and Bennett strongly object to ascribing psychological predicates to the brain. Instead, they think that we are constrained by logic to focus on the person as a whole. Hacker and Bennett warn against committing the mereological fallacy, or taking the part for the whole.[59] This idea is further developed by those who contemplate the "extended mind," which does not stop at the end of our bodies.[60]

Whatever validity this critique may have in particular cases, I do not think that it necessarily affects the importance of an emphasis on the central role of the brain in connection with conscious experiences, or with respect to the subjective sense of well-being. It seems highly plausible that the brain does play a central—if not exclusive—role in either promoting or inhibiting the project of the enlargement of life.

A third objection to highlighting the brain in connection with sport and the good life is that no particular gain accrues from doing so, beyond what is available by restricting ourselves to psychological considerations.[61] For example, one might argue that we already know that psychological abuse of athletes by coaches is wrong apart from any reference to the brain; hence, giving focused attention to the brain in this context is superfluous. But I think that this view is mistaken. By understanding the central role of the brain in living the good life we broaden and deepen our understanding of "the fragility of goodness," to borrow from Martha Nussbaum. We broaden our grasp of the vulnerability of the athlete. We may also be led to a more empathic understanding of others as we consider the stages of brain development, the receptivity and vulnerability of the brain to social influences, and the vulnerability of the brain to trauma. Psychologist Steven Pinker captures this broad sentiment in poignant fashion.

> This power to deny that other people have feelings is not just an academic exercise but an all-too-common vice, as we see in the long history of human cruelty. Yet once we realize that our own consciousness is a product of our brains and that other people have brains like ours, a denial of other people's sentience becomes ludicrous. 'Hath not a Jew eyes?' asked Shylock. Today the question is more pointed: Hath not a Jew—or an Arab, or an African, or a baby, or a dog—a cerebral cortex and a thalamus?
>
> If that sounds mechanistic, if it makes us seem like transitory things, what of it? Think about why we sometimes remind ourselves that 'life is short.' It is an impetus to extend a gesture of affection to a loved one, to bury the hatchet in a pointless dispute, to use time productively rather than squander it. I would argue that nothing gives life more purpose

> than the realization that every moment of consciousness is precious and a fragile gift.[62]

Is the brain the whole story? By no means. But the brain appears to be a critical part of the story of a good life, and of the role of sport in a good life.

Conclusion

If V. S. Ramachandran is correct, we are on the verge of a great scientific revolution—indeed the greatest revolution we have yet experienced. No doubt it will unfold with anxiety as well as excitement. If it fulfills its promise it is likely to have far-reaching implications, including implications fraught with ethical significance. Emerging social and affective neuroscience may broaden our conception of the ethics of neuroscience and of the neuroscience of ethics. Reflection on neuroethics and its connection to "consciousness ethics" may help us understand how the neuroscientific revolution can contribute to the project of "the enlargement of life."

How coaches interact with athletes has mattered ethically in the past. Ethical concerns about coach-athlete interactions did not surface for the first time in thinking about the potential for brain change that comes from these interactions. But in another sense much changes when we place the athlete's brain in the foreground. In the *Apology* Socrates intimated that real harm is moral harm. As a result he was less concerned about his body.[63] But this may have been a false dichotomy, or at least an exaggerated distinction. If we accept the claims of social neuroscience, then coaching surely involves teaching and learning that changes brains and, in turn, the quality of consciousness.

This suggests a neglected sense in which we are vulnerable human beings. Within our skulls lies a vital organ that is fragile, vulnerable, and responsive to others at its microscopic level of organization. This recognition of the social brain gives added meaning to the insights of Anthony Skillen.[64]

In an insightful and moving article, "Sport Is for Losers," Skillen writes that sport can teach us (and thus, as we have seen, change our brains) "to live within the limits of a human fellowship informed by awareness of common frailty."[65] Part of this frailty consists of our fragile brains and of our neural vulnerability to one another.[66]

Questions for Review and Discussion

1. What does it mean to say that the brain is "plastic," and what is some of the evidence for this plasticity? Why is this plasticity both good news and sobering news?

2. What roles do mirror neurons play? How do you feel about the fact that when you mirror others, you become like them to some extent?

3. Given that exposure to coaches may change your brain, what kinds of coaches would you want and not want to play for?

4. If coaches can or do have an impact on the brains of athletes, especially young developing athletes, what are the implications for the ethics of coaching, since it is already generally accepted that coaches can affect the character of their players?

Suggestions for Further Reading

Agassi, Andre. *Open: An Autobiography*. New York: Vintage, 2010.

Bennett, M. R., and P. M. S. Hacker. *Philosophical Foundations of Neuroscience.* Malden, MA: Blackwell, 2003.

Bennett, Maxwell, et al. *Neuroscience and Philosophy: Brain, Mind, and Language*. New York: Cambridge University Press, 2007.

Blackmore, Susan. *Consciousness: An Introduction.* 2nd ed. New York: Oxford University Press, 2011.

Clark, Andy, and David J. Chalmers. "The Extended Mind." In *Philosophy of Mind: Classical and Contemporary Readings,* 643–651. Edited by David J. Chalmers. New York: Oxford University Press, 2002.

Clifford, Craig, and Randolph Feezell. *Coaching for Character: Reclaiming the Principles of Sportsmanship*. Champaign, IL: Human Kinetics, 1997.

Doidge, Norman. *The Brain That Changes Itself: Stories of Personal Triumph from the Frontiers of Brain Science*. New York: Penguin, 2007.

Hardman, Alun R., and Carwyn Jones, eds. *The Ethics of Sports Coaching*. London: Routledge, 2011.

Lazenby, Roland. *Mindgames: Phil Jackson's Long, Strange Journey*. Chicago: Contemporary, 2002.

Leamnson, Robert. *Thinking About Teaching and Learning: Developing Habits of Learning with First Year College and University Students*. Sterling, VA: Stylus, 1999.

Nussbaum, Martha C. *The Fragility of Goodness: Luck and Ethics in Greek Tragedy and Philosophy*. Cambridge: Cambridge University Press, 1986.

Omalu, Bennett. *Play Hard, Die Young: Football, Dementia, Depression, and Death*. Lodi, CA: Neo-Forenxis, 2008.

Pinker, Steven. "The Riddle of Knowing You're Here." In *Your Brain: A User's Guide,* 12–19. New York: TIME Books, 2009.

Plantinga, Alvin. *Where the Conflict Really Lies: Science, Religion, and Naturalism*. New York: Oxford University Press, 2011.
Ramachandran, V. S. *A Brief Tour of Human Consciousness*. New York: PI Press, 2004.
Strauch, Barbara. *The Primal Teen: What the New Discoveries About the Teenage Brain Tell Us About Our Kids*. New York: Anchor, 2004.

Eleven

Competition, Ethics, and Coaching Youth

CESAR R. TORRES AND PETER F. HAGER

Although organized youth sports in the United States date back to the nineteenth century, it was in the last fifty years or so that the experience became prevalent in the life of youths and their families.[1] One indication that youth sport has become a significant phenomenon in society is the widespread use since the 1990s of the term "soccer mom," which designates those mothers who coordinate the sport schedules of their children. One study indicates that in the year 2000, the number of youths "who played on at least one organized sport team was found to be 54% of kids ages 6 and 17."[2] A 2005 study shows that "among a slightly older age group of 10- to 17-year olds, participation had jumped to 59%."[3] According to Ronald B. Woods, "Participation in youth sport [is] at an all-time high."[4] Along these lines, Christina Theokas reported in 2009 that "frequency of engagement in sports is extremely high for children and youth" and that "for the 19th consecutive year (2007–2008), the number of students participating in high school athletics increased."[5] Participation in youth sports is so extensive in the United States that Mark Hyman believes the country is obsessed with it.[6]

Hyman's characterization is meant as an indictment of the problems besetting it, not a citation of its merits. Competition, which typically plays a prominent role in youth sports, is at the center of this indictment. The condemnation of competition in this setting is nothing new. For example, the New York State Public High School Athletic Association temporarily abolished its state championships in the early 1930s "due to charges of overemphasis and overspecialization."[7]

While some critics simply oppose participation in competitive youth sports programs, others have taken a reformist approach.[8] This chapter analyzes the role of competition in youth sports and the ethics of coaching in such programs. Our approach will not focus on the consequences, negative or positive, of sports competition, but on its intrinsic character. We begin with an exploration of the most common criticisms of youth sports and of some of the reforms proposed to improve it. We then present an interpretivist account of competitive sports and its central purpose, which establishes a framework through which (1) a case can be made for competition in organized youth sports, (2) proposed reforms can be analyzed, and (3) an ethics of coaching that respects competitive sports' central purpose while advancing youth's interests, needs, and welfare can be proposed. We intend to demonstrate that, understood from an interpretivist perspective, competition in youth sports is morally defensible and coaches have a pivotal role to play in promoting and designing morally beneficial competitive experiences.

Problems and Reform Within Organized Youth Sports in the United States

The landscape of youth sports in the United States is haunted by a variety of ethical problems, many of which are related to those manifesting themselves at the elite level. Examples of on-field and off-field cheating and poor sporting behavior can be found in both media reports and the discussions of coaches, administrators, parents, and young athletes. Recruiting and eligibility violations, deceptive on-field rule breaking, the use of illegal performance enhancing substances and methods, intimidating and threatening forms of trash talk, and disrespectful behaviors toward coaches and teammates, as well as opponents and officials, are just some of the issues challenging proponents of youth sports today.

Many of these problems are grounded in the attitudes and tendencies of individuals within sports and society in the United States. One such tendency is what R. Scott Kretchmar has referred to as runaway individualism—an extreme form of individualism in which "individual rights, interests, and activities dominate and overwhelm social duties and concerns."[9] Among other things, runaway individualism "can lead to an insensitivity regarding the rights of others" and "can cause a person to lose touch with his or her cultural roots and shared community values."[10] This tendency can be observed more generally in people's habits of seeking their own interests through activities of their choice, without consideration for others participating in the activities or for the activities themselves.

Runaway individualism is evident at all levels of sports in the United States, where the members of sporting communities often seek personal gain in the form of achievement, advancement, financial profit, and legacy, without much thought for their moral obligations to other community members or for their sport as a unique type of activity. In the words of Alasdair MacIntyre, the reasoning of these individuals is instrumental rather than practical in nature—focused on goods external to their sport (e.g., fame, fortune, status, recognition, etc.) rather than on its internal goods (i.e., the challenges, skills, and strategies that make sports unique social practices) or the virtues that should be cultivated and employed in determining and overseeing their sport's best interests and interpretations.[11]

Two subcategories of runaway individualism have been identified. The first, which Kretchmar seems to recognize,[12] is a tendency to overemphasize personal achievement and personality; the second[13] is what appears to be an escalating obsession with advantage seeking. These tendencies toward egregious self-aggrandizement and obsessive advantage seeking have become so habitual for many athletes, coaches, and administrators that they have formed cults to rationalize the tendencies and act as apologists for them and for the poor sporting conduct they encourage and facilitate.

While the cult of egregious self-aggrandizement operates most visibly at the professional level, it is clearly at work at the youth and amateur levels, where young athletes toil diligently to earn recognition for their talent and gain advancement. In youth sports and interscholastic and intercollegiate athletics, it is not uncommon for such athletes and their parents to lobby coaches for more playing time, for the chance to play a specific position, or for the opportunity to play a more substantial role on their team.

The cult of obsessive advantage seeking has also fastened its talons on each level of sports in the country. Because of the strong emphasis on winning and the belief in doing whatever it takes to win, athletes, coaches, and administrators feel the need to spend increasing amounts of time working to secure as great an advantage (or as small a disadvantage) as possible. The escalation in analysis of game films, in the advance scouting of opponents, and in coaches' expectations regarding the amount of time young athletes should spend on conditioning, strength training, and sport-specific skill development are just a few examples of how obsessive advantage seeking is reshaping the landscape of youth sports.

A further indicator of this cult's influence is the willingness of athletes, coaches, and administrators to ignore or intentionally violate the rules of their sport and/or the regulations established by that sport's governing body or bodies. Although the majority of rules and regulations have been set in place to maintain sports as unique social practices and/or maintain conditions of fairness within their contests and practice communities, many tend to view competitors simply as obstacles to be circumvented on the road to victory. The violation of recruiting and eligibility rules and the doctoring of equipment to illegally enhance performance are two examples of rule breaking practices that place strategic advantage ahead of fair play in athletic competition.

The tendencies toward obsessive advantage seeking and egregious self-aggrandizement and their respective cults have developed to the point that they have become resistant to simple reforms. This is why simple appeals to fair play and good sportsmanship have done little to stem the tide of negative consequences flowing from them. Several attempts to reform youth sports have been employed to counteract the effects of these cults and tendencies, as well as the inclination to overemphasize winning and outcomes. For instance, the typical approach to reform utilized at the initial levels of youth sports (ages 5–11) has deemphasized competition, eliminating such elements as scorekeeping, standings, play-off and championship tournaments, and even organized teams and leagues.[14] These kinds of reforms were crafted by well-meaning individuals who were concerned that youth sports had been corrupted by coaches, administrators, and even parents, whose win-first approach to sports had marginalized the more traditional values of youth sports participation, such as skill learning and mastery, moral and social character development, and fun.

The problem with reforms that deemphasize competition in youth sports is that they stifle attempts to teach youths how to compete in a good and decent manner. We believe that competitive youth sports, when well organized and well led, can play an important educational role by teaching youth how to compete strongly against one another in the spirit of cooperation and friendship, without animosity or jealousy. Reforms that remove competitive aspects of sports or strongly deemphasize them jeopardize sports' ability to actualize its educational potential. Such reforms do not provide youngsters with a view or account of competition and value-based habits of action that will help them compete ethically in sport. Without tools of this kind, young athletes will not be well prepared to be competent contestants in sports and beyond. In the section that follows, we will examine an account of sports (interpretivism) which offers a different type of youth sports reforms (mutualist reforms) that maintain the competitive aspects of youth sports while increasing the moral accountability of participants as members of sports practice communities.

Interpretivism and Competitive Sport's Central Purpose

Interpretivism is a theory of sports that falls under the larger conceptual umbrella that Robert L. Simon calls "broad internalism," which is "the view that in addition to the constitutive rules of sport, there are other resources connected closely—perhaps conceptually—to sports that are neither social conventions nor moral principles imported from the outside."[15] According to Simon, interpretivism "derives the principles and theories underlying sport . . . from an appeal to the best interpretation of the game or an inference to the best explanation of its key elements."[16] Furthermore, for him, interpretivism maintains that:

> Certain principles and theories must be *presupposed* if we are to make sense of key elements of sport, such as the rules, the skills that are tested, and possibly the history, traditions, and central elements of the ethos of particular sports. . . . The form of the argument [that an interpretivist might employ] is that a particular activity, competitive sport, would lack a point, be not fully intelligible, or make no sense (or at least less sense than otherwise) were not certain underlying principles taken as normative or as applying to the activity in question.[17]

At its core, interpretivism holds that moral deliberation and assessment in sports should be guided by rationally grounded interpretations of its central purpose and features. An interpretation here means the rational articulation of sports as a comprehensive, coherent, and principled activity, not just as an intelligible activity. What is at stake in an interpretation of sports in general, and of a specific one in particular, are its defining point and most prominent characteristics. An interpretation, then, is not based on preference, thoughtless agreement, or tradition, but rather on carefully constructed arguments that ultimately render it legitimate. As Nicholas Dixon argues, "Whether a position on a debate about sport—be it about a particular issue or about fundamental principles—is defensible depends on the quality of the supporting arguments, not on whether it has the assent of the relevant athletic community."[18]

Interpretivists have explained, following the work of Bernard Suits, that a sport is a game—or artificial problem—created by rules and governed by a "gratuitous logic" that puts a premium on the execution of physical skills. The gratuitous logic is a fundamental element of sports and all games because it refers to the restriction of the means available to accomplish the stipulated goal.[19] This restriction, as detailed by rules, requires the use of less efficient rather than more efficient means to pursue those goals (e.g., hitting golf balls with clubs rather than just carrying them to the target). It is the gratuitous logic of each sport that distinguishes one from the other, equipping each with its distinctive characteristics and charm. In the process, the rules that codify the gratuitous logic of each sport facilitate the emergence of a set of highly specialized skills that Cesar Torres has referred to as constitutive and restorative skills. The former are meant to be tested and are typically implemented during open play; the latter are those that are implemented to restore sports after an interruption.[20] For instance, in basketball, the jump shot, the layup, screening, and rebounding are examples of constitutive skills while the free throw and in-bounding of the ball are examples of restorative skills. From an intepretivist perspective, both constitutive and restorative skills and the strategies used in conjunction with them form the basis of a sport's overall standard of excellence.

J. S. Russell holds that interpretivism presupposes two related principles. The first requires that the rules are interpreted "to generate a coherent and principled account of the point and purpose that underline the game, attempting to show the game in its best light."[21] The second states that "rules should be interpreted in such a manner that the excellences embodied in achieving the lusory goal of the game are not undermined but are maintained and fostered."[22] What these two principles indicate is that for Russell intepretivism demands that sports (and different sports in particular) be articulated as comprehensive, coherent, and principled activities. For him, an interpretivist account of sports requires the virtue of integrity: intepretivism looks for the most coherent version of sports' defining point and most prominent characteristics.

In the philosophy of sports, interpretivism was developed as a theory meant to explain the relationship between sports and moral values.[23] For instance, "Simon's main thesis is that the moral evaluation of sports should be rooted in the best interpretation of its main point and purpose."[24] Thus scholars working within the tenets of interpretivism have emphasized its normative implications. In this sense, Russell notes that interpretivism, especially in light of its commitment to the virtue of integrity, is a theory of sports "informed by basic considerations of moral equality" and that it implies "duties to foster a context of competition."[25] Consequently, participants in competitive sports are entitled to equal concern and respect, and have the obligation, for example, to "pursue genuinely worthy adversaries" and to "take reasonable measures to promote conditions that would allow competitors to function as worthy adversaries."[26] Deliberately avoiding worthy adversaries or attempting to tamper with their training would represent moral failures in competitive sports. The notion that interpretivism demands moral equality and the fostering of genuine competition conforms to the principles expounded above: an integrated account of sports requires making the best sense of its point, purpose, and distinguishing features as much as a commitment to advance that best sense.

Although intepretivism has emphasized the moral dimension of sports, it has distinctive aesthetic connotations. Torres has recently argued that interpretivism takes a combined moral-aesthetical point of view.[27] Interpretivism's moral demands are grounded in a systematic characterization of the point, purpose, and defining features of sports, in an effort to display them at their best. Such a characterization requires making reference to the intrinsic properties of sports, from which aesthetic predicates emerge and to which they refer back, considered worthy of sustained attention. These properties are related to the constitutive and restorative skills and the strategies used in conjunction with them that constitute the basis of a sport's overall standard of excellence. This means that an interpretation of sports involves deliberation and the construction of defensible arguments about the standards of excellence worthy of repaid attention that portrays them in their best light. Sporting communities engage in this kind of exercise when specifying their sport's best version. Any such specification comprises making aesthetic judgments. For example, soccer has been described the world over as "the beautiful game," and actions that dishonor such a view are typically labeled as "ugly."[28]

"The most cogent version of a sport requires that contestants treat each other as moral equals, and that they honor and foster the intrinsic properties worthy of repaid attention that characterize it."[29] Contestants, then, have simultaneous moral and aesthetic obligations; moreover, these obligations appear to be intertwined. Moral equality in competition is coupled with the "duties to foster a context of competition" in a practice that is defined by its intrinsic properties and standards of excellence. All this suggests that interpretivism presupposes that the central purpose of competitive sports is not simply to beat one's opponent but rather to accurately measure and compare contestants' athletic excellence. Simon and Russell, among others, recognize that competitive sports are best thought of "as a mutual striving for excellence."[30] This does not deny the zero-sum quality of competition, but rather puts it in the context of the best interpretation of sport. As Russell argues,

> The value of winning seems to lie, then, in its contribution to constructing certain competitive contexts that will foster the exercise and display of distinctive sporting excellences, particularly contexts that attempt to measure and record superior displays of excellence.[31]

Clearly the mutualist defense of the central purpose of competitive sports can be understood as relying on interpretivism's interdependence of the moral and the aesthetic. The moral dimension necessitates fairness, the aesthetic dimension necessitates embodying intrinsic properties, and together they signify a mutual effort as well as a commitment to promote and honor excellence and the integrity of sports' best interpretation. Competition does not disaggregate contestants but rather binds them together in a mutual striving for excellence with moral and aesthetic connotations.

An Interpretivist Case for Competition in Youth Sports

In order to make an interpretivist case for competition in youth sports, it is appropriate to note that the term "youth" refers to the period between childhood and adulthood. More generally, the term is often used as a synonym for "youngster." This varied usage makes it difficult to determine precisely who should be labeled youths. For instance, the World Health Organization defines young people as those between the ages of ten and twenty-four.[32] The United Nations includes only "those persons between the ages of 15 and 24 years."[33] Acknowledging the significant differences among the people encompassed in this large age bracket, the United Nations distinguishes between "teenagers" (those between the ages of 13 and 19) and "young adults" (those between 20 and 24).[34] It is important to note, however, that the United Nations also considers teenagers to be "children," a group that includes "persons up to the age of 18."[35]

Regardless of the legal parameters of the definition of youth, the differences in the social, cultural, and political undertones and understandings that the term takes in different countries, and its specific age delimitations, the term unmistakably refers to the relatively lengthy period of time immediately prior to adulthood. As mentioned above, the term "youth" also encompasses the early stages of adulthood. This implies that the period of youth ranges roughly from the age of twelve to the age of legal adulthood, and that it shares some of the attributes of childhood. However, as youths are closer to adulthood than younger children, the difference is not of kind but of degree. Some youths are children who are closer to adulthood but have not yet reached that stage of life. This is the conceptualization of youth referred to in this chapter.

What typifies the youth traversing the last part of the path to adulthood? In her influential article "What Is a Child?" Tamar Schapiro, inspired by Kantian ethics, argues that "the condition of childhood is one in which the agent is not yet in a position to speak in her own voice because there is no voice which counts as hers."[36] For Schapiro, childhood is a normative predicament in which persons are in a state of underdevelopment: "the undeveloped agent, unlike the developed agent, is unable to work out a plan of life 'all at once.'"[37] Schapiro is aware of the enormity of the normative predicament in which children find themselves and believes that such a condition excuses a paternalistic attitude toward children if their ability to work out a plan of life all at once is not yet developed. Thus she proposes that adults have a duty to help children overcome this normative predicament, but realizes that only they can do so. In other words, children have to develop a voice that counts as legitimately theirs that will assist them in conceiving a broad life plan. Schapiro supports a principle stating that adults should, to the best of their ability, help children become developed agents. To do so, she contends that adults must recognize both negative and positive obligations to children:

> Our negative obligation as adults must be to refrain from hindering them [children] in this effort [of developing a perspective they can endorse as their own].We do this by not treating children as if they belonged to a distinct and permanent underclass. . . .
>
> The second part of the principle, which prohibits us from treating children as a permanent underclass, determines both positive and negative duties. Negatively, it implies that we must refrain from acting in ways which hinder children's development as deliberators. . . . Positively, the principle demands that we make it our end to help children overcome their dependent condition. In nurturing, disciplining, and educating children, we must strive as far as possible to make them aware of their natural authority and power over themselves and of its proper exercise.[38]

For Schapiro, the negative and positive obligations adults have to children, whose ultimate goal is to facilitate the latter's most exigent quest to become developed agents who can authoritatively rule over themselves, "all stem from the idea that in order not to abuse our privilege as adults, we must make children's dependence our enemy."[39] This view indicates that paternalistic attitudes toward children are only temporarily justified. It also recognizes that children develop a capacity to authoritatively rule over themselves as they grow. Finally, it suggests that adults should allow this developing capacity to be exercised in matters that children are capable of facing and handling, especially those that affect them directly. As youths' dependence shrinks, the domains over which they exercise and rely on their own authority expand.

The interpretivist account of the central purpose of competitive sports articulated above is compatible with and advances youths' interests and needs. Specifically, it assists youths on the last part of their journey to adulthood by respecting their emerging authority over themselves, which includes providing opportunities to exercise, consolidate, and expand this capacity. First, by arguing that competitive sports are best construed "as a mutual striving for excellence,"[40] interpretivism compels youths to ponder their place in this mutuality. Since competitive sports is never an individual endeavor, but rather, as Simon maintains, a cooperative one, it provides youths with valuable opportunities to carve out their own space among themselves, which demands deliberation to find their own voices and make them public.[41] In carving out their own space, youths situate themselves not only in relation to peers but also relative to coaches, administrators, and parents, among other social actors involved in competitive sport.

This point is driven home by Edwin J. Delattre, who maintains that "the testing of one's mettle in competitive athletics is a form of self-discovery, just as the preparation to compete is a form of self-creation."[42] He further argues that "the claim of competitive athletics to importance rests squarely on their providing for us opportunities for self-discovery which might otherwise have been missed."[43] Under this view, sports is a rich terrain for youths to practice in a rather intense fashion their ability to responsibly decide for themselves among peers.

The mutualist approach to competitive sports demands that youths recognize the value of opponents not just for self-development, but instead as moral equals who are also searching for, and affirming, themselves through the quest for excellence. This recognition is important because it implies the realization that treating opponents in this way means also recognizing that the latter "are capable of forming and acting on intelligent conceptions of how their lives should be lived."[44] And this realization, in turn, might prevent competitors from using others simply to satisfy personal sporting ends or advance their own self-development. In addition, this realization might prevent youths from instrumentalizing themselves to secure victory in a sporting contest by dubious means. Likewise, this realization might assist youths in resisting attempts by others (e.g., opponents or coaches) to instrumentalize them for their own benefit. By conceiving of contestants as partners in a cooperative effort toward excellence, competitive mutualism overcomes the notion that "opponents are at best means to one's own ends, and at worst obstacles to be surmounted."[45] Through mutualism in sports, youths might learn that respecting themselves necessitates respecting opponents.

Conceiving competitive sports from a mutualist perspective promotes another relevant benefit for youths. As seen above, youths who engage in competitive sports are introduced to a practice with a set of intertwined moral and aesthetic values. Broadly speaking, the former are related to issues of fairness while the latter are related to the intrinsic properties and standards of excellence definitive of any particular sport. To accurately measure their relative athletic merit, contestants are obliged not only to recognize each other as equals but also to foster a context of competition that is conducive to excellence. This requires, for example, finding worthy opponents, following the rules, and demonstrating concern for excellence and self-control, among other qualities. As Simon explains, "The practice of competitive sports and athletics is value laden in important ways. Some values . . . are traits that all competitive athletes have strong reason to commend and act upon themselves."[46] What can be labeled, paraphrasing him, as the inner moral-aesthetic compound of competitive sports comprises the normative features that are indispensable to the attainment of athletic excellence.[47] The inner moral-aesthetic component of competitive sports exemplifies a form of life worth aspiring to with undeniable educational characteristics and the potential to positively influence the development of character. When introduced to and maturing into competitive sports, youths are confronted with the decision to embrace this form of life and its ensuing inner values. Whether or not they decide to do so, the deliberation is beneficial in itself as it represents an opportunity to practice their emerging autonomy. This development of autonomy is essential to human flourishing; a mutual understanding of competitive sports offers youths a way to foster it.

There is at least one more reason why the interpretivist account of competitive sports' central purpose advanced here is significant to youth, which is related to the previous point: it demonstrates what a good life entails and at the same time offers a route to pursue it. By a good life we have in mind what William J. Morgan calls a life of wholehearted engagement, which is characterized by an "active, passionate engagement in some enterprise, of engagement that is more mindful and self-conscious than habitual and unreflective, and more touched by elan because of the higher sense of purpose and aspiration it embodies."[48] Wholehearted engagement stands in contrast to mundane engagement, which is epitomized by the taking up of different pursuits simply to be occupied and avoid being bored. Morgan claims that sports "is one form of life in which such full engagement is called for."[49] Indeed, he believes that it "is one of a select few human undertakings in which full-blown engagement is a characteristic rather than uncharacteristic feature of the actions of its participants."[50] This is the case because of sports' distinctive and attractive gratuitous logic, which inverts the instrumental rationality of ordinary living and its concern for excellence. To be wholeheartedly engaged in sports portends to value and commit to its defining point and standards of excellence. What this all means for youths is that competitive sports serve as a potent exemplar of not only the substance of a good life but also of what it takes to achieve it.

While the mutualism articulated by the interpretivist account of competitive sports attends to and serves the interests and needs of youths, it also helps in responding to the general problems in youth sports noted earlier in the chapter. Mutualism requires bestowing equal concern to all contestants and fostering a competitive context in which excellence flourishes. As already noted, these broad requirements take different normative form: contestants are obliged to follow the rules of the sport, seeks out worthy opponents, make their best efforts in competition, recognize their strengths and weaknesses as well as those of their opponents, train and perform to the best of their ability, respect opponents and referees, wish and honor excellence, and so on. Undoubtedly, if competitive sports is understood and experienced in its mutualist version, egregious self-aggrandizement and obsessive advantage seeking would have no place in youth sports. As subcategories of runaway individualism, they are in stark contrast to the tenets of mutualism in sports. By overly stressing the advancement of self-interest, even to the expense of the interests of others, egregious self-aggrandizement denies the cooperative aspect of competitive sports and its ensuing duties. On the other hand, obsessive advantage seeking typically implies a "do whatever it takes" or "win at all costs" attitude that often leads to dubious actions that instrumentalize opponents and rebuff excellence. Mutualism in sports does not accept self-aggrandizement but rather self-discovery and self-creation as well as its collective dimension. In competitive sports one needs others to fully know one's caliber and to create excellence. As for advantage seeking, mutualism does not disapprove it altogether but only when it is contrary to the quest for excellence and the virtues needed to foster a competitive context. Mutualism in sports responds to the general problems in youth sports and presents a direction for more sensitive reforms. In the final section we make suggestions to reform coaching youth sports consonant with this view.

Suggestions for Strengthening Youth Coaching

Given the discussion throughout this chapter, it seems reasonable to argue that the overarching goal of youth sports coaches should be, paraphrasing Schapiro, to make young athletes' dependence their enemy. Coaches are positively obligated to comport themselves in a manner that is conducive for the young athletes they are working with to develop their own voice. This implies a careful evaluation and respect of what the young athletes are capable of doing at any given moment and their interests as well as what they will need in adulthood to conceive and pursue a broad life plan. Youth sports coaches should match these elements with coaching practices that promote their athletes' authority to rule over themselves. This requirement will often demand the implementation of paternalistic attitudes. For instance, as Dennis Hemphill illustrates, "it is justifiable for coaches or parents to insist that young athletes wear protective equipment or sit out of competition due to an injury that, if left unattended, might result in a more serious injury."[51] However, paternalism is limited to circumstances in which youths are unable to decide for themselves. This is because coaches are also negatively obligated to refrain from practices that will hinder youths' development of their authority over themselves. That youth sports coaches should make young athletes' dependence their enemy means negative and positive duties. While asking young athletes to cheat exemplifies a breach of the former duties, neglecting to confront a young athlete who intentionally harms an opponent exemplifies a breach of the latter duties.

We find it reasonable to conceive of youth sports coaches as individuals who open a path to a good life. This is no trivial matter. The role of youth sports coaches is of paramount importance as they are not simply technicians who facilitate skill acquisition and mastery, but rather individuals who introduce and mentor young athletes into a social practice with internal goods and standards of excellence. As such, youth sports coaches are initiators and facilitators of "a life of wholehearted engagement."[52] While it is only a possibility that young athletes would embrace sports wholeheartedly, coaches should realize that, as Morgan states, sports is a social practice that calls for full engagement.[53] They should also realize that coaching calls for such engagement and that consequently they represent role models for their young athletes. Coaches have a chance to start and guide their young athletes along a road that not only leads to but constitutes a good life.

What follows is a series a of suggestions for youth sports coaches that stem from the two general responsibilities that coaches have as individuals assisting youths and the interpretivist framework discussed in this chapter. Far from recipes, these suggestions should be taken as broad guidelines to organize and reform youth sports in a way that respects both their protagonists and the mutualist approach to competitive sports and its central purpose defended here. There is, of course, much latitude for coaches and administrators to develop their own strategies. While there is some necessary overlap among the suggestions, each one stresses a distinctive and important element in coaching youth sport.

Youth Sports Coaches Should Adopt a Mutualist Perspective on Competition

By focusing youths on achieving excellence in sports rather than simply winning, the mutualist perspective can help coaches teach athletes appropriate ways to approach competition. By distinguishing between excellence and winning and emphasizing the former rather than the latter, coaches can help their young charges learn to view the competitive process as one in which it is imperative to respect the internal goods of the sporting practice (i.e., the highly specialized skills and strategies that make their sport the unique type of activity it is), the standards of excellence of that practice, the opponents who provide them with opportunities to test themselves and quest for excellence in the sporting context, and others (e.g., officials, coaches, athletic trainers, administrators, and parents) who provide them with support within that context. Once learned, the mutualist view of sports competition will help young athletes develop an awareness of their moral obligations as athletes collectively striving for excellence within a particular sport, and, in turn, will help them to learn to compete in a good and decent manner within that sport.

The mutualist coach is able to impart to youth the moral duties that they owe to their opponents. Since mutualism recognizes opponents as partners in the competitive process rather than obstacles or enemies to be overcome or dominated, coaches can help young athletes understand why their opponents are worthy of respect, even when unsporting or aggressive behavior may make it seem otherwise. The mutualist coach will also be well positioned to explain to young athletes why they should respect and adhere to the rules of their sport, especially the constitutive rules that establish the means through which excellence in the sport is to be achieved.

Youth Sports Coaches Should Focus Young Athletes on the Goods Internal to Their Sports, Their Standards of Excellence, and the Virtues That Foster Their Attainment

Coaches should teach their young athletes to be strong and vigilant stewards of their sport by encouraging them to consistently strive for excellence in ways that respect and honor their sports' internal goods and standards of excellence, the constitutive rules, the means that are supported by these rules, and the gratuitous logic in which they are grounded. In MacIntyrean terms, coaches should instruct their athletes on how to be caretakers of the internal goods and standards of excellence of their sports and dissuade them from focusing on the subsidiary external goods, such as fame and advancement, that can accompany successful youth sports participation. By emphasizing the goods internal to the sport, its standards of excellence, and the virtues that facilitate their achievement, coaches emphasize the inner moral-aesthetic compound that makes excellence in each sport a unique entity and help their athletes to realize that athletic excellence cannot be achieved without moral responsibility. Such emphasis on these fundamental elements also points to the reason why sports invites a wholehearted engagement. That is, these fundamental elements are related to "the good of a certain kind of life"[54] that is realized when they are embraced. Coaches working in this spirit, then, open up possibilities for their young athletes to exercise and be inspired by that good.

Youth Sports Coaches Should Seek to Develop Resolution Seekers, Not Outcome Seekers

If coaches adhere to the first two recommendations above, they will help young athletes develop a view of competition that clearly places the pursuit of excellence through the moral and aesthetic process of sports competition ahead of the outcome of winning or competitive sport's external goods. In doing so, they should, in the words of Cesar R. Torres and Douglas W. McLaughlin, help athletes develop as resolution seekers rather than outcome seekers.[55] Coaches and athletes who place too much emphasis on winning are often outcome seekers who "are not ultimately interested in *how* they solve athletic challenges or in establishing valid differences in performances."[56] These individuals often find themselves mired in the practice of obsessive advantage seeking as they go to great lengths to pursue victory within their sports.

While the lure of winning can be strong, it should not override the moral and aesthetic obligations athletes have within their sports if those athletes learn to adopt a mutualist perspective that will, in turn, help them to prioritize the internal goods and the standards of excellence of their sports and their supporting values over the external goods that can come with winning. Young athletes accomplishing these two objectives stand out as resolution seekers, who are further characterized by Torres and McLaughlin as contestants who "do not merely hunt for favorable results regardless of athletic merit. Rather, they consider sporting contests as the sites in which athletic superiority is determined through testing excellences."[57]

To emphasize resolution seeking over outcome seeking, mutualist coaches will focus more on constitutive and restorative skill mastery as a means to athletic excellence, and less on it simply as a means to winning and its subsidiary rewards. While coaches typically stress the importance of skill execution in the pursuit of victory, many competitive foibles are forgiven and forgotten by outcome seeking coaches in winning's afterglow. Those same mistakes remain visible to vigilant mutualist coaches, who focus athletes on correcting them out of a sense of duty to the sporting practice and its standards of excellence rather than a base appetitive desire to win. It is this sense of obligation to sporting practice that mutualist coaches should strive to pass on to their young athletes, thus helping them to develop as both resolution seekers and as wholeheartedly engaged athletes.

Youth Sports Coaches Should Seek to Provide Young Athletes with Opportunities to Develop Their Authority over Themselves

Coaches often fail to give youths the opportunities they need to develop as autonomous individuals. Many coaches hesitate to share power with their young athletes or turn leadership roles or decision-making responsibilities over to their charges because they are afraid the young athletes will make significant mistakes that may lead to losses in competition. As are result, they are frequently stingy when it comes to providing such opportunities to young athletes. However, if competitive youth sports are to help young athletes move out of their state of dependence as both athletes and human beings, coaches must begin to allow their athletes to make more of their own decisions on the playing surface and during training sessions. Such a shift in responsibility will help the athletes develop their abilities to think critically and imaginatively, and to take greater ownership in their decisions and the consequences that stem from them. This does not mean that youth sports coaches should relinquish their authority; rather, they should change their outlook on how they exercise it in order to "contribute to the development of personhood by gradually expanding and supporting opportunities for athletes to develop decision-making abilities and commitments to meaningful engagement."[58] This does not mean that young athletes should be left in the lurch either. Again, the provision of opportunities for youths to develop their own authority demands that youth sports coaches gradually withdraw their authority. But they should remain available, supportive, and even protective of their young athletes as required by the situation.

Mutualist coaches who take this recommendation seriously will give their athletes more decision-making responsibilities and leadership roles to assist them in achieving greater autonomy and overcoming dependence. These roles and responsibilities might include play calling responsibilities in sports like soccer, football, and basketball, pitch calling duties in baseball and softball, or game and even practice planning opportunities in a variety of sports. Such opportunities will help young athletes develop as athletes and as human beings, and will allow them to take greater ownership of the decisions and consequences that help shape their sports experiences. Youth sports coaches should be wary of demanding that their young athletes blindly follow their orders.

Conclusion

In this chapter we have defended competition in youth sports and argued that coaches in this setting should be seen as individuals whose main role is to introduce and guide their young athletes in a social practice that, given its structure, leads to a fully engaged form of life while providing them opportunities to develop their own authority over themselves. Based on these general responsibilities, we have provided a number of suggestions to organize and reform coaching youth sports that also respect competitive sport's central purpose as mutualistically conceived. We believe our analysis shows how competition in youth sports and youth sports coaching can be carried out as ethically sound pursuits. While it does not escape us that, when understood in this way, youth coaching is a remarkably difficult pursuit, we would argue that it is extremely important and could also be a gratifying experience. Contributing to the moral growth of young athletes through meaningful engagement in sports would unavoidably test coaches in more than one way. This should make the sporting community more tolerant and respectful of coaches involved in youth sports, but should also make coaches more tolerant, understanding, and respectful of their young charges, together with their abilities, interests, potential, and future.

Questions for Review and Discussion

1. Describe the reforms proposed to improve youth sports in the United States.

2. What are major criticisms of and problems with the reforms proposed to improve youth sports in the United States?

3. How does interpretivism (also called broad internalism) explain competitive sports and its central purpose?

4. How does interpretivism's account of competitive sports and its central purpose help advance youth's interests, needs, and welfare?

5. Given the tenets of interpretivism and the interests, needs, and welfare of youth, articulate a defensible ethics of coaching youth sport.

Suggestions for Further Reading

Dixon, Nicholas. "Sport, Parental Autonomy, and Children's Right to an Open Future." *Journal of the Philosophy of Sport* 34:2 (2007): 147–159.

McNamee, Mike. "Beyond Consent? Paternalism and Pediatric Doping." *Journal of the Philosophy of Sport* 36:2 (2009): 111–126.

Russell, J. S. "Children and Dangerous Sport and Recreation." *Journal of the Philosophy of Sport* 34:2 (2007): 176–193.

Shields, David L., and Brenda L. Bredemier. *True Competition: A Guide to Pursuing Excellence in Sport and Society.* Champaign, IL: Human Kinetics, 2009.

Simon, Robert L. *Fair Play: The Ethics of Sport.* 3rd ed. Boulder, CO: Westview, 2010.

Torres, Cesar R. "The Danger of Selectively Changing the Rules in Youth Sport: The Case of the Strike Zone." *Journal of Physical Education, Recreation and Dance* 81:5 (2010): 29–34.

Torres, Cesar R., ed. *Niñez, deporte y actividad física: Reflexiones filosóficas sobre una relación compleja.* Buenos Aires: Miño y Dávila Editores, 2008.

Torres, Cesar R., and Peter F. Hager. "De-emphasizing Competition in Organized Youth Sport: Misdirected Reforms and Misled Children." *Journal of the Philosophy of Sport* 34:2 (2007): 194–210.

Tymowski, Gabriela. "Rights and Wrongs: Children's Participation in High Performance Sport." In *Cross Cultural Perspectives in Child Advocacy*, 55–94. Edited by Ilene R. Berson, Michael J. Berson, and Bárbara C. Cruz. Greenwich, CT: Information Age, 2001.

PART 4

Coaching, Compliance, and the Law

ROBERT L. SIMON

While the discussion so far has focused on ethical issues in coaching, remember that coaches have legal responsibilities as well. What are a coach's legal responsibilities in regard to the health and safety of players? How far are coaches legally required to go to prevent injury to their athletes, particularly in contact sports where the players apply physical force to each other's bodies? Does a coach have legal as well as moral responsibilities with regard to gender equity? What contractual obligations does a college coach incur when recruiting athletes for his or her institution? Perhaps most vexing of all, what is the relationship, if any, between a coach's legal responsibilities on the one hand and moral ones on the other?

Here I offer an overview of each chapter and then make a few remarks about the relationship between legal and moral responsibilities. That issue is complex and has generated an extensive literature of its own, in both jurisprudence and philosophy of law, but perhaps I can provide a brief guide that will help readers understand the broader intellectual context of these chapters.

In Chapter 12, Nancy Hogshead-Makar explains and defends Title IX, which prohibits gender discrimination in federally funded educational programs. Title IX is widely credited with ending the era in which women were basically excluded from most areas of organized competitive athletics, leading to an enormous expansion of women's participation in sports.

However, as Hogshead-Makar points out, there are also criticisms of Title IX, especially relating to the manner in which it has been interpreted by the government agencies charged with enforcement. Hogshead-Makar explains and examines these criticisms and finds them seriously flawed. She concludes her chapter by discussing the responsibility of coaches not to exploit, abuse, or discriminate against individual players. She argues that sexual relationships between coaches and players are unethical because they are exploitative, especially in view of the differences in power relationships between coaches and the athletes under their responsibility.

The question of what the law requires of coaches may be controversial. Individuals, including judges and lawyers, often disagree about what the law on a particular matter is, especially in hard cases where apparently reasonable arguments can be presented by opposing sides. In Chapter 13, Matthew Mitten presents a number of fascinating, controversial cases where courts have adjudicated issues involving the coach's responsibilities for the players' health and safety.

Clearly coaches have both legal and moral responsibilities to protect the health and safety of their athletes. But how far do these responsibilities extend? In particular, what does *the law* require of coaches? Can such requirements be morally justified?

Mitten suggests that the law in this area is not completely settled since courts in different jurisdictions have imposed different standards of care that yield contrary results when applied to the same case.

The first standard, roughly stated, is that coaches are bound by ordinary standards of negligence and due care and must take reasonable steps to protect the health and safety of their players. However, some courts worry that this negligence–reasonable care approach imposes too strict a standard on coaches, especially those who coach at very competitive levels. Coaches may become so afraid of violating the standard that they coddle their teams and are inhibited from requiring the kind of tough conditioning that prepares players for demanding competition. Even worse, fear of liability may prompt institutions such as high schools to limit participation to reduce the possibility of lawsuits. These courts recommend a looser standard, requiring only that coaches not have malicious intent to promote injury and not be reckless in their behavior.

Mitten, however, argues that the first standard is ethically superior and that the kind of consequences or utilitarian considerations proponents of the second standard are concerned about are neither sufficiently weighty nor sufficiently probable as to override protecting players from serious harm. Mitten is making in part a moral point that the first, stricter standard is more morally defensible than the second.

In Chapter 14, Timothy Davis explores the legal and moral conundrums that may arise during the recruitment of college athletes. How binding are the commitments coaches make to recruited athletes? For example, what if a coach promises more scholarships than are actually available, anticipating that some athletes will drop out? But what if they don't drop out? Do all prospective players have a right to a scholarship? If not, what legal recourse, if any, is available? Davis explores these and other related issues that may arise in the recruiting process and suggests how it might be carried out in an ethically acceptable fashion.

Morality and Law

The chapters in Part 4 explore important and often controversial legal cases bearing on the duties, rights, and responsibilities of coaches. They also examine the reasoning behind these decisions and argue for a conclusion about what standards courts should employ in deciding cases in the areas under discussion. But isn't it the job of judges to enforce the *law as it is* rather than impose their own moral standards about *what the law should be*?

Philosophers, jurists, and other theorists, as well as practicing lawyers and judges, have long debated the relationship between law and morality. Their discussions and debates are far too complex for me to fully cover here. What follows is a guide to the discussion that I hope lays a framework for evaluating the theses advanced in this section. Although some important positions are not covered in this discussion, the views considered have been influential in the theory of jurisprudence. Readers uninterested in exploring these complexities can simply take the chapters in this section as offering a moral critique of the law or recommendations about what the law should be.

The conclusions found in these chapters may be viewed as *recommendations,* either to legislators who draft statutes or to judges who interpret and apply them, as to the morally best way of deciding cases in this area. Court decisions, of course, are not always ethically sound. Thus in *Plessy v. Ferguson* (1896), the Supreme Court of the United States upheld racially segregated facilities under the infamous idea that they could be "separate but equal." That decision, reversed in *Brown v. Board of Education* (1954), upheld the immoral practice of racial segregation and was rightly criticized on moral grounds.

An intuitively justifiable view is that what the law is, is one thing; what it should be is another, a view known as legal positivism. It asserts that there are no significant moral tests for law. The most influential version of positivism, advanced by the distinguished twentieth-century legal theorist H. L. A. Hart, views sophisticated legal systems as bodies of rules of different kinds (criminal law, law of wills, and tax law are all derived from a supreme rule, called the rule of recognition).[1] Perhaps the rule of recognition in the United States is the US Constitution, although some have argued that (1) it is the original intent of the founders, and (2) the Constitution must be read as a flexible document that can be applied pragmatically to resolve contemporary issues. Hart's version of legal positivism resembles the idea that a game is defined by its constitutive rules, which emanate from a supreme rule—the official rule book applying to the game or sport in question.

On Hart's version of legal positivism, the judge applies the rules. But what about hard cases where rules require interpretation? Or were not anticipated by the rule makers? Suppose, to borrow a kind of example used by Hart himself, that a college administration passes a rule prohibiting the use of "vehicles" in the college quad, presumably in order to encourage pedestrian traffic. What should the campus safety officers do about students who skateboard in the restricted area? Is a skateboard a "vehicle" in the meaning of the statute? Some would say that we need to follow the original intent of the rule makers. But they may never have considered such a case or, if they had, might have different views of it. Similarly, the plain words of the rule may provide insufficient guidance, since "vehicle" may be a term with fuzzy edges. In such cases, Hart suggested that judges are forced to use their discretion. But in my view just which factors should legitimately influence their judgment is left unclear. In any case, readers sympathetic to positivism's separation of law and morality can view the recommendations in these chapters as arguments for how judges should use their discretion in hard cases involving coaching.

But perhaps there is a closer connection between law and morality than legal positivists acknowledge. An alternate view is often called the natural law approach because a major version of natural law theory arises from Aristotelean accounts, often mediated through Christian and particularly Catholic theology. It postulates that there are natural conditions necessary for human flourishing. Law is an instrument for promoting and protecting these conditions. On this view, as thinkers ranging from Thomas Aquinas to Martin Luther King have argued, an "unjust law" is not a genuine law and imposes no legal or moral duty to obey. Although the idea that "an unjust law is not a law" is puzzling, even sounding contradictory to many, it may be rendered more plausible by considering whether a game with arbitrary or changing rules is a genuine game.[2] In such a case, we can say plausibly that arbitrary or ever-changing rules are not true rules; similarly, an arbitrary or unjust law would not be a true law. This reasoning suggests that the immorality of a statute or judicial ruling counts against it being legally valid.

A different version of natural law, especially relevant to this book, has been proposed by legal theorist Ronald Dworkin and has had a major influence on the development of broad internalist or interpretive views of sport, as discussed in several chapters in this book and in the philosophy of sport literature generally.[3] On Dworkin's view, when a judge must apply such abstract legal requirements as that of equal protection of the laws (guaranteed by the Fourteenth Amendment to the US Constitution) or a requirement to avoid negligence, the judge must develop and rationally defend a theory of equal protection or negligence as the case may be. Interpretations are justified by their "fit" or ability to explain existing law in the form of statutes and significant judicial decisions (precedents) and also must be the morally most defensible interpretation available. Thus *Plessey v. Ferguson*, which upheld racial segregation in southern states, was later rightly rejected by the Supreme Court because it did not fit the language of equality in the US Constitution, Declaration of Independence, and other court decisions about equal protection, and because it surely is not a morally acceptable interpretation of equal protection. Dworkin's interpretivist approach has been criticized on a variety of grounds, for example, that it gives too much power to judges to come up with philosophical interpretations of legal terms that in reality only reflect their political leanings. Similarly, according to broad internalism, making moral judgments in sports requires a theory that makes sense of a sport's key features, such as provisions of the rules and interpretations of principles presupposed by the rules that present the sport in its morally best light.

Although the versions of legal positivism and natural law roughly described above do not exhaust all the alternative theories of the relation of law to morality, they do provide a framework for understanding the chapters in Part 4. Those sympathetic to positivism can simply view the recommendations of Mitten and Davis largely as theses about what the law ought to be, although both authors also describe existing law as it has evolved in court decisions. Those more inclined to agree with the natural law approach can take their arguments as establishing moral criteria for determining what the law is. For example, on a reading of Mitten's article that is sympathetic to the natural law approach, one might argue that a test for the legality of laws in the area of a coach's responsibility for the health and safety of athletes is whether the law reflects a *moral* standard of reasonable care and avoidance of negligence in treating players. On a view like Dworkin's, this does not involve judges imposing their own personal morality on the rest of us but rather searching for the best interpretation or theory of evaluative concepts already in the law such as "negligence" and "reasonable care."

Interested readers can explore the issue of the relationship of law to morality in the works cited in the endnotes. In any case, the chapters in Part 4 should acquaint readers, especially athletes and coaches, with some of the controversies involving their legal rights, duties, and responsibilities and, in addition, raise important questions about how the relevant law is best formulated and understood.

Twelve

The Ethics of Title IX and Gender Equity for Coaches: Selected Topics

NANCY HOGSHEAD-MAKAR

Title IX of the Education Amendments of 1972 expresses the nation's collective aspirational belief that girls and boys, women and men, deserve equality in educational experiences and opportunities. Our country has been shaped by ethical guidelines of equality, tolerance, freedom, and rule of law. By contemporary standards, it seems almost peculiar that equality for males and females in federally supported education was ever considered a radical idea.

Despite the progress of the past forty years, athletic departments remain an area of ongoing resistance to equity for men and women in higher education. The battle for gender equality in athletics is befuddling; athletic participation is characterized by ennobling ideals that transmit values of fair play, teamwork, sportsmanship, and compliance with the rules.[1] Yet full compliance with these values cannot be said to have been widely embraced where women seek parity of athletic opportunities in their individual schools.[2] Although athletic gains have been sweeping, women continue to lag behind men by every measurable criterion, including participation opportunities, scholarships, budgets, facilities, and recruiting.

The statutes, case law, and regulations interpreting Title IX may seem daunting, but they all arise from a simple ethical point that is relevant to every question raised today: whether girls and boys, men and women, are receiving equal educational opportunities in athletics.[3] The NCAA put it this way when it adopted Operating Principle 3.1: "An athletics program can be considered gender equitable when the participants in both the men's and the women's programs would accept as fair and equitable the overall program of the other gender."[4] Reflecting this view is that treating female athletic programs as second-class sends a visible message to everyone, on-campus and off-campus, that formal discrimination is acceptable. This chapter explores the responsibilities of coaches and athletic administrators to view gender equity in athletics not just as a matter of legal or technical compliance, but as a matter of ethical responsibility. In doing so, this chapter shares the goal of other feminist ethicists to eliminate or at least ameliorate oppression, particularly of women.[5]

Beyond basic concepts of fairness, Title IX can be defended on utilitarian principles. A large body of research tends to show that, despite the dumb jock myth, interscholastic sports participation provides boys and girls (from diverse socioeconomic, racial, and ethnic backgrounds) measurable positive educational impacts, including improvements in self-concept, higher educational aspirations in their senior year, improved school attendance, increased math and science enrollment, more time spent on homework, and higher enrollment in honors courses.[6] A sports experience provides a positive health trajectory for girls, including reducing the risk for obesity, heart disease, breast cancer, osteoporosis, tobacco and drug use, unwanted teen pregnancy, sexually transmitted diseases, depression, and suicide.[7]

Similarly, research by Professor Betsey Stevenson at the Wharton School of the University of Pennsylvania found that Title IX was responsible for one-fifth of the rise of female educational attainment for the generation that followed the new policy, as well as a 10 percent increase in women working full-time and a 12 percent spike in women in traditionally male-dominated occupations, such as accounting, law, and veterinary medicine.[8] While her research focused on girls, and comparisons just before and after the legislation passed, there is no reason to think that these benefits wouldn't be just as applicable for boys. In short, from a utilitarian perspective, sports make both boys and girls more productive members of society, thereby providing a justifiable investment of public tax dollars.

Coaches are uniquely positioned to advocate for the women and men in their programs, which includes providing gender equitable sports programming, setting ethical boundaries for sexual and romantic relationships, and ensuring ethical treatment for gender equity advocates complaining about sex discrimination in their departments. The coaching profession has been described as a "moral enterprise" that involves the transmission of values and ethics.[9] Yet when professors Ellen Staurowsky and Erianne Weight polled over one thousand coaches about their knowledge of Title IX requirements, they found that most college coaches lack the basic knowledge of the law and its application; coaches simply have not been educated about Title IX through reliable educational mediums.[10] The mainstay of Title IX advocacy and compliance should be coaches.

Ethical Underpinnings of Title IX

Congress passed Title IX on June 23, 1972.[11] Other than the constitutional right to vote, possibly no other piece of legislation has had a greater effect on women's lives than Title IX. Education has been this country's primary method to improve income potential and social class mobility. Yet for most of American history, women were formally excluded or limited in higher education opportunities, thereby blocked from improving themselves economically and socially. It was Title IX that cracked the barriers to women's ability to have equal opportunity to pursue education. As Senator Birch Bayh, one of the drafters of the legislation, stated:

> What we were really looking for was . . . equal opportunity for young women and for girls in the educational system of the United States of America. Equality of opportunity. Equality. That shouldn't really be a controversial subject in a nation [that] now for 200 years has prided itself in equal justice.[12]

Since its adoption, Title IX has become an iconic symbol. The statute is widely recognized as the source of a vast expansion of athletic opportunities for women in the nation's schools and universities. For example, in 1970–71, only 300,000 girls (compared to 3.7 million boys) participated in interscholastic sports. After the passage of Title IX, 2 million girls were participating by 1978–79, and the number of participating girls passed the 3 million mark in 2007.[13] Some laws have an expressive or transformational quality that transcends their remedial purposes; Title IX is one of those laws.[14] Indeed, Title IX's commercial panache has resulted in a company that sells women's athletic apparel marketing itself under the same name: www.titlenine.com.[15]

Four statutes require equality based on receipt of federal funds. Title IX was premised on the first statute passed, Title VI of the Civil Rights Act of

1964, which bars race discrimination in schools receiving federal funds. Title VI reads, "No person in the United States shall, on the ground of race, color, or national origin, be excluded from participation in, be denied the benefits of, or be subjected to discrimination under any program or activity receiving Federal financial assistance." Note that Title IX merely substituted the word "sex" in place of "race, color and national origin." The two other are Section 504 of the Rehabilitation Act of 1973, which banned discrimination against qualified handicapped persons in federally assisted programs or activities; and the Age Discrimination Act of 1975, which banned age discrimination in federally assisted programs or activities. These four statutes are almost identical, but it is Title IX alone that garners any significant pushback.

Other sources provide excellent overviews of the law, the legislative history, and its technical requirements as well as the uniform judicial rejection of legal attacks on Title IX.[16] This chapter discusses some of the ethical underpinnings of Title IX and gender equity that complement the laws.

Sports Are Uniquely Sex Segregated

After Title IX was passed, legal compliance in classrooms, membership in the marching band, and other school-sponsored activities were relatively straightforward. Schools could seek to comply with gender-neutral standards of merit—whether students had specified SAT scores or grade point averages, whether students could play instruments proficiently while marching, and so on.[17] What makes sports programs unique is that they are one of the few activities left in American college life that are formally sex segregated. After puberty, male and female physical differences warrant sex segregation in athletics in order to give girls and women equal educational opportunities to participate.

Interestingly, early discussions of Title IX compliance favored equal budget allocation between men's and women's programming. There are many attractive features in this proposal, not the least of which is its simplicity. Under an "equal budgets" regime, men and women could have adopted their own model of sport, rather than providing women and men with the right to a sports experience similar to each other. In other words, men and women could have chosen independently which model of sport to adopt: a high school–type broad-based participation at a relatively low cost, or the Division I model of a small number of participants with very large budgets. This equal budget option was scuttled by the passage of the Javits amendment that was approved by Congress in 1974 and remains in effect. The Javits amendment required the administrative agency to prepare and publish regulations covering intercollegiate athletics, and those implementing regulations "shall include with respect to intercollegiate athletics . . . reasonable provisions considering the nature of particular sports."[18] The published regulations ultimately became the 1975 Regulations.[19] These regulations allow different amounts of money to be spent on different sports, depending on the distinct needs of the sport. It recognizes that some sports, such as football and equestrian, are inherently more expensive than other sports, requiring costlier equipment or larger budgets for big spectator events. Other sports are relatively inexpensive to operate, such as cross-country. But if both genders are being provided the best equipment or if both genders are being provided barely functional equipment, it is not a violation of Title IX despite large discrepancies in spending, because both genders are considered to be receiving the same educational experience. Ultimately the Javits amendment preserved the ability of schools to fund men's football and basketball budgets because administrators can choose to retain sports that inherently require larger budgets.

Title IX, as applied to athletics, could not be accomplished by merely integrating existing programs, like the classroom or the band. Instead, schools had to create entirely new sports programs. It is the sex segregation that determines equality measurements; athletics require a comparison to men's sports programs with those made available to women. This comparison necessitates reviewing the equality of opportunities, facilities provided, the number of scholarships, and many other indicia, such as equipment, uniforms, access to tutors and medical treatment, coaching, scheduling, publicity, locker rooms, and competitions.[20] It's why courts hold that comparing men's and women's athletic programs is an "unavoidably gender-conscious comparison [that] merely provides for the allocation of athletics resources and participation opportunities between the sexes in a non-discriminatory manner."[21] And determining whether women are being discriminated against in athletics requires a comparison of the new and existing women's programs with the men's program. It was the first part of the 1975 Regulations that gave schools the most trouble—whether the school was providing girls with the proper number of sports opportunities. This led to the creation of the three-part test in the 1979 Clarification.[22]

The Ethics of the Three-Prong Test

A 1979 Policy Interpretation of the Department of Education created three independent ways for schools to demonstrate that students of both genders have equal opportunities to participate in sports. I've paraphrased for simplicity:

- Under prong 1, a school can show that the percentage of male and female athletes is about the same as the percentage of male and female students enrolled in the school (the proportionality test); *OR*

- Under prong 2, the school can show it has a history and a continuing practice of expanding opportunities for female students; *OR*

- Under prong 3, the school can show it is fully and effectively meeting its female students' interests and abilities to participate in sports.[23]

If a school meets any one of these tests, it will be found to be providing equal athletic participation. This three-part test has been in effect for more than three decades. It has been heavily litigated and has been upheld by the eight federal appeals courts that have considered it.[24]

Legality aside, why is the three-prong test ethical? Prong 1 is premised on the principle that a school should provide athletic opportunities so that students, regardless of gender, have an equal opportunity to play sports. If a school has 1,000 students, evenly split between males and females, but offers only 500 participation opportunities, that school should offer 250 of those opportunities to males and 250 to females. Each male and female would have an equal opportunity of playing in a sports program. Creating 300 sports participation opportunities for males versus 200 for females disproportionately favors men, and it is thereby unfair, without some justification.[25] So long as female students have the same chance of participating in athletics as male students, prong 1 is satisfied and the ethic of equality is met. Prong 1 also allows for administrative efficiency by adopting a strict numerical standard, thereby avoiding competing advocacy from men (or women) about whose programs are more important and worthy of scarce athletic department dollars. This is particularly true at larger schools with small percentages of the student body participating in athletics, like schools in the BCS. In 2010 just 1.7 percent of the student body at the University of Florida could participate in college athletics, just 1.6 percent at the University of Texas, and just 2.5 percent at Ohio State.[26] The ease of prong 1 compliance keeps the men's and women's programs from having to justify which sports are inherently more deserving of a team.

The ethics underlying prong 1, though powerful in vision and application, are not compelled. An alternative ethic is permitted under prong 3. Even if a school cannot meet the proportionality requirement of prong 1, it can provide fewer athletic opportunities to girls if the school can show it meets the "interests and abilities" of its female students. In other words, schools do not have to provide sports opportunities to females if they can show that their students are not interested in playing sports. This prong can, in application, effectively require girls to prove their interest in sports, whereas boys are presumed to be interested.[27] Prong 3 thereby presupposes that females are not as interested in sports, exactly the sort of gender stereotype that equality laws were designed to combat. In practice, however, prong 3 has not proven to be the brake on girls' participation that its promoters thought it would be. The reason is simple: the more sports that females are provided, the more sports participation has become normalized, and the less hesitant girls have become to ask for even more. As schools have made opportunities available, girls have rushed to fill them.

This leads to the ethics reflected in prong 2, which is the notion of continuous improvement for women's sports opportunities. The idea is although a school has not met the equality required by law, it can show significant strides toward doing so. Thus if a school has a history and continuing practice of program expansion, it can provide fewer than numerically equal opportunities, yet still be in compliance. This prong raises serious ethical questions. While it might make sense in the short term to allow compliance under prong 2, it makes little sense in the longer term. Forty years have passed since the passage of the law. The 1975 regulations required compliance in high schools and colleges within three years,[28] placing every institution on notice of what is required since at least 1975. Yet a school can deny willing and able females sports participation opportunities simply by making slow, incremental progress. No other area of civil rights law allows for this sort of dilatory practice on an ongoing basis; instead, they require equality in the here and now.

The three-prong test has been subject to steady vilification for over thirty years, typically by those who erroneously claim that strict proportionality (prong 1) is required under Title IX. They typically make no mention of the other two ways of achieving compliance, both of which can, in practice, work to reduce the level of sports opportunities for girls and women.[29] Thereby, the three ways of achieving compliance are not in ethical unison. Indeed, it can be argued that prongs 2 and 3 can undermine the basic ethic of equality depending on the manner by which schools, colleges, and universities implement the legal test.

Ethics of Sex Segregated Athletics: Why Title IX Is Not a Quota Law or Affirmative Action

Ongoing data collection concludes that high schools and higher education institutions have responded to Title IX by increasing overall the level of female participation rather than by decreasing male participation.[30] Opportunities for sports participation by girls and boys, men and women, are increasing.[31] (See Figure 12.5 at the end of the chapter.) This expansion might not always prove to be true in the future. What if men's sports were losing at the expense of women; would Title IX become a quota system? In a true quota system, the law gives some type of preference to certain group members. Quotas are legally permissible (and fair) only for the purpose of correcting historical practices engaged in by the entity now wishing to provide the preference. Courts regularly identify quotas and quickly prohibit practices that don't meet remedial legal standards. For example, if a city were to be found to have intentionally discriminated against minorities in its contracting, a legal remedy to counteract such discrimination is a quota of contracts that are earmarked specifically for the excluded minority. It is not enough that the subcontractors have engaged in systemic discrimination, or that the overall environment for minorities in the field is fraught with discriminatory practices that work to prevent full economic participation by the minority; it must be the city itself that has engaged in discrimination, or the court will strike it down as unconstitutional.

Athletic departments, by contrast, are not providing females with sports in order to overcome past discrimination but to allocate scarce resources fairly. Because athletics are sex segregated, "determining whether discrimination exists in athletic programs requires gender-conscious, group-wide comparisons."[32] In other words, sex segregated athletics aren't about quotas so much as about comparing resources and sharing them. The only standard to determine whether there has been discrimination is to review what resources are provided to the opposite gender as a comparison.

When Congress was considering limiting the scope of Title IX and weakening regulations interpreting the law, it considered those arguing that requiring equal opportunity in athletics would impose quotas and result in reverse discrimination against men. Yet Congress specifically rejected these arguments.[33] The quota and affirmative action arguments fail for the same reason that equitable sharing of scarce resources does not equate to a quota or reverse discrimination within a family.

The ethics of sharing scarce resources plays out daily in families across the country, which struggle to fairly allocate financial and other resources to their children's education. For example, our son was born five years ahead of our twin daughters. Prior to their arrival, he was the center of our universe and, naturally, received a high level of family resources. When his sisters were born, he got less of the shared family resources, particularly the most valuable commodity every child covets: his parents' time. His portion of the family time and budget would now be shared with his sisters. He did not receive the same level of family resources as he did before his sisters were born, but that is not reverse discrimination or affirmative action. It is the natural and expected result of limited family budgets. While we increased our family budget to accommodate having three children, it still was not enough proportionally to ensure our son the same levels of programs and activities he previously enjoyed. Similarly, schools cannot necessarily increase the size of their athletic department budgets to maintain preexisting levels of spending pro rata. When a school decides that it will not increase its athletic budget but will share the overall resources equally among men's and women's sports, it is not discrimination against men or engaging in quota fulfilling activities. Instead, it is simply assuring that everyone in the family is treated equally.

This ethic is reflected in the Department of Education's 2003 clarification letter, which confirmed that "nothing in Title IX requires the cutting or reduction of teams in order to demonstrate compliance with Title IX, and . . . the elimination of teams is a disfavored practice."[34] Cutting teams will not help a team comply with prongs 2 or 3. Moreover, there is no economic defense to discrimination.[35] "A school may not skirt the requirement of providing both sexes equal opportunity in athletic programs by providing one sex more than substantially proportionate opportunity through the guise of 'outside funding.'"[36]

In short, schools face the same ethical conundrum that millions of families face: what to fund and what to cut to balance the family budget? Ideally, resources would be available to increase, at least incrementally, the school's athletic budget so that no sports opportunities need to be cut.[37] Sharing resources presents difficult choices that are not unlike ones that the parents of the student athletes have already had to make in raising their families.

Another illustration comes from a similar civil rights context from the 1960s, when new desegregation laws required cities to integrate public parks and swimming pools. Some communities closed these facilities rather than integrate them, akin to "cutting off the nose to spite the face." In *Palmer v. Thompson*[38] the Supreme Court upheld the city's racially motivated choice to close public pools, holding it was permissible because the closure placed whites and blacks in the same access to public facilities, or no access.[39] The analogy isn't completely accurate; *Palmer* is much more egregious. When schools close men's sports teams, they are not doing so in order to spite females or to express hostility toward either males or females. Rather, they are doing so to rectify a budget imbalance, replace it with another men's sport, or to shift resources elsewhere within the institution.

While this discussion has assumed a static or limited budget, most NCAA institutions are not cutting their budgets; they have been growing at a robust 7 percent over the past ten years. Over the same time period, academic budgets have not risen appreciably. Most of the new growth in athletics budgets has gone to other men. Between the 2005–06 and 2009–10 academic years, men's budgets increased by $5.2 million, while women's budgets increased by just $1.8 million.[40] Interestingly, two men's sports, football and basketball, make up 78 percent of the entire men's budget, leaving 22 percent for all other men's sports.[41] Title IX does not protect a sport, does not distinguish between sports, and does not favor or disfavor any particular sport. It protects men and women from discrimination, regardless of what uniform the athlete is wearing or the size of the team that the school has decided to offer.[42] Football is allowed eighty-four scholarships according to NCAA rules, which is typically far more than half of all scholarships offered to men.[43] Title IX allows schools to decide what sport model to adopt and which sports they choose to emphasize, and merely requires an equitable allocation between these educational opportunities.

Coaches and athletic administrators can be advocates for gender equity within their departments from both equality and utilitarian perspectives. When doing so, coaches could either tell athletes and department officials that their decisions are required by Title IX, or they could assume responsibility for creating a gender equitable environment within their department. If a school funds football for men and lacrosse for women, the school cannot ethically blame Title IX for the decision not to fund a male lacrosse team. They should instead explain how they've assumed the responsibility to distribute resources equitably between males and females within the athletics department.

The Ethics of Romantic or Sexual Relationships Between Coaches and Athletes

Athletics creates opportunities for sexual harassment due to the close relationship of team members with their coaches and the physical nature of sports. The Supreme Court has noted that different standards of behavior exist for classroom and athletics. If the coach smacks a professional football player on the buttocks as he heads onto the field, it is not sexual harassment, even if the same behavior would reasonably be experienced as abusive by the coach's secretary (male or female) back at the office.[44] Title IX also prohibits sexual harassment in education as a form of sex discrimination, including athletics. Four features of athletics that affect sexual harassment and assault include the coach-student relationship, the increased opportunity for harassment, the physical nature of sports, and the focus on the athlete's body.[45]

A coach's authority over athletes cannot be overestimated. They decide playing time, playing positions and possibly scholarship amounts. They exert power through praise, criticism, or withholding either; they grant or deny leadership opportunities. They exert a special power over an ambitious athlete by holding out the prospect of greater athletic accomplishments. They frequently impose restrictions on the athlete's personal life such as curfew, dress code, or membership in a sorority or fraternity.[46] Yet a coach may reach the elite coaching ranks without knowing about power: how it can be used and abused, and may have never had a course on ethics.

In a typical academic setting, students often have limited opportunity for one-on-one contact with professors. In the athletic context, by contrast, opportunities for such contact are common, and often arise in places conducive to sexual behavior. Most athletic teams travel overnight with their coaches to attend away games. Even without travel, coaches and athletes can spend over a third of all waking hours together. Coaches and trainers commonly work on and off the field to massage athletes' sore muscles and rehabilitate common sports injuries. In addition, sports are inherently physical, and many coaches apply a hands-on approach to demonstrate athletic moves. Coaches and athletes regularly use physical contact, such as a pat on the back or a hug, to convey praise and acknowledge success. Some coaches help athletes stretch before a workout or rub stiff muscles. Athletes and coaches regularly discuss the body as a tool; the status of injuries, the effect of prior workouts on specific body parts, and weight as it relates to performance. Such behavior can be entirely proper in the context of athletics, but would be inappropriate in the classroom. These special circumstances, including the authority of the coach, together with the coach's one-on-one contact, amplify the potential for harassment.

Title IX also protects lesbian, gay, bisexual, and transgender (LGBT) students from discrimination, particularly when the abuse and bullying centers around the athlete's sexuality, or the athlete's failure to conform to sex stereotypes. Typical forms of harassment involve epithets or abuse that would not be used if the athlete were of the opposite gender.

The culture of athletics has not protected athletes from sexual harassment from their coach in the way employees are protected from similar conduct from their manager. The boundaries of workplace harassment have normalized the impermissibility of quid pro quo sexual harassment and hostile environment harassment,[47] but many still view sexual and romantic relationships as permissible, so long as both parties are above the legal age of consent, and there is no overt coercion. In recognition of this permissive culture, many sports organizations have developed ethical policies that explicitly prohibit romantic and sexual relationships between coaches and athletes, regardless of the age of the athlete and coach, or whether the athlete consents to the attention. Like other professional settings marked by an imbalance in power and a duty of care, the ethical standards governing coaches should be designed to safeguard the well-being of persons for whom they are responsible, rather than for the benefit of those in power.

The United States Olympic Committee's (USOC) policy is a model for its breadth and clarity.[48] It leaves no scenario unaddressed. Romantic and sexual relationships are addressed under the heading "exploitative relationships," and the ethics policy flatly prohibits them. "(b) Coaches do not engage in sexual/romantic relationships with athletes or other participants over whom the coach has evaluative, direct, or indirect authority, because such relationships are likely to impair judgment or be exploitative." The USOC policy goes on to prohibit sexual intimacy with current athletes, sexual intimacies with former sexual partners, as well as reviewing boundaries for starting a sexual relationship with a former athlete.

Unfortunately the USOC ethics policy for coaches does not apply to the national governing body (NGBs) of each sport unless the coaching association adopts it. Consequently many NGBs do not ban these types of relationships, or have no mechanism to remove coaches for having a romantic or sexual relationship with someone of age.[49] The Ted Stevens Olympic and Amateur Sports Act does have a nondiscrimination clause,[50] but because these disputes go through AAA arbitration rather than through the court system, they have not provided as effective protection as has Title IX. The USOC recently released materials that deal with misconduct directed toward athletes, including emotional, physical, sexual, bullying, harassing, and hazing.[51] It similarly prohibits relationships between coaches and athletes.[52]

The NCAA policy "Staying in Bounds: A Model Policy to Prevent Inappropriate Relationships Between Student-Athletes and Athletic Department Personnel" is similarly thorough. It addresses the fact that romantic relationships are still common between coaches and athletes and pulls no punches.

> Some will argue that coach-athlete liaisons are not "abusive." Some will maintain that (as many coaches have told us) "you can't control the heart," or "you can't legislate against love," or "as long as the two people are adults, no one can stop them from dating." These comments are self-justifying and, frankly, self-delusional. When coaches enter into sexual relationships with student-athletes, they almost always try to keep these liaisons secret—even if both parties are unmarried—because coaches are well aware that such relationships are inappropriate and unethical. They know deep down that infatuation, sexual attraction,

> and loving feelings do not, in fact, justify an authority figure in a sports program becoming sexually involved with a young adult who plays sports in that program. This is a violation of professional boundaries, and a violation of trust.[53]

In higher education, a typical amorous relationship policy will remove the supervisory capacity between consenting adults.[54] Other professional and ethical standards of conduct also prohibit sexual and romantic relationships between those in a power differential, such as doctors, lawyers, judges, and clergy. All regard it as unethical to have sexual relationships with those they treat, counsel, and appear before. In this way, middle-aged employees are better protected by cultural norms and formal ethical standards than are young athletes participating in club sports.

Retaliation, Commercialism, and Ethical Considerations

Coaches advocating for gender equity in their departments have never had the legal support they are currently enjoying. In 2005 the Supreme Court held that coaches who suffered retaliation for speaking up about gender inequity in their athletics department could sue under Title IX.[55] This makes sense; otherwise institutions could continue discrimination merely by firing or demoting people working to eliminate discrimination. Since that time, numerous women and men working in collegiate athletics have successfully sued their athletic department, alleging they were retaliated against for their advocacy for the women athletes. Juries continue to send decisive verdicts to women and men shown unfair treatment. Listed below are a few of the more recent cases.

- Fresno State lost three retaliation claims by former athletic department employees. Lindy Vivas, a onetime Fresno State women's volleyball coach, was awarded $5.85 million by a jury, later reduced to $4.52 million plus $660,000 in legal fees. Stacy Johnson-Klein, a former women's basketball coach, was awarded $19.1 million; her verdict later was reduced to $6.6 million, plus $2.5 million in legal fees. Fresno State settled with Diane Milutinovich, Fresno's former associate athletic director, for $3.5 million.[56]

- California-Berkley paid $3.5 million to its former women's swimming coach and athletics administrator, Karen Moe Humphreys. She filed a discrimination and retaliation suit alleging she was fired because she complained about treatment of women in the athletics department.[57]

- Florida Gulf Coast University paid $3.4 million in 2008 to two former women's coaches, Jayne Flood and Holly Vaughn, to settle their lawsuit alleging retaliating against the women after they voiced concerns about gender inequity in the school's athletic programs, and were fired shortly thereafter.[58]

- San Diego State University announced it would pay $1.45 million to former swimming and diving head coach Deena Deardurff Schmidt, in a settlement of her Title IX retaliation case. Schmidt's lawsuit alleged that the university had unrealistic expectations for her performance, as her team had lacked a swimming facility since 1999.

- Iowa State awarded $287,000 to former softball coach Ruth Crowe. In her Title IX retaliation suit against the university, Crowe had alleged that after nine years in the head coach position, the university dismissed her before her contract expired because she had complained about salary discrimination and the university's failure to allocate comparable money for recruiting female athletes.

In the past I have put this jury hostility into context by comparing a death from a medical malpractice case that averages just over $1 million in final verdicts.[59] Jury verdicts in Title IX retaliation claims, by contrast, involve a multiple of that amount in part because of the intentional and overt conduct on the part of the defendants.

These cases are also valuable in revealing obstacles to women's leadership in athletics. As a broad generalization, it's fair to say that athletic departments do not value the power of dissent. This can make it hard for advocates of gender equity. They have become a touch-point on the conflict between the educational mission of athletics and the commercial enterprise, particularly in Division I athletics.

Despite large television contracts, sponsorships, and ticket sales at the highest levels of sports, high school and collegiate sports are not for-profit businesses. Taxes are not imposed on revenues from corporate sponsorships, ticket sales, or donor contributions, and athletic facilities are built with tax-free bonds. Students are often forced to pay for athletics as part of their student fees, even for the few sports programs whose income exceeds expenses. The public forgoes taxes on the NCAA multibillion-dollar-basketball championship television contract with CBS and Turner Sports, as well as on billions more in guaranteed payouts from current media football contracts to the top five major conferences.[60] Even the tiny minority of schools actually operating at a profit[61] cannot deny their heavy reliance on public tax dollars that flow from their educational enterprise.

In addition, collegiate athletics receive direct subsidies from their institutions. The latest report from the Knight Commission on Intercollegiate Athletics found that roughly 80 percent of the football bowl subdivision programs averaged a net operating deficit of nearly $10 million. That's money coming from academics to athletics, not the other way around.[62] For public schools in particular, it is another source of tax dollars for athletics. Finally, businesses must pay their employees, while educational institutions do not pay student athletes. Schools are relieved of this obligation because of the athlete's status as a student. If the economic model of high school and intercollegiate sports is founded on utilitarian concepts, forgoing tax revenue as an investment in education for future health benefits and economic productivity for the country, women have an equal right to a fair share of the benefits arising from participation in sports.

The successes of the retaliation cases give advocates of gender equality grounds for cautious optimism. In the battles between the educational mission of athletics and the commercial enterprise, retaliation cases give men and women in athletics more reason to act ethically and champion women within the department; championing women's athletics provides job security. The momentum of multimillion-dollar verdicts and settlements on their side, coaches are better situated now than ever before to seek remedies that will help ensure that college athletic department values include equal opportunity for women's athletics, including its leadership.

Conclusion

Implicit in this chapter has been the notion that the conduct of coaches raises ethical as well as legal issues. Coaches are uniquely positioned to advocate for women and men in the athletic department. They can be forceful advocates for providing men and women with equitable sports programming, including participation, treatment, and scholarships. Coaches, through their coaching associations, must collectively decide to enforce ethical boundaries for sexual and romantic relationships between coaches and athletes. The athletic department may be sex segregated, requiring a different type of thinking than that applied to the classroom, but they collectively comprise one family of athletes, and all need to be provided for equitably. As transmitters of values and ethics, their unwillingness to tolerate inequity speaks loudly to their athletes and to the athletic community.

THE UNITED STATES OLYMPIC COMMITTEE COACHING ETHICS CODE

Readers interested in the discussion issues of harassment and romantic and sexual relationships between coaches and athletes may consult the Coaching Ethics Code, which follows.

1.08 Sexual Harassment

(a) Coaches do not engage in sexual harassment. Sexual harassment is sexual solicitation, physical advances, or verbal or nonverbal conduct that is sexual in nature, and that either:

1. is unwelcome, is offensive, or creates a hostile environment, and the coach knows or is told this;
2. is sufficiently severe or intense to be abusive to a reasonable person in the context.

Sexual harassment can consist of a single intense or severe act or of multiple persistent or pervasive acts.

(b) Coaches accord sexual-harassment complainants and respondents dignity and respect. Coaches do not participate in denying an athlete the right to participate based upon their having made, or their being the subject of, sexual harassment charges.

1.13 Multiple Relationships

(a) In many communities and situations, it may not be feasible or reasonable for coaches to avoid social or other nonprofessional contacts with athletes and other participants. Coaches must always be sensitive to the potential harmful effects of other contacts on their work and on those persons with whom they deal. A coach refrains from entering into or promising another personal, professional, financial, or other relationship with such persons if it appears likely that such a relationship reasonably might impair the coach's objectivity or otherwise interfere with the coach's effectively performing his or her functions as a coach, or might harm or exploit the other party.

1.14 Exploitative Relationships

(a) Coaches do not exploit athletes or other participants over whom they have supervisory, evaluative, or other authority.

(b) Coaches do not engage in sexual/romantic relationships with athletes or other participants over whom the coach has evaluative, direct, or indirect authority, because such relationships are likely to impair judgment or be exploitative.

3.04 Sexual Intimacies with Current Athletes

Coaches do not engage in sexual intimacies with current athletes.

3.05 Coaching Former Sexual Partners

Coaches do not coach athletes with whom they have engaged in sexual intimacies.

3.06 Sexual Intimacies with Former Athletes

(a) Coaches should not engage in sexual intimacies with a former athlete for at least two years after cessation or termination of professional services.

(b) Because sexual intimacies with a former athlete are so frequently harmful to the athlete, and because such intimacies undermine public confidence in the coaching profession and thereby deter the public's use of needed services, coaches do not engage in sexual intimacies with former athletes even after a two-year interval except in the most unusual circumstances. The coach who engages in such activity after the two years following cessation or termination of the coach-athlete relationship bears the burden of demonstrating that there has been no exploitation, in light of all relevant factors, including:

(1) the amount of time that has passed since the coach-athlete relationship terminated,

(2) thc circumstances of termination,

(3) the athlete's personal history,

(4) the athlete's current mental status,

(5) the likelihood of adverse impact on the athlete and others, and

(6) any statements or actions made by the coach during the course of the athlete-coach relationship suggesting or inviting the possibility of a post-termination sexual or romantic relationship with the athlete or coach.

Source: USACoaching.org. www.usacoaching.org/resources /Coaching%20Ethics%20Code_new.pdf

Data on Gender Equity in Sports

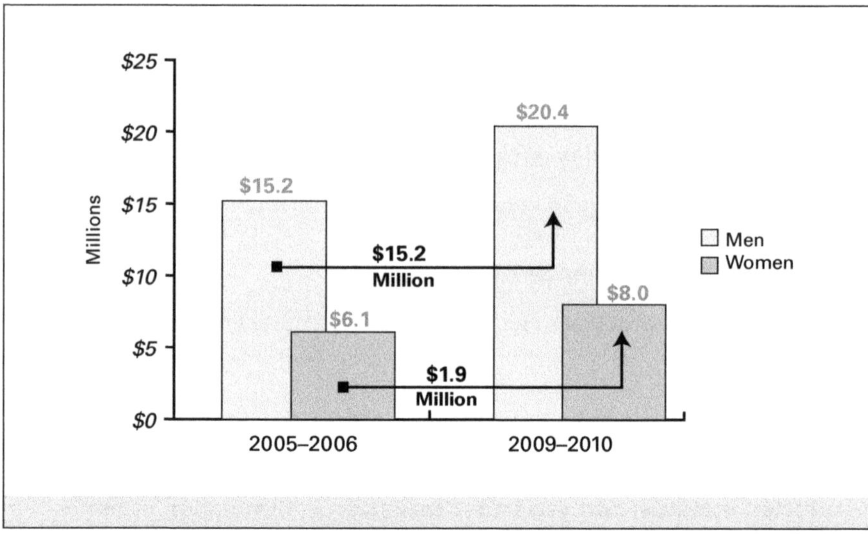

Figure 12.1. Median Total Expenses in Women's and Men's Athletic Programs: Football Bowl Subdivision

Source: NCAA Gender Equity Report, 2004–2010, p. 37

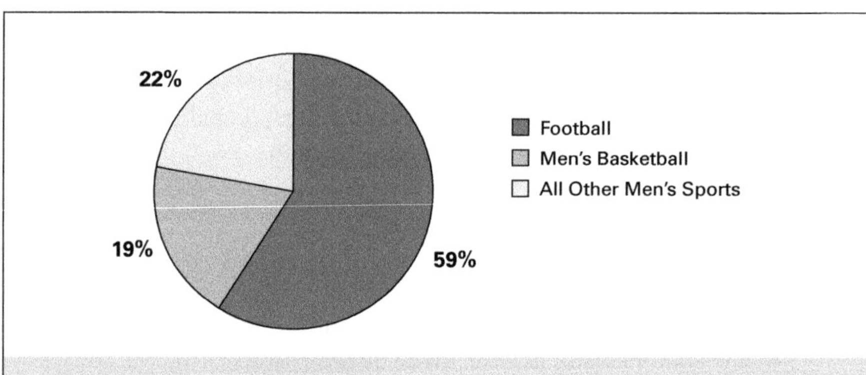

Figure 12.2. Percent of Expenses for FBS Men's Sports, 2009–2010

Source: NCAA Gender Equity Report, 2009–2010, p. 35

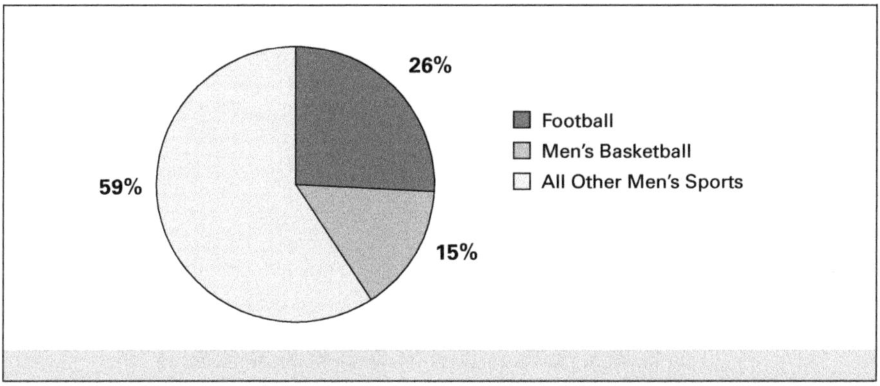

Figure 12.3. Percent of Expenses for Division III Men's Sports, 2009–2010

Source: NCAA Gender Equity Report, 2009–2010, p. 35

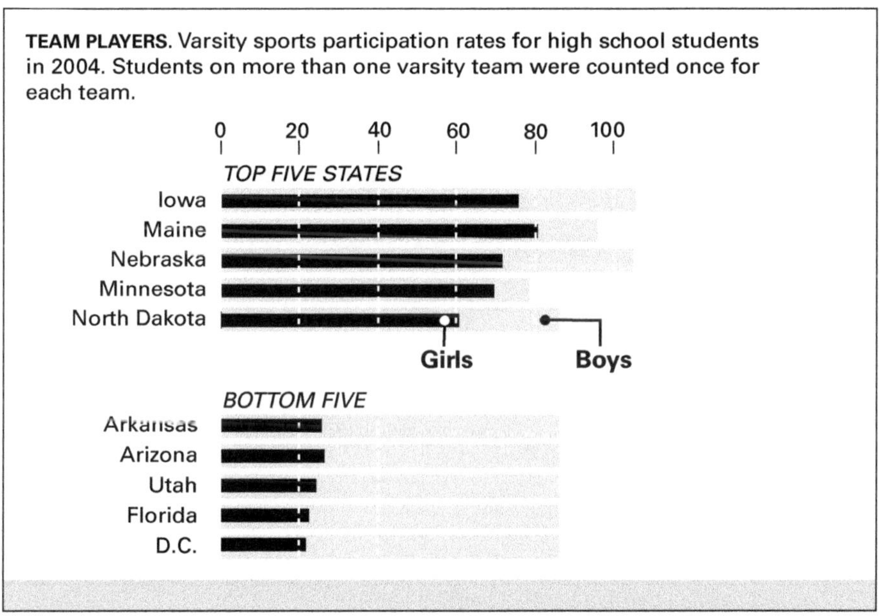

Figure 12.4. Interest in Sports Is Dictated by Opportunities

Source: Professor Betsy Stevenson, http://well.blogs.nytimes.com/2010/02/15/as-girls-become-women-sports-pay-dividends/

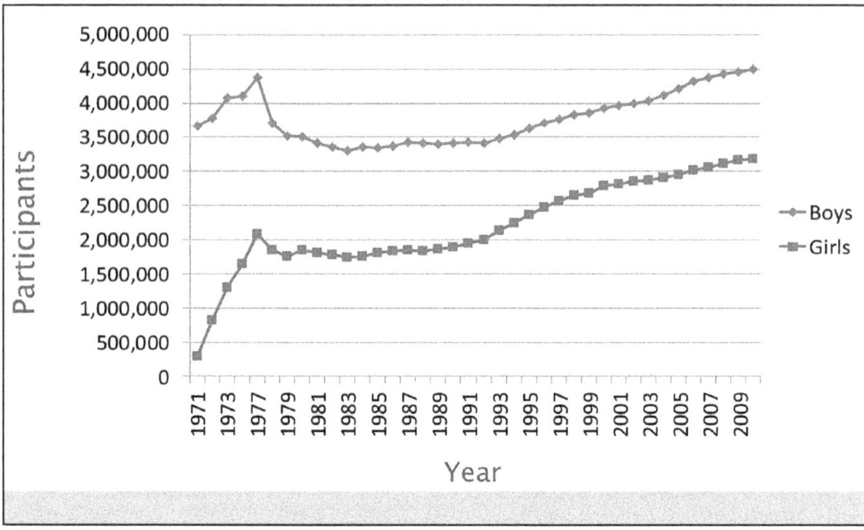

Figure 12.5. High School Athletics Participation Survey Totals, 1971–2012 (Boys' High School Sports Participation, 2010–2011 = 4,494,406, the Highest in History)

Source: National Federation of State High School Associations, 2010–2011 Athletics Participation Summary

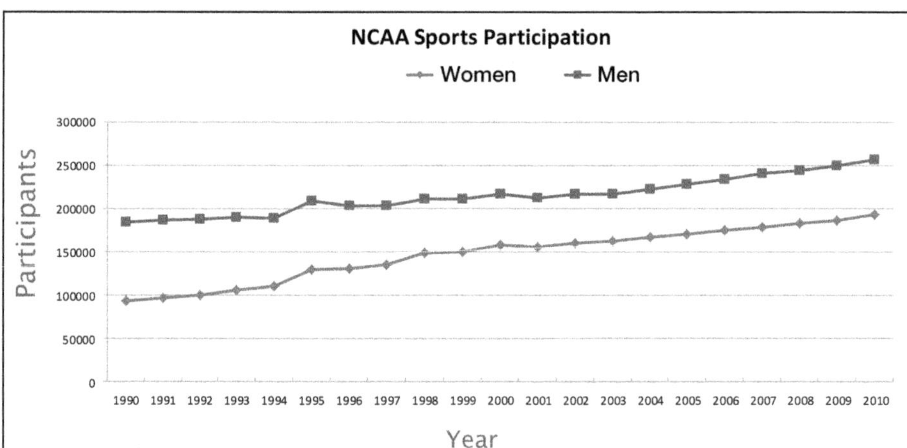

Figure 12.6. Sponsorship Levels: Total Participants, 1990–1991 and 2010–2011 (Includes Emerging Sports and Nonchampionship Sports)

Source: NCAA Sponsorship and Participation Rates Report, 1981–1982 and 2010–2011

Questions for Review and Discussion

1. Explain the three-part test for participation compliance with Title IX in athletics.

2. Why did some critics of Title IX argue that it implemented a quota?

3. What according to the author distinguishes a quota from Title IX and athletics?

4. Does Title IX protect men?

5. Look up your school's data on the Equity in Athletics Disclosure Act website: http://ope.ed.gov/athletics. Does your school satisfy any prongs of the three-part test? If so, which ones?

6. What utilitarian principles justify providing males and females with equal educational opportunities?

7. In addition to legal entanglements, what ethical problems are raised when coaches have sexual or romantic relationships with athletes? Do you agree that such relationships always are improper? How would you defend your view?

8. Why is a cause of action for retaliation an important right for advocates for gender equity? What would happen if advocates were unprotected?

Suggestions for Further Reading

Anderson, Elizabeth S., and Richard H. Pildes. "Expressive Theories of Law: A General Restatement." 148 *U. Pa. L. Rev.* 1503 (2000).

Brake, Deborah L. *Getting in the Game: Title IX and the Women's Sports Revolution.* New York: New York University Press, 2010.

———. "The Struggle for Sex Equality in Sport and the Theory Behind Title IX." 34 *U. Mich. J.L. Reform* 13, 16–18 (2001).

Buzuvis, Erin. "Sidelined: Title IX Retaliation Cases and Women's Leadership on College Athletics." 17 *Duke J. Gender L. & Pol'y* 1 (2010).

Chalenor v. Univ. of N.D., 292 F.3d 1042 (8th Cir. 2002).

Cohen v. Brown Univ., 101 F.3d 155 (1st Cir. 1996), cert. denied, 520 U.S. 1186 (1997).

Geisinger, Alex. "A Belief Change Theory of Expressive Law." 88 *Iowa L. Rev.* 35, 37 (2002).

Hogshead-Makar, Nancy. "Attitudes, Platitudes, and the Collegiate Sports Arms Race: Unsustainable Spending and Its Consequences for Olympic and Women's Sports." *Journal on Intercollegiate Sports.*

McAdams, Richard H. "An Attitudinal Theory of Expressive Law." 79 *Or. L. Rev.* 339 (2000).

Neal v. Bd. of Trs., 198 F.3d 763 (9th Cir. 1999).

Sabo, Don, and Phil Veliz. "Go Out and Play: Youth Sports in America." East Meadow, NY: Women's Sports Foundation, 2008. www.womenssportsfoundation.org/home/research/articles-and-reports/mental-and-physical-health/go-out-and-play.

Thirteen

The Coach and the Safety of Athletes: Ethical and Legal Issues

MATTHEW J. MITTEN

Regardless of the level of athletic competition, a coach is not at fault or legally responsible for an athlete's injury simply because it happens. By voluntarily choosing to participate in a sport, student athletes assume the inherent risk of injury during training, conditioning drills, practices, and athletic competitions, which coaches do not have a legal duty to eliminate or reduce. An inherent risk is one that is "part of the game," and it is an obvious or known risk that is among the potential consequences of normal competition in a sport. Suffering an eye injury from an elbow to the face while rebounding during a basketball game, receiving a knee injury when kicked by an opponent while playing soccer, or suffering a broken arm while being tackled during a football game are all inherent risks of playing these sports.

Although coaches generally are not liable for athlete injuries that are part of the game, there is potential legal liability if a coach's action or inaction increases the inherent risks of injury in a sport. To recover damages for an injury, an athlete is required to prove tortious (i.e., wrongful) action or inaction by a coach caused his injury. Negligence, which is the failure to use reasonable care to protect against foreseeable harm under the circumstances, is the legal theory generally relied on by athletes who have sued coaches for sports-related injuries. The reasonable care standard requires that coaches take appropriate measures to prevent or minimize the risk of injuries (particularly serious or permanent ones) or death during athletic competition. Consistent with the legal duty of reasonable care established by the negligence standard, a coach has an ethical obligation to not create an unsafe environment by enhancing a sport's inherent risk of injury and to take affirmative steps to protect their athletes from suffering serious injuries or death.

In some instances, the coach's legitimate objectives of maximizing athletic performance, maintaining discipline, and winning games or competitions conflict with the legal and ethical duty to protect the health and safety of athletes under his or her supervision and control. Some recent deaths and serious injuries suffered by young athletes during athletic competition or training illustrate this inherent tension and raise red flags. In August 2008 Max Gilpin, a fifteen-year-old Kentucky high school football player, died of complications from heatstroke during a practice at which David Stinson, the head football coach at Pleasure Park High School, required players to continue running in helmets and pads in 94 degree weather, although some were gasping for breath and/or vomiting. Stinson had decided he would not stop this conditioning drill until someone quit the team. Olivia Kahn, a fourteen-year-old novice member of the junior varsity swim team at East Union High School in California, broke her neck during an unsupervised practice dive into a shallow pool without adequate safety instruction, allegedly after her coach told her minutes before a swim meet that she would be required for the first time to dive into the pool rather than starting a relay race in the water. In February 2011 thirteen University of Iowa football players were hospitalized after suffering a muscle disorder known as exertional rhabdomyolysis, which can cause kidney failure in serious cases, as a result of grueling off-season conditioning workouts.

In this chapter I provide an overview of developing law regarding the nature and scope of a coach's duty to protect the health and safety of athletes participating in youth and high school sports (who generally are minors entrusted to coaches' custodial care) or college sports (who generally are adults not having a custodial relationship with their coaches) and illustrate a coach's ethical obligation to do so. State statutes and judicial decisions may immunize coaches at public educational institutions from liability for negligence that causes injury to athletes, and preinjury releases and waivers may protect both private and public school coaches from liability for their negligence.

This discussion is based on the premise that coaches have an ethical obligation to protect their athletes' health and safety, regardless of the level of athletic competition. Rather than being uniform nationwide, the governing law regarding a coach's legal obligation to protect athletes' health and safety varies from state to state. However, consistent with their ethical obligation, the law generally requires (or should require) coaches to exercise reasonable care to protect athletes' health and safety with liability for negligence if this duty is breached and they are injured.

Youth and High School Sports

One of a coach's primary responsibilities is to provide players with appropriate instruction regarding how to properly play and safely participate in a sport, which requires a coach to use reasonable care to protect athletes from foreseeable harm while playing the particular sport to avoid potential liability for negligence. In *Vendrell v. School District No. 26C, Malheur County*,[1] the plaintiff, a fifteen-year-old freshman who suffered a broken neck when tackled during a high school football game, claimed that his coaches' negligent instruction and training caused his injury. The Oregon Supreme Court ruled that a "coach or physical education instructor is required to exercise reasonable care for the protection of the students under his supervision," but determined that the coaches were not liable for his injury because they provided "adequate, standard instruction and practice" to their football team:

> No one expects a football coach to extract from the game the body clashes that cause bruises, jolts and hard falls. To remove them would end the sport. The coach's function is to minimize the possibility that the body contacts may result in something more than slight injury. The extensive calisthenics, running and other forms of muscular exercise to which the defendant's coaches subjected the defendant's squad were intended to place the players in sound physical condition so that they could withstand the shocks, blows and other rough treatment with which they would meet in actual play. As a further safeguard for the players' protection the defendant provided all of the players with protective equipment. Each player was taught and shown how to handle himself while in play so that a blow would fall upon his protective equipment and not directly upon his body. We have also noticed the fact that every player was instructed in the manner of (1) running while carrying the ball, (2) tackling an opposing player, and (3) handling himself properly when about to be tackled.

Based on different facts, a coach may be liable for negligently failing to provide adequate instruction necessary to protect players' health and safety. In *Thompson v. Seattle Public School District 47*, a Washington high school football player was awarded damages for injuries caused by his coach's negligent failure to warn him of the risks of lowering his head to ward off tacklers while carrying the football, which increased the risk of serious neck injuries.[2]

Courts also have held that a coach's legal duty to properly instruct and supervise young athletes in connection with a sport includes the obligation to provide them with appropriate protective equipment and to ensure its usage during athletic competition or to adequately warn them about the health and safety risks of not using it. For example, in *Baker v. Briarcliff School District*,[3] a New York court held that a coach's failure to properly warn students about the risks of not wearing a mouthpiece during a girls' high school field hockey practice "unreasonably increased [their] risks of injury" and created possible liability for a mouth injury suffered by a girl who was not wearing her mouthpiece as a result.

Although coaches do not ensure the health and safety of students entrusted to their care, they have a legal duty to adequately supervise them and to provide a reasonably safe practice environment. In *Stirgis v. St. John the Baptist Parish School Board*,[4] a Louisiana appellate court explained that a coach should provide "reasonable, competent supervision appropriate to the age of the children and the attendant circumstances," which includes "protecting against unreasonable risk of injury from dangerous or hazardous objects in the school buildings and on the grounds." The court ruled that conducting football throwing drills requiring players to make quick pivots and turns on a wet gymnasium floor may constitute negligent conduct by a football coach.

A coach also breaches the negligence standard of care by pushing an athlete beyond his or her endurance level and creating exposure to an unreasonably enhanced risk of injury above the sport's inherent risks. In *Vargo v. Svitchan*[5] a Michigan appellate court held that urging a high school football player to push "himself to and beyond his limits" with resulting injury may establish negligence liability. During the first of a scheduled series of weight lifting sessions to prepare him for high school football team tryouts, while being urged by the football coach "to perform to the utmost," a fifteen-year-old high school student fell while lifting a 250- to 300-pound weight and suffered injuries resulting in paraplegia.

Although Coach David Stinson did not acknowledge any liability for Max Gilpin's August 2008 death from heatstroke and was acquitted of criminally reckless homicide and wanton endangerment charges, Stinson's deposition testimony in a wrongful death suit filed by the boy's parents (settled for $1.75 million) evidences his negligence. Stinson testified he would not have stopped a grueling series of sprints by his players in football helmets and full pads in 94 degree weather even if players were vomiting, passing out, and calling for water. During this running drill Stinson apparently was more concerned with instilling discipline in his players than preventing them from overheating.

Another area in which coaches have a legal duty is the provision of emergency care. Coaches should promptly obtain emergency medical care for an injured athlete. In *Mogabgab v. Orleans Parish School Board*[6] two high school football coaches were found negligent for failing to obtain medical care for a student for almost two hours after he exhibited symptoms of heatstroke during practice, which caused his death. Although coaches are not required to have the same degree of knowledge as medical experts, they must recognize a medical emergency and act reasonably under the circumstances (e.g., by seeking prompt medical treatment for an ill or injured student).

Courts also have found coaches liable for improperly providing first aid that worsens an injured athlete's condition by, for example, moving the athlete before medical personnel arrive to provide treatment.[7] In *Halper v. Vayo*[8] an Illinois appellate court ruled that a coach may be liable for aggravating a high school wrestler's knee injury by attempting to treat the injury by manipulating his knee. The court explained: "Because of the substantial risks involved, we believe it can be reckless for an individual with no medical training to pull on the leg of a person with a knee injury and attempt to manipulate the knee assuming no exigency exists which necessitates such treatment."

Although coaches are not required or expected to be able to diagnose the nature and extent of a player's injury, in *Jarreau v. Orleans Parish School Board*[9] a Louisiana court observed "they should recognize their limitations in this regard and seek expert medical advice" before permitting an injured athlete to return to play. The failure to do so gives rise to potential liability for aggravated injuries. The court upheld a jury's finding that a coach negligently allowed a highschool student to continue playing football with an injured wrist despite his persistent complaints of pain and swelling.

On the other hand, a coach is not liable for an aggravated injury from continued play if it is not foreseeable under the circumstances or if reasonable care was used in determining its severity. In *Zemke v. Arreola*[10] a California appellate court ruled that a coach is not liable for a high school football player's severe and debilitating brain injury caused by second impact syndrome when he was permitted to return to a game after suffering a dislocated finger. His brain injury was not foreseeable because the player apparently suffered only an injury to his finger, and he did not appear to have or report any symptoms of an initial head injury. Similarly, in *Cerny v. Cedar Bluffs Junior/Senior Public Sch*ool[11] a coach exercised reasonable care by properly evaluating a high school football player for symptoms of a concussion before allowing him to resume play and was not liable for a subsequent injury causing severe brain injury.

An Alternative Liability Standard: Intentional or Reckless Conduct

The foregoing cases adopt a negligence standard of legal liability and require coaches to exercise reasonable care to protect youth and high school athletes under their custody and control from foreseeable harm while participating in a sport. However, some courts recently have refused to impose a legal duty on coaches to use reasonable care when instructing and supervising athletes participating in youth and high school sports. In other words, a coach is not liable for negligent instruction or supervision that causes injury to athletes. Rather, injured athletes must prove the coach's conduct was more culpable than a mere failure to use reasonable care to protect them against foreseeable harm under the circumstances. These courts require proof that a coach intentionally or recklessly injured an athlete. This alternative standard makes it more difficult to hold coaches legally liable for injuries.

In *Kahn v. East Side Union High School District*[12] a fourteen-year-old freshman girl broke her neck during an unsupervised practice dive from a starting block into three and a half feet of water in the racing pool at her high school. She alleged that her coach negligently directed her to practice shallow water diving for the first time shortly before a competitive swim race without giving her adequate training or supervision. Because of her fear of suffering a traumatic head injury from diving into shallow water, the coach had allowed her to start two prior meets in the water rather than by diving into the pool, but he told her she would not be permitted to start her relay in the pool this time.

While recognizing that a coach has a legal duty not to increase the risks inherent in the process by which a young athlete learns a sport, the California Supreme Court expressed concern about imposing "a duty to mitigate the inherent risks of learning a sport by refraining from challenging a student" because it "could have a chilling effect on the enterprise of teaching and learning skills that are necessary to the sport." The court stated that "pushing an athlete to compete, excel, or move to the next level of competence ordinarily does not form a basis for liability on the part of athletic instructors and coaches." Rather than requiring that coaches use reasonable care when doing so, a majority of the court's judges adopted a much lower legal standard of care:

> [I]n cases in which it is alleged that a sports instructor has required a student to perform beyond the student's capacity or without providing adequate instruction, it must be alleged and proved that the instructor acted with intent to cause a student's injury or that the instructor acted recklessly in the sense that the instructor's conduct was 'totally outside

the range of the ordinary activity' involved in teaching or coaching the sport.

All of the *Kahn* judges concluded that the coach may be liable for reckless conduct causing the girl's injury:

> If a jury were to find that defendant coach directed plaintiff (a novice on the swim team) to perform a shallow racing dive in competition without providing any instruction, that he ignored her overwhelming fears and made a last-minute demand that she dive during competition, in breach of a previous promise that she would not be required to dive, we believe the trier of fact properly could determine that such conduct was reckless in that it was totally outside the range of the ordinary activity involved in teaching or coaching the sport of competitive swimming.

Expressing concern that this legal standard places greater emphasis on enhancing athletic performance than on protecting young athletes' safety, Justice Werdegar asserted that a coach should be subject to liability if his conduct "constitutes a gross or extreme departure" from "the range of ordinary instructional activities, increasing the risks of injury beyond those inherent in teaching a sport." Advocating that this standard "will provide sufficient protection against unfair second-guessing of the instructor's judgment and, therefore, will not unduly chill participation in sports instruction," he explained that "society expects—legitimately, in my view—more from instructors and coaches than merely that they will refrain from harming a student intentionally or with wanton disregard for safety. An instructor's gross or extreme lack of care for student safety is not an inherent risk of school athletics programs."

Justice Kennard, another *Kahn* case judge, would require high school coaches to conform to the negligence standard of ordinary care:

> Coaches of student athletes teach them the skills necessary to perform their sport of choice safely and effectively. Because student athletes, particularly minors, often consider their coach a mentor or role model, they trust the coach not to carelessly and needlessly expose them to injury. The majority's decision puts an end to that trust. . . .
>
> Applying the negligence standard here would leave coaches free to challenge or push their students to advance their skills level as long as they do so without exposing the student athletes to an unreasonable risk of harm.

> High school shop instructors who teach students how to operate a power saw or repair a car, and chemistry teachers in their laboratories, are held to a standard of ordinary negligence. Why should a different standard apply to an instructor who teaches students competitive swimming?

At this point, it is uncertain whether the *Kahn* majority's ruling that a coach is not liable for negligent instruction or supervision that causes injury is representative of a developing national judicial trend. South Dakota,[13] New York,[14] and Connecticut[15] courts have rejected it. However, in *Karas v. Strevell*[16] the Illinois Supreme Court followed *Kahn* in ruling that a coach is liable for an injury to a young athlete participating in an organized contact sport only if he intended to cause the injury or engaged in conduct "totally outside the range of the ordinary activity" involved with coaching the sport. The court expressed concern that applying an ordinary negligence standard to the numerous subjective decisions coaches make during a fast-paced game would open the door to litigation and unfairly burden them with potential liability. However, Justice Kilbride cautioned: "We cannot legitimately ignore younger athletes' greater physical vulnerability or their limited autonomy from their coaches and sporting organizations in assessing the propriety of their conduct toward their young athletes." This judge stated that coaches should be liable for player injuries if their action "was totally outside of the range of the ordinary coaching, instruction, supervision, or organization of *players of a certain age and experience level in a particular sport*."

The danger of permitting "the range of the ordinary activity" involved in teaching or coaching the sport to establish a coach's legal duty of care is that it conclusively establishes customary practices in the coaching profession as the appropriate standard for protecting athletes' health and safety. In most instances, this standard probably achieves the desired level of safety and provides an adequate level of protection to youth and high school athletes. It is, however, an inappropriate legal and ethical standard of care when customary coaching practices unduly emphasize winning or athletic performance and expose young athletes to the risk of serious injuries. Surely we do not want to characterize a practice as ethically permissible just because everyone does it, which is what the customary practices standard in effect does. On the other hand, the negligence standard, which requires coaches to use reasonable care to protect against foreseeable harm *under the circumstances*, is a flexible and better means of ensuring that coaches adequately protect the health and safety of athletes under their supervision and control. It also ensures that they do not increase a sport's inherent risks of injury.

In some instances, federal or state laws may immunize coaches from negligence liability for policy reasons. Congress enacted the Volunteer Protection Act of 1997[17] to encourage the provision of voluntary service on behalf of nonprofit organizations and governmental entities by limiting the tort liability of volunteers. This federal statute generally provides that a volunteer is not liable for harm caused by negligence. In *Avenoso v. Mangan*[18] a Connecticut court held that the Volunteer Protection Act immunized a volunteer coach for a local nonprofit soccer club who has never received compensation for any of his activities from negligence liability for an injury suffered by one of his players during a soccer practice. Similar to the Volunteer Protection Act, some states immunize volunteer coaches for nonprofit organizations from negligence liability.[19] Other states (e.g., Massachusetts)[20] have statutes specifically immunizing volunteer coaches who provide services to nonprofit associations that operate sports programs primarily for children under eighteen years of age from liability for negligence.

In some jurisdictions, the doctrine of qualified immunity, which may be established by a state statute[21] or by the state's courts, protects public school employees, including coaches, from negligence liability when they are engaged in *discretionary acts*. For example, in *Gasper v. Freidel*[22] a student was injured while training in a public high school's weight facilities and sued his coaches. The South Dakota Supreme Court ruled that coaches are immune from liability for negligence:

> [C]oaches were carrying out the important function of conditioning student/athletes for all sports. For this court to second-guess Freidel's and Meyer's judgment on how to supervise and train athletes would infringe on the executive branch of the government. Most importantly, imposition of liability would impair the free exercise of discretion. No person will want to be a coach if his or her judgment in supervising athletic training is continually open to lawsuits. . . . No matter how well a coach trains an athlete, there are always unexpected events which may produce an injury. This court does not want to position itself to continually decide whether the string of athletic injuries that occur every year are the result of coaching negligence. . . . [S]tudent athletes who go out for sports know there are attendant dangers. Injury is one of those risks and athletes accept that as part of the price of participating in sporting events.

Mississippi courts also have ruled broadly that coaches act in a discretionary capacity when conducting practices, including making decisions about health-related matters involving student athletes entrusted to their care, and are immune from negligence liability. In *Prince v. Louisville Municipal School District*[23] a high school football player suffered heatstroke during practice requiring hospitalization and causing permanent injuries, allegedly because of two coaches' negligence. He alleged they negligently failed to keep a proper monitor on his health and condition, failed to provide necessary liquids, and failed to provide necessary medical care in a timely manner. The Mississippi Supreme Court held:

> [H]igh school football coaches Bowman and Chambliss were responsible for coordinating and supervising the football program at NanihWaiya High School. . . . In a typical practice there are strains, sprains and complaints from a coach's players. A coach must consider the good order and discipline of the team when confronted with situational complaints by the players. A coach must use his discretion in judging whether or not an individual player is injured and then, whether the player should report to a trainer or seek other medical aid. There was no evidence presented in the lower court to show that either Bowman or Chambliss did anything beyond exercising ordinary discretion in supervising the NanihWaiya football practice on August 29, 1991. Prince produced no facts that evidenced any disregard for his health or any other outrageous action on the part of Bowman or Chambliss that might have warranted a departure from our previous holdings.[24]

In *Harris v. McCray*[25] the Mississippi Supreme Court explained the adverse consequences that would result if public school coaches are not immune from negligence:

> High school football coaches around the state would lose their ability to control their football teams. Discipline of a football team would become non-existent. If a coach refused a player's request to have a water break—to see a trainer—to not have to run any more wind sprints—to not have to do any more one-on-one blocking drills, because of that player's complaint of "feeling weak" or "not feeling good" or simply "not feeling like it," that coach would be very much aware of the fact that he/she would be running the risk of being successfully sued . . . should that player later suffer physical/medical problems related to the coach's failure to cow to the player's every whim and wish. On the other hand, if the coach, in fear of a successful lawsuit, should cow to the player's every whim, wish and demand, then the coach would lose the respect of the players, and discipline and morale would be lost.

Mississippi law is troubling because it gives coaches broad latitude to maintain team discipline and eliminates any legal duty to use reasonable care to protect their players' health and safety. It permits utilitarian or instrumental concerns about interfering with coaches' autonomy to outweigh legitimate concerns about the protection of the health and safety of players entrusted to their supervision and control. In my view, it is legally and ethically better to require a standard of care that minimizes the likelihood of deaths or serious injuries during athletic competition or training, even if doing so may limit a coach's disciplinary authority.

Observing that qualified immunity's primary objective is to prevent governmental legislative, judicial, and executive policy decisions from being legally challenged and judicially second-guessed, other courts have recognized that coaching decisions generally do not involve the exercise of "policy-making, planning, or enforcement powers" involving "the exercise of a high degree of official judgment or discretion."[26] In *Hacking v. Town of Belmont*[27] the New Hampshire Supreme Court ruled that the decisions of coaches during the course of games are not entitled to immunity against negligence claims because they do not concern municipal planning and public policy that "involve the weighing of competing social, economic, or political factors." This judicial view, which refuses to apply the doctrine of qualified immunity to coaching decisions, would align the law consistent with a coach's ethical duty to protect student athletes' health and safety.

It also is important to understand that a coach's negligent *ministerial acts* (i.e., failing to comply with or to ensure players comply with the applicable sports-governing body or school rules) are not immunized from tort liability. In *Yanero v. Davis*[28] a high school baseball player who was not wearing a batting helmet was injured after being struck in the head by a ball thrown by a teammate. The Kentucky Supreme Court ruled that the doctrine of qualified immunity does not shield a coach from the negligent failure to require that players wear a batting helmet. They concluded: "The performance of that duty in this instance was a ministerial, rather than a discretionary, function in that it involved only the enforcement of a known rule requiring that student athletes wear batting helmets during baseball batting practice. The promulgation of such a rule is a discretionary function; the enforcement of it is a ministerial function."

Similarly, in *Felix v. Spaulding High School Union District*[29] a Vermont trial court determined that a high school football coach's decision to permit a student to play in an interscholastic game before attending ten practices as required by the Vermont Principals' Association bylaws and policies concerning athletics was a ministerial act. The student suffered a catastrophic spinal injury because he tackled an opposing player with his head down, allegedly because of his coach's negligent failure to provide him with proper instruction regarding how to tackle.

The doctrine of qualified immunity also does not protect coaches from liability for intentional, reckless, willful and wanton, or grossly negligent conduct, which is more culpable than simply failing to exercise reasonable care. In *Koffman v. Garnett*[30] the Virginia Supreme Court held that the following allegations, if proven, constitute gross negligence: "[Coach] Garnett ordered Andy to hold a football and 'stand upright and motionless' so that Garnett could explain the proper tackling technique to the defensive players. Then Garnett, without further warning, thrust his arms around Andy's body, lifted him 'off his feet by two feet or more,' and 'slam[ed]' him to the ground. Andy weighed 144 pounds, while Garnett weighed approximately 260 pounds. The force of the tackle broke the humerus bone in Andy's left arm. During prior practices, no coach had used physical force to instruct players on rules or techniques of playing football."

In some jurisdictions, courts have enforced preinjury liability waivers absolving educational institutions from negligence liability for a minor student's injuries while participating in extracurricular activities, which effectively also immunize coaches from negligence liability for injuries to student athletes. For example, in *Sharon v. City of Newton*[31] the Massachusetts Supreme Court rejected the argument that enforcement of a preinjury liability waiver would violate Massachusetts public policy by, among other things, undermining the legal duty of reasonable care that public high schools owe to their students. It explained:

> Our views with respect to the permissibility of requiring releases as a condition of voluntary participation in extracurricular sports activities, and the enforceability of releases signed by parents on behalf of their children for those purposes, are also consistent with and further the public policy of encouraging athletic programs for the Commonwealth's youth. This policy is most clearly embodied in statutes that exempt from liability for negligence: nonprofit organizations and volunteer managers and coaches who offer and run sports programs for children under eighteen years of age (*G. L. c. 231, § 85V*). . . .
>
> To hold that releases of the type in question here are unenforceable would expose public schools, who offer many of the extracurricular sports opportunities available to children, to financial costs and risks that will inevitably lead to the reduction of those programs. . . .
>
> [The student athlete] contends that to enforce the release would convey the message that public school programs can be run negligently, in contravention of the well-established responsibility of schools to

> protect their students. We disagree. There are many reasons aside from potential tort liability why public schools will continue to take steps to ensure well-run and safe extracurricular programs—not the least of which is their ownership by, and accountability to, the citizens of the cities and towns they serve.

In contrast to *Sharon*, the Washington Supreme Court held that requiring a student and his parents or guardian to sign a standard form releasing a public school district from liability for negligence in connection with the student's participation in interscholastic athletics violates the state's public policy. In *Wagenblast v. Odessa School District*[32] the court ruled that the existence of the following factors invalidated the waiver: interscholastic sports were extensively regulated in Washington; interscholastic sports were "a matter of public importance"; participation in interscholastic sports was open to all students with the requisite skills and eligibility; there was "no alternative program of organized competition" for interscholastic sports; no sports participation was allowed unless the waiver was signed; and the student was under the coach's "considerable" control and subject to the risk that reasonable care would not be used to protect him from harm.

A Brief Defense of the Negligence Standard of Reasonable Care

Although the avoidance of both litigation and potential loss of athletic participation opportunities are legitimate concerns justifying judicial enforcement of preinjury liability waivers, it is questionable whether these policy objectives outweigh the need for application of a negligence standard of care. The negligence standard would encourage coaches to appropriately safeguard the health and safety of student athletes participating in interscholastic athletics. These three objectives are not necessarily mutually exclusive. A coach's exercise of reasonable care will reduce the number of student athlete injuries, thereby also reducing lawsuits and avoiding the loss of interscholastic sports participation opportunities caused by the costs of tort judgments and liability insurance.

Because the important goals identified by courts are not necessarily incompatible and dangerous customary coaching practices that cause injury should not be legally excused, there is strong justification for generally requiring coaches to adhere to the negligence standard of exercise reasonable care in carrying out their duties. Moreover, if we take into consideration the argument of other contributors to this volume, such as Simon and Boxill, that coaches are educators, the view that coaches should be held to the same legal and ethical standards as other teachers appears even stronger. Holding coaches legally liable only for intentionally or recklessly caused injury does not further other important goals of sport and eliminates a necessary level of protection for the health and safety of young athletes.

College Sports

In contrast to youth and interscholastic athletes, intercollegiate athletes generally are adults eighteen years of age or older who are not entrusted to the custodial care of their coaches. Like athletes competing at other levels of competition, college athletes assume the inherent risks of injury from participating in a sport. Similar to youth and high school sports coaches, those coaching intercollegiate sports have a legal duty not to increase a sport's inherent risks of injury to participating players; for example, by supplying defective equipment causing injury to intercollegiate student athletes, which may create negligence liability.[33] Like public high school coaches, public university and college coaches may have qualified immunity from negligence liability.[34] Unlike some youth sports organizations and high schools, universities and colleges generally do not require student athletes to sign preinjury waivers absolving the educational institution or its coaches from negligence causing injury while participating in intercollegiate athletics.[35]

There are relatively few cases in which college coaches have been sued for negligent instruction or supervision that causes injury to their own players, but coaches at this level of competition should use reasonable care to minimize the risks of injury, particularly death or serious harm. In *Moose v. Massachusetts Institute of Technology*[36] a Massachusetts appellate court ruled that two university track and field coaches were liable for negligently supervising and instructing a pole vaulter during practice, which contributed to his suffering a skull fracture and brain contusions when he fell into an improperly padded vaulting pit after a vault. However, *Crace v. Kent State Univ*ersity,[37] a recent case involving serious injury to a college cheerleader, suggests that some courts may follow the *Kahn* majority and refuse to hold a coach liable for negligent instruction or supervision that causes injury to an intercollegiate athlete. Because injuries from falls while performing mounted stunts are an inherent risk of cheerleading that a coach has no legal duty to protect against, an Ohio appellate court ruled that a coach is liable only for intentionally or recklessly caused injuries to cheerleaders, which effectively means that injuries caused by a coach's negligence are inherent risks that must be assumed by cheerleaders. The *Moose* court's negligence standard requiring coaches to use reasonable care to protect against foreseeable harm under the circumstances is a better means of protecting the health and safety of intercollegiate athletes under his or her supervision and control.

Courts also have ruled that college coaches owe a legal duty not to increase the inherent risks of injury in a sport to opposing players as well as their players. But courts have narrowly construed the scope of this duty by holding that coaches are liable for injuries to opposing players caused by their own players' aggressive play only in limited circumstances. In *Avila v. Citrus Community College District*[38] the California Supreme Court ruled that a coach has no legal duty to prevent a pitcher on his team from intentionally throwing at the head of an opposing team's batter because "being intentionally thrown at is a fundamental part and inherent risk" of baseball. Similarly, in *Kavanagh v. Trustees of Boston University*[39] the Massachusetts Supreme Court held that a coach is liable for injury to an opposing player only if he expressly instructed or encouraged his players to intentionally or recklessly harm their opponents, not merely for encouraging their aggressive play. It reasoned, "With respect to any reasonable expectations as to who will protect competitors from excessively rough play or violence during a game, one would ordinarily expect that the referees would perform that function, not the opposing coach, team, or school."

Even if a college coach is not responsible for an intercollegiate athlete's original injury, there is potential liability for an aggravated injury that a coach could have prevented or reduced by using reasonable care. In *Kleinknecht v. Gettysburg College*,[40] the United States Court of Appeals for the Third Circuit held that a university, including its coaches, has a legal duty to use reasonable care to protect its recruited athletes from foreseeable harm and may be liable for negligent action or inaction in connection with the operation of its intercollegiate athletics program. This case involved allegations of negligent emergency medical assistance procedures, which delayed the administration of first aid care to an athlete who collapsed and died from cardiac arrest during an off-season varsity lacrosse practice in which players participated only in "skills and drills." The decedent had no medical history of heart problems and had been medically cleared to play lacrosse by both a team physician and his family physician. An autopsy failed to discover any heart abnormality, and it was uncertain what caused his cardiac arrest. The team's coaches were present during the practice, but they were not certified in cardiopulmonary resuscitation (CPR) and had never discussed how to respond to an emergency during off-season practices. No athletic trainer attended practice, and the nearest telephone was approximately 200 to 250 yards away from the practice field.

Although the victim's heart attack was unforeseeable under the circumstances, the court held that the possibility of severe and life-threatening injury is foreseeable during intercollegiate contact sports and there is a legal duty to have an appropriate university medical emergency response plan and to provide reasonable emergency care to injured athletes.

Consistent with *Kleinknecht*, courts have held that a coach has a legal duty to require an intercollegiate athlete to seek medical treatment for an injury. Courts have held that a coach has a legal duty not to pressure or permit an injured athlete to return to play without medical clearance. In *Lamorie v. Warner Pacific College*[41] a college basketball player asserted that his coach negligently required him to play with a nose and eye injury in violation of a physician's orders. Because the plaintiff feared losing his scholarship if he did not play, he participated in a team scrimmage and reinjured his eye. An Oregon appellate court ruled that the university could be held liable for the coach's negligence because the player's reinjury was a foreseeable risk of being directed to resume playing basketball without physician medical clearance.

However, in *Orr v. Brigham Young University*[42] a federal appellate court narrowly construed the legal duty of care that a university (and by implication, its coaches) owes to an injured college football player. Although the court held that a university is liable for negligent medical care provided by its sports medicine personnel, it refused to rule that coaches have a legal duty not to establish a win-at-all-costs mentality, to pressure student athletes to increase their performance at the risk of their health, and to create disincentives to report injuries or seek medical attention. It characterized the legal relationship between a university and its student athletes as contractual rather than custodial in nature and declined to find that its coaches "assumed the responsibility for his safety and deprived him of the normal opportunity for self protection" by recruiting him to play football.

Orr holds that a coach's legal duty of reasonable care to prevent an intercollegiate student athlete from aggravating an injury or potentially exposing himself to a risk of serious injury does not extend beyond simply following the recommendations of sports medicine care providers. It creates a questionable legal precedent that is inconsistent with our proposed ethical obligation of coaches: to avoid creating or facilitating harm to student athletes by discouraging them from disclosing injuries or encouraging them to sacrifice their health in the pursuit of individual athletic performance and/or the team's on-field success. Even adult student athletes may not have the maturity and judgment necessary to make sound athletic participation decisions consistent with their long-term health interests and place intercollegiate sports, which are an amateur, extracurricular activity that is a part of their college education (at least in theory), in proper perspective.

In 1990 Hank Gathers, Loyola Marymount University's star forward and a prospective National Basketball Association player, collapsed and died from cardiac arrest while playing in an intercollegiate basketball game in California. Before his death, Gathers had been diagnosed as having a potentially life-threatening heart rhythm disorder known as cardiomyopathy, but chose to continue playing college basketball. Gathers's death spawned the filing of multimillion dollar lawsuits by his mother, minor son, and other heirs against Loyola Marymount, its coach, and athletics trainer as well as several physicians participating in Gathers's care and treatment. Plaintiffs alleged Gathers was not fully informed of the seriousness of his heart condition, should not have been medically cleared to continue playing college basketball, and was given a nontherapeutic dosage of heart medication to enable him to perform at a higher level. The lawsuits further contended that defendants conspired and fraudulently failed to inform Gathers of the seriousness of his heart condition and the danger of continuing to play competitive basketball. Plaintiffs also alleged that, at the urging of Loyola Marymount's coach, Gathers's heart medication was reduced below therapeutic levels to enable him to play better. In sum, plaintiffs contended that Gathers was "sacrificed on the altar of basketball" in Loyola Marymount's quest for basketball success, notoriety, and economic gain.[43] These lawsuits ultimately were settled without any finding or admission of liability on the part of any defendants.

Marc Buoniconti, a former linebacker for The Citadel, sued the university along with its team physician and athletic trainer, seeking damages for permanent paralysis suffered while making a tackle during a 1985 college football game. Buoniconti had injured his neck during three prior games. Daily heat packs and whirlpool treatments did not improve the condition of his neck. In the game before he was paralyzed, Buoniconti suffered a sprained neck that prevented him from practicing, inhibited his sleeping, and required him to wear a soft collar for neck support. Believing that Buoniconti had suffered an extension injury to his neck, the team's athletic trainer fixed a ten-inch elastic strap to the face guard of Buoniconti's helmet and connected it to the front of his shoulder pads. The device prevented Buoniconti's head from going back and was approved by the team physician. The athletic trainer tightened the strap downward, causing Buoniconti to walk "like a robot . . . with his head down." While making a tackle with his head constrained by this device, Buoniconti broke his neck and was rendered a quadriplegic. Buoniconti asserted that the team trainer and physician were negligent for permitting him to play with a serious neck injury and with equipment that placed his neck in a position making it vulnerable to being broken. Before trial, Buoniconti settled his claims against The Citadel and its trainer for $800,000.

The *Larmorie* and *Orr* cases suggest that a coach has no legal duty to protect intercollegiate athletes' health and safety beyond acting in accordance with recommendations made by sports medicine personnel. Intercollegiate athletes often feel invincible, have a strong desire to play a sport for psychological or economic reasons, narrowly focus on their athletic objectives, and are willing to sacrifice their bodies and risk long-term adverse health consequences. A coach's ethical obligations to student athletes, which are broader than the legal standard of care, require more than simply following medical clearance recommendations. Although both of them were medically cleared to participate, perhaps the tragedies suffered by two former intercollegiate athletes, Hank Gathers and Nick Bouniconti, could have been prevented if their long-term health interests had been the coaches' top priority rather than the team's need for their services or their strong desire to play with a serious medical condition or significant injury that was not fully healed.

A coach has broad autonomy regarding playing decisions and the authority to refuse to permit an injured or otherwise physically impaired student athlete to play in a game or participate in an athletic event (even if he or she has been medically cleared) to prevent exposure to potentially serious harm. Surely one of a coach's primary ethical responsibilities is to protect the health and safety of his or her players. Our review of the foregoing cases suggests that the flexible negligence standard of reasonable care best furthers this important moral duty of the coach.

Questions for Review and Discussion

1. What factors justify holding coaches legally responsible for injuries to youth and high school athletes caused by their negligence?

2. Why do some courts refuse to hold coaches liable for negligent instruction or supervision injuring youth or high school athletes?

3. What legal standard provides the best means of ensuring that coaches conform to their ethical obligation to protect the health and safety of youth and high school athletes?

4. Should coaches have the same legal duty to protect the health and safety of intercollegiate athletes as they do for youth and high school athletes?

5. Should coaches have the same ethical obligation to protect the health and safety of intercollegiate athletes as they do for youth and high school athletes?

Suggestions for Further Reading

In addition to the works listed below, the author suggests that those interested in exploring the issues raised in this chapter consult the cases cited in the notes.

Benard, Howard P. "Little League Fun, Big League Liability." *Marquette Sports Law Review* 8 (1997): 93.

Brown, Jamie. "Legislators Strike Out: Volunteer Little League Coaches Should Not Be Immune from Tort Liability." *Seton Hall Journal of Sport Law* 7 (1997): 559.

Davis, Timothy. "*Avila v. Citrus Community College District:* Shaping the Contours of Immunity and Primary Assumption of the Risk." *Marquette Sports Law Review* 17 (2006): 259.

Doleschal, Janice K. "Managing Care in Interscholastic Athletic Programs: 14 Duties of Care." *Marquette Sports Law Review* 17 (2006): 295.

Fitzgerald, Timothy B. "The 'Inherent Risk' Doctrine, Amateur Coaching Negligence, and the Goal of Loss Avoidance." *Northwestern University Law Review* 99 (2005): 889.

Hurst, Thomas R., and James N. Knight. "Coaches' Liability for Athletes' Injuries and Deaths." *Seton Hall Journal of Sport Law* 13 (2003): 27.

Lake, Thomas. "The Boy Who Died of Football." *Sports Illustrated,* December 6, 2010, 131.

McCaskey, Anthony S., and Kenneth W. Biedzynski. "A Guide to the Legal Liability of Coaches for a Sports Participant's Injuries." *Seton Hall Journal of Sport Law* 6 (1996): 7.

Mitten, Matthew J. "Emerging Legal Issues in Sports Medicine: A Synthesis, Summary, and Analysis." *St. John's Law Review* 76 (2002): 5.

Fourteen

The Coach and Athlete Recruitment: Ethical and Legal Dimensions

TIMOTHY DAVIS

The real and perceived benefits that are derived from successful intercollegiate programs contribute substantially to the intense recruitment of high school athletes to participate in intercollegiate athletics. As colleges increase their athletic expenditures and search for new revenue streams, the competition among institutions for the best athletes is likely to intensify. At the center of college recruitment efforts are head and assistant coaches who are principally responsible for persuading high school students to attend their institutions. Coaches resort to various strategies in selling their athletic programs and institutions to recruits. In this chapter we will examine three aspects of coaching behavior during the recruitment process: conduct by coaches that violates National Collegiate Athletics Association (NCAA) rules and regulations, withdrawing scholarship offers that coaches make to student athletes, and coaches extending scholarship offers to student athletes that exceed what NCAA regulations permit them to honor.

We will consider standards of accountability that potentially govern these recruitment-related activities. I describe and assess legal norms and regulatory processes, both internal and external to intercollegiate athletics, which either regulate or potentially regulate coaches' recruitment behavior.

I conclude that some of these behaviors violate NCAA regulations and expose coaches, athletes, and their institutions to NCAA sanctions. There is considerable uncertainty, however, as to whether specific conduct in which coaches engage during recruiting will expose coaches or institutions to legal liability.

Apart from legal liability, however, we will examine the ethical dimensions of coaches' recruitment activities, with a focus on whether the coach-athlete relationship imposes ethical responsibilities on coaches to refrain from certain conduct during the recruitment process. I propose that the sports culture in which student athletes become inculcated prior to enrolling (and continuing into college) renders athletes vulnerable to false representations and other recruitment devices that coaches employ during the recruitment process. We will also consider whether the multiple roles that coaches may play in athletes' lives, such as teacher and transmitter of moral values, support imposing obligations on institutions to protect the interests of student athletes, even in the absence of legal liability requiring that they do so.

The Coach-Athlete Relationship

As is true for coaching, which is a multifaceted and complex endeavor,[1] complexity resides in the coach-athlete relationship. Given this complexity, the following discussion is intended only to provide limited insight into this relationship. Its focus is on the salient features of the coach-athlete relationship that lend context to the legal and ethical issues that resound in the recruiting process.

A principal role of a coach is to provide the instruction that enables athletes to maximize their athletic abilities.[2] In their role as educator, coaches impart technical expertise for improved individual performance and strategies for maximizing opportunities for competitive success.[3] Yet the role of the coach extends beyond merely conveying to athletes practical skills to improve athletic proficiency.[4] As explained below, their interpersonal interaction with athletes positions coaches to exert influence over matters ranging from athletes' values to their decision making.

Because it involves interpersonal interaction, coaching has been described as "fundamentally a moral practice."[5] As a "moral enterprise,"[6] coaching involves the transmission of values and ethics.[7] In fact, the ethical dimension of the coach-athlete relationship has been defined as pervasive.[8] As transmitters of values, coaches play an important role in identifying the "values, aims and objectives [that] ought to be pursued by athletes."[9] Thus coaches seek to instill values that may lead to athletic success, such as loyalty, hard work, enthusiasm, and confidence.[10]

There exists, however, another dimension to the coach as a transmitter of values. One scholar noted the attribute of practical wisdom—the ability to act in consonance with "virtues such as justice and fairness, temperance and enthusiasm, empathy and understanding."[11] Others have stated that "morally praiseworthy coach-athlete relationships that aim to be honest and sincere and to promote autonomy should be the gold standard."[12]

The extent to which coaches achieve the "gold standard," particularly as it relates to contributing to athletes' development of personal autonomy, may be inhibited by the power dynamic of the coach-athlete relationship. Coaches exert varying degrees of power over athletes.[13] However, athletes are not without power in their relationships with coaches.[14] Nevertheless, the coach-athlete relationship tends principally to be an asymmetrical relationship[15] in which coaches exert control over athletes.[16]

This power dynamic is exacerbated by the emotional bonds and trust that are critical aspects of the coach-athlete relationship.[17] The emotional bond, often manifested in a youth's admiration for the coach, can become a principal reason why athletes remain involved in sports.[18] As for trust, by the time most elite athletes play sport at the collegiate level, they would have developed relationships with coaches premised on the expectation that a coach would act to protect and promote the interests of the athlete.[19] Consequently athletes, particularly youngsters, are vulnerable to the influence of their coaches.[20] Therefore, the coach-athlete relationship is a quasi-fiduciary one in which athletes are particularly susceptible to the influence of coaches.

In varying contexts, courts have recognized the numerous roles coaches play in the lives of athletes.[21] In some instances, the influence wielded by coaches enhances their ability to exploit an athlete's vulnerability. For example, certain rules promulgated by interscholastic athletic associations seek to prohibit the exercise by coaches of undue influence in the high school recruiting process. These rules recognize the extent of the influence that coaches may exercise over athletes.[22]

A 2010 NCAA survey of approximately 20,000 collegiate student athletes provides some evidence of the influence coaches exert over student athletes during the recruitment process. Many of the athletes surveyed stated that they probably would not have chosen the college at which they matriculated if a different coach had been in place. For example, close to 60 percent of Division I men's basketball players responded that they would more than likely not have attended their institution had another individual been the coach.[23] Many athletes also reported that coaches had been overly aggressive—contacting them too often—during the recruiting process.[24]

The multiple roles assumed by coaches contribute to their ability to exert influence over athletes. Consequently, no matter how savvy athletes may believe themselves to be, by the time they become active participants in the college recruitment process, they are likely to have spent years in a system in which they have been inculcated with the multiple dynamics of the coach-athlete relationship. This alone renders athletes vulnerable to the conduct in which coaches may engage during the recruiting process.

Coaches, Athletes, and Recruiting

The emergence of highly commercialized college athletics over the past century and the concomitant pressure on college coaches to field successful sports programs have created an intense pursuit by colleges of high school athletes.[25] The factors that propel recruiting have been adroitly described by one commentator as follows:

> The pressure to produce winning teams increases efforts to recruit for athletic purposes. "Recruiting is the name of the game" is the cliché reflecting the necessity to have a team of superior athletic ability to win. The important variable is likely to be the ability of team members rather than the quality of the coaching or the desire to win. The coach's desire to excel, to do a superior job in training, to have players who achieve distinction, all can incline him to recruit. Yet, the primary pressure is usually external, from the institution or its alumni or supporters, in a "job-on-the-line manner."[26]

Although this opinion was expressed several decades ago, it is just as relevant today. Indeed, during this period the process by which colleges procure the services of these athletes has become more sophisticated and costly, devouring substantial amounts of athletic department resources.[27] Recruiting often becomes a college coach's number one priority, eclipsing leading and teaching.

Given these dynamics, encouraging high school athletes to attend his or her college is one, if not the most critical, function of the college coach. Indeed, coaches have been described as salesmen whose job is to convince high school seniors to sign the Letter of Intent signifying the prospective student-athlete will compete for their college.[28] As expressed by a sports journalist: "Coaches, after all, are salesmen. Their jobs depend mainly on convincing high school seniors to sign on the dotted line the first Wednesday in February."[29]

The recruitment efforts of athletic departments are also influenced by the student athlete's professional aspirations. High school recruits are interested in attending a school that will enable them to enhance their opportunity to compete professionally. These professional aspirations play a significant role in the athletes' school selection decision. For instance, because of professional aspirations, the amount of playing time likely to be afforded becomes a key consideration in a high school athlete's selection of a college sports program.[30] In addition, many high school athletes believe that starting as freshmen on a winning team will afford the maximum amount of playing time and television exposure. All of this will presumably improve their preparation and chances for the illusive yet coveted professional career. Coaches will exploit this goal by emphasizing the number of athletes from their program who have signed professional contracts. In short, the pressure on institutions to field winning teams and professional aspirations among student athletes serve as important elements of the context for the discussion that follows.

There are several problematic aspects of the process whereby promising high school student athletes are recruited to attend and participate in intercollegiate athletics at colleges and universities. These include the risky behaviors (e.g., drinking, going to bars and off-campus parties) in which many prospective student athletes engage during recruiting visits,[31] the use of female hostesses in the recruiting of male athletes, and the lack of adult supervision of recruits during their visits. In the following discussion we will focus on three specific aspects of the recruiting process in which coaches are intimately involved: the commission of NCAA rules violations during recruiting, revocation of scholarship offers, and oversigning.

NCAA Rules Violations

All too frequently, coaches commit recruiting violations as they seek to sign the most promising student athletes and thus gain an advantage over their competitors. This problem is illustrated by a celebrated example of rules violation. In 1987 the NCAA's enforcement arm imposed a one-year prohibition on Southern Methodist University's (SMU) football program from engaging in games against outside competition. The SMU case constitutes the only instance in which the NCAA has imposed the "death penalty" against a Division I intercollegiate athletics program. The conduct that led to the imposition of this sanction included the involvement of football coaches in facilitating cash payments to football recruits. Some of these payments continued after players matriculated at the university. In its report on the matter, the NCAA's Division I Committee on Infractions stated: "Past efforts at the university to design a program to gain a competitive advantage over the university's competitors by cheating did achieve its apparent goal—a winning record and national prominence for its football program."[32]

College coaches have engaged in a range of improper recruiting activities in violation of NCAA rules. At one end of the continuum is conduct not viewed as serious but nevertheless inappropriate, for example, a coach giving a recruit an item of clothing during recruitment, unknowingly making impermissible contact with a recruit, and engaging in limited but impermissible off-campus conduct with a recruit.[33]

At the other end of the spectrum are major violations.[34] These include, for example, offering or giving a student athlete money as an inducement to matriculate at the coach's institution, providing free lodging and airline tickets to a recruit or family and friends, making tuition payments at a junior college on behalf of a recruit, allowing a student athlete to use a vehicle, and arranging for someone to take a standardized college admissions test on behalf of an athlete. In a typical case involving a major violation of NCAA recruiting rules, some combination of the foregoing conduct and other impermissible inducements is present.[35]

Major violations of NCAA recruiting rules, specifically those involving improper offers and inducements,[36] typically result in colleges and universities self-imposing penalties and the NCAA imposing additional penalties. Both types of penalties have ramifications not only for culpable coaches but also for student athletes and their institutions. The following cases illustrate serious recruitment-related violations committed by coaches, with implications for coaches, student athletes, and their colleges or universities.

In a 2005 NCAA infractions case involving Baylor University,[37] a former head coach and assistant coaches of Baylor's men's basketball violated several NCAA rules, including those relating to impermissible inducements to prospective student athletes and attempts to cover up those violations. The coaches provided cash, clothing, tuition payments at a community college, meals, cost-free travel arrangements (e.g., airline tickets and lodging), and transportation (e.g., use of vehicles) to student athletes and their families. To explain their involvement in these violations, the assistant coaches cited, in part, loyalty to the head coach.

In addition, the NCAA Committee on Infractions (COI) found that the head coach engaged in unethical conduct. He did not act with high standards of honesty, attempted to conceal his violations and encouraged student athletes to engage in deceptive behavior, and provided false and misleading information to Baylor and to NCAA enforcement staff. In its report the COI stated, "In the end, the former head coach and his assistants' blatant disregard for NCAA rules brought incalculable disgrace to themselves, the university and intercollegiate athletics as a whole."[38]

The repercussions of this conduct were substantial. The head coach and his entire staff were replaced. In addition, the NCAA issued a show cause order that effectively prohibited the head coach from coaching at another NCAA member institution for ten years. Other penalties included a five-year probationary period, a one-year prohibition on postseason play by the men's basketball team, a reduction in the number of scholarships that could be awarded to basketball players, and restrictions on recruiting by the men's basketball coaches.

Recruitment violations by coaches can also result in vacating wins and revenues generated from conference and NCAA-wide championship events. This will occur if the coach's impermissible activities render an athlete ineligible to participate in intercollegiate competition. When an ineligible student athlete participates in intercollegiate contests, the NCAA's rule of restitution is triggered, which can lead to the vacation of wins and the records an athlete compiles while ineligible.[39] An athlete ruled ineligible may also be required to seek reinstatement before being permitted to participate in intercollegiate athletics.[40]

This is what transpired in an NCAA infractions decision involving violations of NCAA recruitment rules at Boise State University.[41] In 2011, the NCAA launched an investigation revealing that coaches of Boise State's women's tennis and women's and men's track programs had provided impermissible inducements, including cash and free lodging and meals, to prospective student athletes. In addition, the NCAA found that the coaches' intentional violation of its prohibitions against improper inducements and, in some instances, providing false information to the NCAA and Boise State, constituted unethical conduct. The COI wrote that the extensiveness of the violations in the women's tennis program resulted in a competitive advantage that warranted penalties in addition to those that Boise State had self-imposed.[42] Ultimately, the penalties included a postseason ban on the women's tennis team, restrictions on the number of available athletic scholarships, a vacation of the wins in which participating athletes were ineligible due to having taken impermissible inducements, vacation of those athletes' records, and a four-year show cause order for the head women's tennis coach.

As was true of its findings in the Baylor decision, the NCAA determined that the coaches not only violated NCAA inducement rules but engaged in unethical conduct. NCAA Bylaw 10.01.1, Honesty and Sportsmanship, imposes a positive duty on coaches and other individuals employed at its member institutions to act with "honesty and sportsmanship at all times so that intercollegiate athletics as a whole, their institutions and they, as individuals, shall represent the honor and dignity of fair play."[43] NCAA regulations also define what constitutes unethical conduct: the "knowing involvement in offering or providing a prospective" with an improper inducement.[44]

Coaches who commit recruiting violations breach their quasi-fiduciary obligations to not engage in conduct harmful to their athletes. This is seen most poignantly when a coach's violations result in penalties that harm athletes who did not behave improperly, such as being banned from postseason play. A coach who violates NCAA recruitment rules also fails to teach and model values such as fair play.

Revocation of Scholarship Offers and Oversigning

Two additional types of misconduct during recruitment present both legal and ethical issues: (1) a coach withdraws an oral scholarship offer made to a student athlete under circumstances that prevent the recruit from obtaining an offer from another college or university; (2) a coach signs more national letters of intent (NLI) or scholarship offers than the coach's college or university can accommodate under NCAA-imposed limitations. A discussion of the legal relationship between student-athletes and their colleges or universities provides a necessary predicate to consideration of revocation of scholarship offers and oversigning.

The Contractual Relationship

The express contractual relationship between a student athlete and a college or university arises out of the NLI, the statement of financial assistance, and various other university publications such as bulletins and catalogs. Several implications flow from a prospective student athlete signing an NLI. By signing an NLI, a prospective student-athlete agrees, for a period of one year, to attend the college or university named in the NLI. Thereafter, other institutions must cease all recruiting contacts with the student athlete. The named institution may freely contact the student athlete and publicly announce the signing. The NLI is not effective unless the student athlete has received a promise in writing from the named institution to provide athletic financial aid for a minimum of one year. In other words, without an accompanying promise of financial aid from the institution that signed the letter of intent, the NLI does not bind a student athlete to attend a particular institution, and the athlete may be recruited by another institution.

As it relates to the statement of financial aid, in exchange for the student athlete's commitment to attend, the college or university promises to provide financial assistance in the form of an athletic scholarship. A statement of financial assistance confirms that the college or university will extend financial aid to the extent of tuition, fees, room, board, and books. Statements of financial aid provide that the purpose of financial aid is to assist and enable student athletes to pursue a program of study and to participate in the educational process of the institution.

Through legislation adopted in 1973, the NCAA restricted schools to awarding one-year athletic scholarships renewable for each year for a period of four years.[45] In an important recent development, heralded by some as shifting the balance of power between coaches and players, NCAA legislation adopted in 2012 jettisoned the one-year limitation on the duration of athletic scholarships. The newly enacted legislation permits, but does not require, conferences and their institutions to award multiyear athletic scholarships.[46]

Revocation of Scholarship Offers

NCAA rules designate specific periods, based on the sport involved, during which a prospective student athlete can sign an NLI and accept a scholarship offer from a college or university. As noted above, the NLI, when combined with an offer of financial assistance, creates a binding contractual commitment between the athlete and the institution. During recruitment, it is common for coaches and athletes to make verbal commitments to each other. The recruit will orally commit to attend a particular college and a coach will orally promise a scholarship to the recruit. Given that a binding express contractual relationship does not arise until the student athlete and an institution's representative sign an NLI and offer of financial assistance, it is not uncommon for either or both parties to fail to honor a verbal commitment. Legal and ethical concerns emerge when the coach withdraws an oral offer previously extended to a prospective student athlete.

Consider the following scenario. Several weeks before they formalize their contractual relationship with a recruit, football coaches at four universities extend scholarship offers to a high school student athlete. Each coach states that his oral offer is contingent on the recruit not entertaining offers or exploring athletic programs at other schools. Nine months before he can sign an NLI, the recruit orally accepts the offer to play football at Big-Time University, one of the four colleges. The recruit discontinues exploring options at the other three universities that had orally extended scholarship offers. As expected, the other three universities withdraw their scholarship offers.

Over the next eight months, Big-Time's football coaches periodically call the recruit to determine if he remains interested its program and to express their interest in him. Three weeks before the date on which the recruit and Big-Time can formalize their agreement, Big-Time's head football coach accepts the head football coach position at another university. Big-Time's assistant football coaches reassure the recruit that the football program will stand by its oral commitment to him and that he has no reason to be concerned. The university promptly hires a new head football coach. A few days before the recruit and Big-Time can sign an NLI with a scholarship offer, Big-Time's newly appointed head football coach informs the recruit that the university has withdrawn its scholarship offer. The recruit requests reconsideration, but the coach informs him that the decision is final. Subsequently the recruit approaches the three other universities that made oral offers but is informed that they no longer have any scholarships to offer. Given how late it is in the season, the recruit receives no scholarship offers from other colleges.

Both student athletes and coaches must anticipate the possibility that one or the other will not abide by their oral commitment. This possibility encourages some student athletes to visit other schools even after making a verbal commitment to attend another institution. Similarly, a coach will continue to recruit for a position even after making a scholarship offer to other recruits who might potentially play at that position.

Several factors prompt coaches to revoke oral scholarship offers. Perhaps the coach receives an oral commitment from an athlete who seems to have greater athletic potential. In such a case, the coach may have viewed the recruit whose offer he canceled as a backup who could be called if the coach did not secure the player he really wanted. Or a coach might revoke a promised scholarship if he discovers that a recruit has expressed an interest in another program even though the athlete did so as a hedge against the possibility that his scholarship offer might be withdrawn. Here the coach likely views the recruit's expression of interest in another program as reflecting a lack of commitment to honor his oral promise.[47]

The same realities do not constrain the conduct of coaches who recruit multiple players for the same position after making an oral promise to other athletes who would also play at that position. Moreover, the consequences for a university when a recruit backs away from an oral commitment are not as severe as when an institution fails to honor an oral promise to a prospective athlete. As stated by one scholar:

> A school that loses a recruit can usually replace him or her with another recruit, someone from the existing roster, or even a recruit from a future year. . . . In short, to use the jargon of risk aversion, recruits suffer more than schools from the possibility of broken yearly commitments because recruits cannot effectively manage the risk of disappointment through diversification. Recruits are one-time players in the early commitment game, and those who try to court multiple prospects actually damage their chances of keeping commitments they have. By contrast, schools are repeat players who easily diversify risk over multiple recruits and multiple recruiting years. Accordingly, coaches

> may worry that early recruits will break their commitments, but they know that they will not suffer catastrophic consequences because alternate plans will have been made. Recruits have no such luxury.[48]

Coaches defend their revocation of oral offers by arguing that prospective student athletes understand how the recruiting game is played, and a part of the game is the reality that no binding deal has been consummated until the required documents are signed. They argue that because both recruits and institutions live in a world in which commitments are often broken, they engage in the process as equals.[49]

These justifications are less than satisfying. No matter how savvy they may consider themselves, recruits are minors and lack the experience and sophistication to fully comprehend the process in which they are engaged.[50] Their youth and inexperience combine to render recruits overly trusting. In addition, recruits often have parents who are unable to protect the recruits' interests. Moreover, most recruits are not blue-chip athletes. Consequently they lack the depth of scholarship options to which coaches point in attempting to justify their revocation of scholarship offers.[51]

Legal Recourse

The substantial harm that prospective student athletes may suffer when scholarship offers are revoked gives rise to the possibility of legal recourse against institutions. To date, the question of institutional legal liability is murky due, in part, to the paucity of lawsuits that have been filed by athletes against colleges and universities. Although coaches frequently revoke scholarship offers, few athletes complain publicly. Most reports of scholarship revocations appear anecdotally in the popular press.[52] The few lawsuits that have been initiated have resulted in settlements.[53]

A recruit alleging that a scholarship was wrongfully revoked would likely assert a variety of legal claims, including breach of contract, a violation of the duty of good faith, and promissory estoppel.[54] Of these claims, promissory estoppel holds the most promise. It provides for the enforceability of a promise based on the promisee's (the person to whom the promise is made) justifiable reliance on that promise. Therefore, if a person makes a promise with reason to know that the promisee is likely to rely on that promise and the promisee does justifiably rely (changes his or her position), the promise is binding based on the promisee's reliance if injustice can only be avoided by enforcing the promise.

In the sporting context, courts have adhered to the conceptualization of promissory estoppel set forth above, which was largely adopted by the court in *Hall v. NCAA*.[55] There, the court stated that the elements for promissory estoppel include (1) a clear and unambiguous promise, (2) reliance on the promise, (3) the promisee's reliance was reasonable and foreseeable by the party who made the promise, and (4) detrimental reliance (an injury sustained by the party asserting the estoppel by reason of his reliance).[56] Other courts, in sports-related cases, expressly add the requirement that the doctrine can only be used when "injustice can only be avoided by the enforcement of the promise."[57]

To date, no court has ruled on whether promissory estoppel provides a basis for imposing liability on an institution where a coach revoked an offer of a scholarship to a recruit. A recent case involves an appropriate vehicle for assessing the viability of the doctrine. Daniel Smith asserted that the University of Hawaii improperly revoked a scholarship offer after the university's head football coach accepted a position at SMU.[58] As it relates to promissory estoppel, Smith alleged:

> On April 26, 2007, UH, through its agent Coach Reinebold, made a promise to provide Daniel a full athletic scholarship to play football at UH beginning in the fall of 2008. . . . Contemporaneously with the promise, UH instructed Daniel to refrain from speaking with any other colleges and universities about football and scholarship opportunities. He was explicitly instructed to inform any and all other colleges and universities who contacted him that he was committed to UH and would be attending UH on an athletic scholarship. . . . UH should have reasonably expected its promise would induce action on Daniel's part. . . . Based solely, on UH's promise, Daniel turned down an athletic scholarship offer from Portland State University. . . . Based solely on UH's promise, Daniel refused numerous offers to visit colleges and universities who were attempting to recruit him for their respective football programs. . . . Because UH abandoned Daniel at the eleventh hour of the recruiting process, just weeks before National Letter of Intent Day, Daniel was unable to secure an athletic scholarship at another college or university.[59]

The case was settled before a court adjudication of the merits of Smith's promissory estoppel claim.[60] The University of Hawaii paid Smith $41,500 and expended over $150,000 in legal fees defending the action.[61]

When student athletes have invoked promissory estoppel, courts have impliedly recognized the viability of the theory but have ruled against athletes on evidentiary grounds. An Illinois court, in *Hall v. NCAA*,[62] dismissed an incoming student athlete's promissory estoppel claim against the NCAA after he claimed that the NCAA promised to give him information that would help make him eligible for his freshman season, yet he still remained ineligible. In granting summary judgment in favor of the defendant university, the court did not reject the viability of promissory estoppel in the university-athlete context. Rather, it concluded that the athlete had failed to offer evidence sufficient to establish the elements of promissory estoppel.

Similarly, an Ohio court dismissed the promissory estoppel claims of a former basketball player at the University of Cincinnati after evidence indicated that he was ruled ineligible "because of his own failures, not because of any . . . unfulfilled promises."[63] The player challenged the decision to rule him ineligible on the basis of the fact that he signed a national letter of intent to play, but was later declared academically ineligible.

The facts as alleged by Daniel Smith could present a viable promissory estoppel claim based on an application of the traditional elements courts employ in assessing such a claim. A university would likely assert that a recruit's reliance was unreasonable given the realities of recruiting, in which both coaches and recruits fail to honor verbal commitments. Once again, the nature of the dynamic athlete-coach relationship lends support for judicial recognition of promissory estoppel if an athlete can establish facts akin to those asserted in the Smith case.

Oversigning of Student Athletes

Oversigning is a recruiting practice connected principally with college football that also raises legal and ethical concerns. It occurs when a college or university signs more student athletes to letters of intent or offers of financial assistance than the institution can honor and remain in compliance with NCAA rules. For example, NCAA rules restrict the number of football scholarships awarded to incoming freshman student athletes to twenty-five per year. This limitation operates in concert with the NCAA limitation on the total number of football scholarships, eighty five, that can be awarded to football student athletes per year.[64]

Coaches willingly run the risk of signing prospective student athletes to more NLIs or offers of financial aid than a college can offer for several reasons. The practice of oversigning (1) provides coaches with a safeguard against a recruited prospect who cannot sign an NLI because he is academically ineligible to receive an athletic scholarship under NCAA rules; (2) allows coaches to hedge against the possibility that a recruited athlete will forfeit his amateur status; (3) affords coaches a supply of incoming student athletes who can replace athletes whose athletic scholarship a coach will not renew based on a coach's assessment that the athlete has underperformed athletically; and (4) facilitates a coach's ability to have players in reserve if a highly desired recruit elects, late in the recruiting season, to attend another college. The desire to gain a competitive advantage also prompts oversigning. "Coaches love over-signing because it gives them more talent to choose from, keeps it out of the hands of competitors."[65] In short, coaches oversign in order to have backup student athletes available if one of the above scenarios occurs.

If the anticipated attrition fails to occur, oversigned recruits as well as student athletes already on the roster from the previous football season are placed in a precarious position. The reality of oversigning is that the coach may have to get rid of players. One way this can be accomplished is for a team to release a recruit from his NLI. A more likely scenario includes a practice known as gray-shirting, which occurs when a coach requests that a recruit delay his enrollment with the hope that a scholarship will become available. Similarly, a coach may request that a recruit matriculate at the college or university and absorb the costs of attendance in anticipation that a scholarship will be awarded in the future. This often occurs in conjunction with a coach asking players to walk on the team without receiving the scholarship the coach promised while recruiting the athlete. Another tactic is to encourage athletes already on the team to take a medical red shirt; this frees up the injured athlete's scholarship while allowing the school to grant him a medical scholarship, which does not count against the NCAA scholarship limits.[66] Finally, the coach can refuse to renew the scholarship of a player on the roster or encourage him to transfer to another institution.

Oversigning has been criticized as being immoral and possibly violating athletes' legal rights.[67] Critics argue that typically a student-athlete is unaware that he is the athlete that may not make the team if one of the scenarios that bring the number of signees within NCAA limits does not occur.[68] As is true when scholarship offers are revoked, a recruit is placed in a particularly precarious position when he is told at the last minute that he will not make a team due to roster limitations. There is often a knowledge gap. In the past, "when top high-school seniors [made] their college commitments, dozens of signees head[ed] to some to the nation's most chronically over-signed schools were either unconcerned, or unaware, that these schools may have to cut some players to balance books."[69] At this point, opportunities for an athlete to visit other schools are extremely limited. Oversigning also jeopardizes the interest of student athletes who are cut to make room for a new recruit.

University of Florida president Bernard Machen has condemned the practice:

> The universities, with full knowledge of what they are doing, extend more athletic scholarships than they have. These schools play roulette

> with the lives of talented young people. If they run out of scholarships, too bad. The letter-of-intent signed by the university the previous February is voided. Technically, it's legal to do this. Morally, it is reprehensible.[70]

It has also been argued that the practice is particularly egregious if a roster athlete is cut after his coach persuaded him not to take a scholarship from a different school the previous year.[71]

Oversigning also fails to comport with good coaching practices. Coaches take advantage of the power and influence that they wield over athletes and exploit the trust the athletes tend to repose in them. It also represents a failure of coaches to act with honesty and integrity and to model such virtues. Particularly as it relates to roster athletes who are cut but have done what was asked of them, oversigning violates the notion that coaches will not act contrary to the interest of athletes.

Legal recourse is a rather dubious option for student athletes to pursue. If an institution and athlete have only signed a national letter of intent, the athlete would have no legal cause of action, such as a breach of contract claim against his institution. On the other hand, if an athlete signed an offer of financial aid and the school refused to honor it because of oversigning, the athlete would have a breach of contract action.[72]

Several factors, however, reduce the likelihood that an athlete would pursue his or her legal rights. First, many athletes may not be aware of their legal options. In addition, the time it would take to pursue an action would inhibit some student athletes. Moreover, under former NCAA rules, the most an athlete would likely recover in damages in a successful breach of contract action would be a monetary judgment equal to the value of a one-year scholarship. (This could change for some athletes with the advent of the possibility of multiyear contracts.) Student athletes would no doubt balance the value of the legal judgment against the stigma that would likely attach to an athlete who challenged the system. Thus from an athlete's perspective, it might be wiser to either accept an offer from another school or simply wait and hope to get a scholarship with the team that subjected him to oversigning.[73]

To address concerns relating to oversigning, the NCAA modified its rules. Effective August 2010 and applicable to bowl subdivision football, the NCAA initially adopted a rule that imposed a yearly limit of twenty-eight on the number of prospective student athletes with whom an institution can enter into a national letter of intent or an offer of financial aid.[74] Realizing that this rule did not completely resolve the problems associated with oversigning, the NCAA subsequently adopted legislation that reduces the number from twenty-eight to twenty-five. In 2012 the NCAA approved legislation intended to curb the practice that is more restrictive. The proposed amendment provides as follows (federated provision, FBS only):

> **13.9.2.3** Limitation on Number of National Letter of Intent/Offer of Financial Aid Signings—Bowl Subdivision Football. [FBS] In bowl subdivision football, there shall be an annual limit of 25 on the number of prospective student-athletes who may sign a National Letter of Intent or an institutional offer of financial aid from December 1 through May 31. [D]
>
> **13.9.2.3.1** Exception—Counter During Same Academic Year. A prospective student-athlete who signs a National Letter of Intent or an institutional offer of financial aid and becomes an initial counter for the same academic year in which the signing occurred (e.g., midyear enrollee) shall not count toward the annual limit on signings.

In articulating the rationale for the rule, the NCAA stated:

> This proposal seeks to address concerns regarding the practice of "over-signing" football prospective student-athletes to National Letters of Intent or financial aid agreements. Reducing the signing limit from 28 to 25 is an appropriate step to focus recruitment and signing of prospective student-athletes to the Football Bowl Subdivision limit on initial counters. By limiting the number of signees, institutions will be encouraged to focus their recruiting efforts on prospective student-athletes with the necessary academic and athletic credentials to succeed at the certifying institution.[75]

The new rule took effect on August 1, 2012.

Conclusion

The coaches' conduct described in the three scenarios presented above raises ethical and legal issues. This assertion is derived from the multiple roles and functions assigned to college coaches that shape their relationships with student athletes and prospective student athletes (as detailed in the chapters in Part 1 of this book). Indeed, attributes of coaching that allow coaches to exert pressure on prospective student athletes during the recruiting process begin during the athletes' initial interaction with coaches. The long-standing nature of these interactions strengthens the influence coaches may wield over student athletes given that an athlete's beliefs, as they relate to the coach-athlete relationship, develop over a period of time extending to and through a coach's recruitment of him or her to play at the collegiate level. Consequently judicial decisions relative to conduct between student athletes and coaches should be considered against the backdrop of the ethical dimensions that arise from the relationships athletes develop with their coaches. Thus judicial consideration of issues, such as the viability of promissory estoppel to the revocation of oral scholarship offers, should not be made without consideration of the social dynamic of the coach-student relationships and how it impacts athletes' decision making. More importantly, institutions should consider the nature of the coach-athlete relationship when impliedly validating conduct by coaches during the recruiting process that harms the interests of student athletes.

Questions for Review and Discussion

1. Explain how the interests of college coaches and those of prospective athletes who are being recruited might conflict.

2. What rationale might coaches offer for offering more athletic scholarships to recruits than are actually available? What criticism(s) can be made of that rationale? In light of the criticisms, is the rationale sound or ethically acceptable?

3. Is it ethically permissible for a recruited high school student athlete to visit a university (in order to attract an offer of an athletic scholarship) after having made a verbal commitment to attend another? Why or why not?

4. What is the doctrine of promissory estoppel and what is its significance for the ethics of athletic recruiting?

5. Do recruited student athletes who lose their athletic scholarships because of oversigning have adequate legal recourse? Are there any nonlegal or moral incentives that might limit oversigning of athletic recruits by Division I colleges and universities?

Suggestions for Further Reading

Bateman, Jonathan D. "When the Numbers Don't Add Up: Oversigning in College Football." *Marquette Sports Law Review* 22 (2011): 7.

Cross, Harry M. "The College Athlete and the Institution." *Law and Contemporary Problems* 38 (1973): 151, 155.

Davis, Timothy. "Student-Athlete Prospective Economic Interests: Contractual Dimensions." *Thurgood Marshall Law Review* 19 (1994): 585, 599.

Doyle, Gregg. "Bad Guys Utilize Over-signing, and It Has to Stop." CBS-Sports.com, April 8, 2010.

Eitzen, D. Stanley. "Social Control and Sport." In *Handbook of Sports Studies,* 376–377. Edited by Jay Coakley and Eric Dunning. London: Sage, 2000.

Karp, Hannah, and Darren Everson. "Alabama's Unhappy Castoffs." *Wall Street Journal,* September 24, 2010.

———. "SEC Coaches Defend Oversigning." *Wall Street Journal,* March 1, 2011.

Nomura, Jamie U. "Refereeing the Recruiting Game: Applying Contract Law to Make the Inter-Collegiate Recruiting Process Fair." *University of Hawaii Law Review* 32 (2009): 275.

Yen, Alfred C. "Early Scholarship Offers and the NCAA." *Boston College Law Review* 52 (2011): 585.

Notes

Part One: Introduction

Chapter 1

1. This TV series, loosely based on the book and movie of the same name, aired from 2006 to 2011.

2. *Report of the Special Investigative Counsel Regarding the Actions of the Pennsylvania State University Related to the Child Sexual Abuse Committed by Gerald A. Sandusky*, 14, www.thefreehreportonpsu.com/REPORT_FINAL_071212.pdf.

3. For details of the investigation of the University of Minnesota men's basketball program, see *NCAA Infractions Report on the University of Minnesota,* October 24, 2000, http://news.mpre.org/features/199903/11_newsroomcheating/infractionsreport.shtml. For a useful discussion of alleged bounty payments for injuring rival players, see Peter King, "Way Out of Bounds," *Sports Illustrated,* March 12, 2012, 34–41.

4. The figures cited are from the article "When Coaches Cross the Line," *USA Today*, December 29, 2011, 3C.

5. Sometimes we can identify egregiously wrong or unjust actions without having a clear positive theory of what is morally right or of the nature of social justice. However, ethical principles and ethical and political theories come into play when we are asked to justify or support our moral judgments or are challenged by whether our judgments concerning some cases are consistent with our judgments on other cases. Moreover, moral intuitions that may serve us well when confronted with clear cases might falter in regard to new or complicated cases. Thus we may all agree that it is wrong for a player to deliberately injure an opponent. But is it also wrong to try to distract an opponent through trash talk? Why or why not?

6. Just because people have a belief, even if firmly held, it does not follow that their belief is correct or that it is supported by good reasons.

Chapter 2

1. Jan Boxill, "Moral Significance of Sport," *in Sports Ethics: An Anthology* (Malden, MA: Blackwell, 2003), 1–12.
2. USADA, *What Sport Means in America: A Study of Sport's Role in Society* (Colorado Springs: U.S. Anti-Doping Agency, Outreach Education Research, 2010).
3. Ibid., 3.
4. Joe Ehrmann, *Inside Out Coaching* (New York: Simon & Shuster, 2011), 9.
5. Ibid., 10.
6. Steve Wieberg, "NCAA Survey Delves into Practice Time, Coaches Trust," *USA Today,* January 15, 2011. http://www.usatoday.com/sports/college/2011-01-14-ncaa-survey_N.htm.
7. Boxill, "Moral Significance of Sport," 1–7.
8. See Robert Simon, *Fair Play: The Ethics of Sports*, 3rd ed. (Boulder, CO: Westview, 2010), 24.
9. Kim Strom-Gottfried, "Ethical Action in Challenging Times," lecture on receiving the Smith P. Thiemann Jr. Distinguished Professor for Ethics and Professional Practice, October 12, 2006, 6–7, http://74.52.28.120/~jdn1754/nbr-content/EthicsLectureBooklet.pdf.
10. Ibid., 8–12.
11. Ibid., 13–14.
12. Robert Simon, "Sports, Relativism, and Moral Education," in *Sports Ethics*, 26.

Part Two: The Coach's Role

1. Some would argue, with justice I think, that such an individual is not really a coach at all but more of an instructor or technical adviser.
2. Readers interested in Dworkin's legal theory might start with Chapters 2 to 4 of his book *Taking Rights Seriously* (Cambridge: Harvard University Press, 1978). His most recent views on ethics and interpretivism are developed in *Justice for Hedgehogs* (Cambridge: Harvard University Press, 2011). My own views on broad internalism were first formulated in "Internalism and Internal Values in Sport," *Journal of the Philosophy of Sport* 27 (2000): 1–16, and were influenced by a number of earlier papers cited in my article. One such influential paper is J. S. Russell, "Are Rules All an Umpire Has to Work With?" *Journal of the Philosophy of Sport* 26 (1999): 27–49. Here Russell explicitly draws on Dworkin's work in legal theory.
3. Of course, professional athletes may engage in sports to make a living, but they do so through accepting and meeting the challenge of their sports;

in that sense meeting the challenge of the sport is fundamental to understanding and developing an ethic of sports.

4. Russell, "Are Rules All an Umpire Has to Work With?" 35.

5. Thus most members of the current basketball community would find nothing morally questionable about a losing team deliberately fouling at the end of a close contest in order to stop the clock and force opponents to hold their lead by making foul shots under pressure. However, a number of writers have raised serious questions about this practice of strategic fouling. For example, some have argued that strategic fouling breaks a tacit contract among competitors to abide by the rules, while others have argued it undermines the game by making less important rote skills, such as foul shooting, more important than primary creative skills like dribbling, shooting over defenders, and passing. While I have doubts about whether these arguments are sound, the critics of strategic fouling have succeeded in showing the prevailing view about strategic fouling is not necessarily acceptable just because it is widely accepted. For a summary of this debate and my own defense of strategic fouling under some circumstances, see Robert Simon, "The Ethics of Strategic Fouling: A Reply to Fraleigh," *Journal of the Philosophy of Sport* 32:1 (2005): 87–95.

6. Indeed, a topic of further discussion is whether the different approaches to the ethics of coaching suggested in this chapter are compatible with one another, at least in an adjusted form, or whether we must choose among them. For example, is the virtue approach suggested by Reid in Chapter 3 compatible with the broad internalism developed in Chapter 4? In other words, does viewing the role of the coach the way that Reid suggests—and taking the main function of sports to be the development of virtue among sports participants—the theory that makes the best sense of sporting practices and presents them in their morally best light? Or do we need a broader conception of sporting practice involving the ideas of challenge, fairness toward, and respect for other competitors, and conceptions of the rights and duties of participants in addition to virtue theory? Are these other values really distinct from virtue or are they examples of virtues themselves? These are complex questions that remain subjects of philosophical debate. For a helpful and quite accessible discussion of different theoretical approaches to ethics, including virtue theory, see James Rachels and Stuart Rachels, *The Elements of Moral Philosophy*, 7th ed. (New York: McGraw-Hill, 2011).

Chapter 3

1. The Greek term *aretē* is difficult to translate. In short, it refers to excellence—a disposition and ability to do great things that includes a moral

dimension. In the language of ethical theory it is usually translated "virtue," although "virtuosity" may better capture the sense in which morality and skill combine to yield exemplary action.

2. For a review, see Sharon K. Stoll and Jennifer M. Beller, "Do Sports Build Character?" in *Sports in School: The Future of an Institution,* ed. John Gerdy (New York: Columbia University Press, 2000), 18–30. Note that the definitions and measurements of "good moral character" used in this social science research are often questioned—and sometimes rejected—by philosophers.

3. For a complete explanation of this approach, see M. Andrew Holowchak and Heather L. Reid, *Aretism: An Ancient Sports Philosophy for the Modern Sports World* (Lanham, MD: Lexington, 2011).

4. Gilgamesh's feat is recounted in *The Epic of Gilgamesh,* trans. N. K. Sandars (London: Penguin, 1960), 69; Shulgi's comes from the "Hymn of Praise to Shulgi," in S. K. Kramer, *History Begins at Sumer* (Philadelphia: University of Pennsylvania Press, 1981), 285–288.

5. This is the argument made by Heather L. Reid, *Athletics and Philosophy in the Ancient World: Contests of Virtue* (New York: Routledge, 2011), 11–21.

6. For a philosophical exploration of the value of Heracles' strength, see H. Reid, "Hercules' Dilemma: Is Strength Really a Virtue?" in *Strength and Philosophy,* ed. M. Holowchak (New York: Mellen, 2010).

7. Homer, *The Odyssey,* trans. Robert Fagles (New York: Penguin, 1990), 8.130–233.

8. Ibid. Books 18–21.

9. For a more complete argument on this point, see Reid, *Athletics and Philosophy,* chaps. 1–3.

10. Nigel James Nicholson, *Aristocracy and Athletics in Archaic and Classical Greece* (Cambridge: Cambridge University Press, 2005), 21, explains that "what motivated anxiety about professional trainers was that, by appearing to add new abilities such as skill to their pupils, they threatened the idea that the qualities on which victory depended were inherited, and, second, that, while the training was traded as a commodity, the relationship between trainer and patron was sufficiently complex that to represent it in other terms was convincing."

11. In contrast to the more liberal and individualistic philosophies of modern times, ancient Greek conceptions of *aretē* always encompass civic responsibility. As Aristotle says, human beings are understood as political animals; human excellence must therefore include political virtues.

12. Kathleen Freeman, trans., *Ancilla to the Pre-Socratic Philosophers: A Complete Translation of Diels, Fragmente der Vorsokratiker* (Cambridge: Harvard University Press, 1948), DK 23 b33, p. 53.

13. The story is told in Iamblichus, *The Pythagorean Life,* trans. Thomas Taylor (London: Watkins, 1818), chap. 5. After watching the student play a complex ball game, Pythagoras concluded that he must also have the ability to learn complex ideas. This student eventually accompanied Pythagoras to the colony of Kroton in southern Italy, where he again recruited students at the gymnasium and founded a community of scholars and athletes renowned in the ancient world, not least for their success at the Olympic Games. Kroton was so dominant in the Olympic Games that the top seven finishers in the sprint race of 576 BCE all hailed from that single city—a phenomenon that gave birth to the proverb that "he who finishes last of the Krotonites is first among the rest of the Greeks" (Strabo 6.1.12).

14. For a fuller discussion, see Heather L. Reid, "Sport as Moral Education in Plato's *Republic,*" *Journal of the Philosophy of Sport* 34:2 (2007): 160–175; and "Plato's Gymnasium," in *Athletics and Philosophy*, 56–68.

15. Plato, Seventh Letter, in *Plato in Twelve Volumes*, trans. R. G. Bury (Cambridge: Harvard University Press, 1966), 7:335d-336b.

16. For a complete argument, see Nicholas Dixon, "On Winning and Athletic Superiority," *Journal of the Philosophy of Sport* 26:1 (1999): 10–26.

17. This argument is made repeatedly by Holowchak and Reid in *Aretism,* for example, page 166. It may also be the case that the beauty we see in athletic movements and perhaps even artistic movements, such as dance, depends ultimately on moral criteria. For a discussion, see Heather Reid, *The Philosophy of Sport* (Lanham, MD: Rowman & Littlefield, 2012), chap. 11.

18. I am not making a consequentialist claim here that the moral value of athletic virtue depends strictly on its beneficial outcomes; rather, I am distinguishing the athletic skill associated with victory from virtue—the latter of which can (and should) be exercised for human benefit beyond sports.

19. Plato *Hippias Minor* 364c–370e.

20. For a comparison of Socratic and Sophistic approaches to argument, see Reid, *Athletics and Philosophy*, chap. 4, especially pp. 46–48.

21. Plato *Apology* 30b. All Plato quotations are taken from the following volume, unless otherwise noted: Plato, *Complete Works*, ed. John M. Cooper (Indianapolis: Hackett, 1997).

22. According to NCAA statistics, the percentage of college athletes who go on to play professionally in the major men's sports of basketball, football, and soccer ranges from 1.0 to 1.7 percent. Since college athletics does not market itself as a preprofessional program, that placement rate is not seen as a failure. National Collegiate Athletic Association, "Estimated Probability of Competing in Athletics Beyond the High School Interscholastic Level," 2011, http://www.ncaa.org/wps/wcm/connect/public/test/issues/recruiting/probability+of+going+pro.

23. Plato *Republic* 413cd.

24. In *Republic,* Socrates' brief discussion of the guardians' dedicated gymnastic period includes the cryptic comment that their performance there "is itself an important test" (537b). In what follows he suggests that the best potential philosophers will be selected, at least partly, on the basis of this test (537c), and, presumably, the also-rans will be weeded out.

25. Plato *Republic* 410b.

26. Plato *Apology* 21d. Socrates is sometimes quoted as saying that the only thing he knows is that he knows nothing, but this exact phrase does not occur in the Platonic dialogues.

27. More precisely, the oracle said no one was wiser than Socrates.

28. Walter Burkert, *Greek Religion*, trans. J. Raffan (Cambridge: Harvard University Press, 1985), 56. For a complete argument about the connection between sports and sacrifice, see David Sansone, *Greek Athletics and the Genesis of Sport* (Berkeley: University of California Press, 1988).

29. Plato *Republic* 424e.

30. At *Gorgias* 463b ff., Socrates calls rhetoric a form of flattery that makes the soul seem healthy when in fact it is not.

31. For more on the role of respect in sports, see Heather Reid, *The Philosophical Athlete* (Durham, NC: Carolina Academic Press, 2002), chaps. 7–9.

32. Plato *Republic* 535bc.

33. The similar proverb, "You can learn more about someone in an hour of play than a year of conversation," is sometimes attributed to Plato, but it does not appear in the extant written texts.

34. Plato *Republic* 535b.

35. Ibid., 504cd.

36. Ibid., 537b.

37. Ibid., 524d ff.

38. The implications of this principle are diverse. One may be a decoupling of athletics and academics during specific time periods—for example, young athletes may devote four years to sporting excellence and another four years to academic excellence. It may also imply a lowering of athletic expectations during times of higher education, or a lowering of academic expectations during times of athletic striving. (I know many athletes who take lower course loads during their competitive season.) It does not imply, however, that individuals should abandon one type of activity in order to pursue excellence in the other. The student who never goes to the gym is just as imbalanced as the athlete who never goes to the library.

39. Coaches should also think of creative ways to align athletic and academic rewards. A student of mine once suggested that college basketball

players receive a score equivalent to their grade point average (instead of the standard 2 or 3 points) for each basket. A radical suggestion, perhaps, but it would motivate students to pay equal attention to athletics and academics.

40. Plato *Republic* 411e: "It seems, then, that a god has given music and physical training to human beings not, except incidentally, for the body and the soul, but for the spirited and wisdom-loving parts of the soul itself, in order that these may be in harmony with one another, each being stretched and relaxed to an appropriate degree."

41. Plato *Republic* 403d.

42. Ibid., 411e.

43. Ibid.,591c.

44. Plato *Phaedrus* 247b.

45. Plato *Republic* 442a.

46. Ibid., 424e.

47. Ibid., 416d.

48. Ibid., 502d–503a.

49. Ibid., 519e.

50. Ibid., 465d.

51. Aristotle, *Nicomachean Ethics*, trans. Terence Irwin, 2nd ed. (Indianapolis: Hackett, 1999), 1098a.

Chapter 4

1. Quoted from "Champions with Character," Utica *Observer-Dispatch*, January 19, 2012, 8A.

2. I borrow this kind of example from Jeffrey Fry, "Coaching a Kingdom of Ends," *Journal of the Philosophy of Sport* 27 (2000): 56.

3. I have argued more fully for such a view in Robert L. Simon, "From Ethnocentrism to Realism: Does Discourse Ethics Bridge the Gap?" *Journal of the Philosophy of Sport* 31:2 (2004). William J. Morgan questions this view in Chapter 5 of the present volume.

4. Of course, when evaluating any group of people, we will find shades of gray. Most coaches, like other people, will be less than perfect without having serious or significant moral flaws.

5. See Scott Kretchmar, "In Defense of Winning," in *Sports Ethics: An Anthology*, ed. Jan Boxill (Malden, MA: Blackwell, 2003), 130–135.

6. Ronald Dworkin, *Justice for Hedgehogs* (Cambridge: Harvard University Press, 2011), 112.

7. See Fry, "Coaching," 59.

8. Someone who reviewed this chapter has suggested, however, that players at elite levels may have implicitly consented to competition for

playing time, and even to coaches using tactics such as those described by Fry if needed to promote competitive success. If the players can be presumed to have consented, perhaps they are not being used as means or exploited after all. However, it is hardly clear that players have consented to the behavior described by Fry or that it would even be rational for them to do so.

9. Here I follow Bernard Gert, who argues that justifiable moral codes must be public or known to all to whom they apply. See Gert, *Morality: Its Nature and Justification* (New York: Oxford University Press, 1998), 191–195.

10. Fry, "Coaching," 59–60.

11. Ibid., 58.

12. A lot hinges on the sport at issue. For example, in cross-country, everyone on the team normally competes so there is no issue of replacing one runner with another.

13. Golf purists might insist on penalizing the offending player, and I would agree if the match in question was a formal, highly competitive one. But what if it is a preseason scrimmage or takes place in a developmental event for inexperienced players? The common courtesies widely recognized by golfers call on them to warn fellow competitors in advance of possible rule violations, so the player who teed the ball ahead of the markers is not the only player at fault in this case.

14. A. Launder, "Coach Education for the Twenty-First Century," *Sports Coach* 16:1 (1993): 1–2; quoted by Oyvind F. Standal and Liv B. Hemmestad, "Becoming a Good Coach: Coaching as Phronesis," in *The Ethics of Sports Coaching,* ed. Alun R. Hardman and Carwyn Jones (London: Routledge, 2011), 50.

15. Reflective equilibrium, following the work of John Rawls, might be thought of as the end result of a process of deliberation—our principles yield results that seem acceptable when applied to particular cases and our judgments about particular cases harmonize with our general principles. Perhaps such a state is an ideal to be aimed at rather than actually achieved, but the attempt to achieve it can, by eliminating incoherencies in our moral perspective, lead to defensible ethical judgments and arguably, if our system stands the test of critical scrutiny, justified moral belief. See John Rawls, *A Theory of Justice* (Cambridge: Harvard University Press, 1971), esp. 46–53, for an influential discussion of reflective equilibrium and its role in moral reasoning.

16. For fuller development of virtue-centered approaches to coaching, see Standal and Hemmestad, "Becoming a Good Coach"; and Alun R. Hardman and Carwyn Jones, "Sports Coaching and Virtue Ethics," in *The Ethics of Sports Coaching,* 45–55; 72–84.

17. For a fuller discussion of "the mutual quest for excellence," see Robert Simon, *Fair Play* (Boulder: Westview, 2010), chaps. 2–3.

18. For a fuller discussion of broad internalism, see Robert Simon, "Internalism and the Internal Values of Sport," *Journal of the Philosophy of Sport* 27 (2000): 1–16, as well as Chapter 5 in this volume. John Russell, "Are Rules All an Umpire Has to Work With?" *Journal of the Philosophy of Sport* 26 (1999): 27–49, has strongly influenced the development of interpretive (broad internalist) positions.

19. This is a principle rather than a rule because in some situations its force may have to be weighed against competing factors. For example, a football coach might not want the challenge of playing a stronger and bigger team because his players might be injured.

20. I have argued for the mutual reinforcement thesis in "Does Athletics Undermine Academics? Examining Some Issues," *Journal of Intercollegiate Sport* 1:1 (2008): 40–58. Critical comments by Drew Hyland and William J. Morgan also appear in that issue, pp. 59–71.

21. Following a different sort of argument to a similar conclusion, based on affinities between athletic and artistic performances in music and dance, is Myles Brand, "The Role and Value of Intercollegiate Athletics in Universities," *Journal of the Philosophy of Sport* 33 (2007): 9–20.

22. For a defense of the view that providing entertainment to large audiences through athletics is a defensible function of big-time intercollegiate sports, see Peter French, *Ethics and College Sports: Ethics, Sports, the University* (Lanham, MD: Rowman & Littlefield, 2004).

23. *Report of the Special Investigative Counsel Regarding the Actions of the Pennsylvania State University Related to the Child Sexual Abuse Committed by Gerald A. Sandusky*, July 12, 2012, p. 14, thefreeh reportonpsu.com.

24. The NCAA vacated the victories of Penn State football from 1998 to 2011, roughly the period when Sandusky committed his crimes and no one reported them to the criminal justice system. Critics of this penalty argue, with some justice in my view, that those victories were earned through the hard work of players who were uninvolved in the scandal and were innocent of any wrongdoing. See Gary Alan Fine, "George Orwell and the NCAA," *New York Times*, July 24, 2012, www.nytimes.com/2012/07/25/opinion/penn-states-vacated-victories.html?_r=1.

25. Other reforms that might help integrate athletics and academics more fully in Division I include restrictions on extended travel that conflicts with class attendance and restrictions on the level of training expected of athletes in the off-season.

Chapter 5

1. Robert Simon, "From Ethnocentrism to Realism: Can Discourse Ethics Bridge the Gap?" *Journal of the Philosophy of Sport* 31 (2004): 122–141.

2. Ibid. 125.

3. Ronald Dworkin, "To Each His Own," *New York Review of Books*, April 14, 1983, 4–6.

4. Simon, "From Ethnocentrism to Realism." Dworkin's normative theory of law is more complicated than I have so far indicated. For while he clearly thinks that a normative theory of law "must be abstract because [it] aim[s] to interpret the main point and structure of legal practice, not some particular part . . . of it," he also holds that "a practical imperative" of any interpretation of the law requires "there is enough initial agreement about what practices are legal practices" in a particular culture if that interpretation is to be successful. See Dworkin, *Law's Empire* (Cambridge: Harvard University Press, 1986), 90–91. That would put his position closer to Simon's normative theory of sport. In the same book, published after the article I cite in the text, he makes it clear that the full-throated abstract position he took in the article is best suited to "justice and other higher-order moral concepts" rather than law because of the former's "global reach" (pp. 424–425). Interestingly, Jürgen Habermas's well-known discourse on ethics, which differs from Simon's by claiming to be ahistorical at both front and back end, also thinks that discourse normative theory is best suited to moral concepts like justice rather than law for the same reason. See Habermas, *Moral Consciousness and Communicative Action* (Cambridge: MIT Press, 1990), 103.

5. Simon, "From Ethnocentrism to Realism," 128.

6. Ibid.

7. As one commentator of the time put it, "What sportsmanlike opponent cares to make his point against a helpless antagonist?" Price Collier, "Sport's Place in the Nation's Well Being," *Outing* 32 (1898): 886.

8. Caspar Whitney, "The View-Point," *Outing* 52 (1908): 766.

9. Benjamin Rader, *American Sports: From the Age of Folk Games to the Age of Televised Sports* (Upper Saddle River, NJ: Prentice-Hall, 2004), 130–131. The seeds of this new, strenuous life were sown at the turn of the twentieth century. Once it attained normative preeminence, however, it held sway until the waning decades of the twentieth century. By that time the market had managed to insinuate itself into the internal affairs of sport, much as it had in just about every organized human enterprise.

10. It is no coincidence that coaches at this time began both literally and metaphorically to sell themselves to the sporting public not as educators, or as stewards of the health of their players, but as "efficient manag[ers] of the

body" whose strategic expertise, they loudly proclaimed, is what separates winners from losers. Donald J. Mrozek, *Sport and the American Mentality* (Knoxville: University of Tennessee Press, 1983), 67.

11. That is not to say that on certain occasions we can't come up with universal negative injunctions against murder, torture, arbitrary imprisonment, and the like. See Michael Walzer's fine book on this point, *Thick and Thin: Moral Argument at Home and Abroad* (Notre Dame, IN: University of Notre Dame Press, 1994). Rather, it is only to say that such wide-ranging agreement, if history is our teacher, is beyond reach when it comes to our own homegrown cultural practices, no matter how much others may seek to emulate our local ways. The most we can expect to derive from such thinning out in this latter sense are abstract platitudes that have little if any normative substance, and thus offer little in the way of ethical guidance or motivation.

12. The sort of argumentative impasse I have in mind here is captured in the book *Chariots of Fire*, later made into a movie, in which Cambridge dons upbraid one of their student athletes, the runner Harold Abrahams, for adopting a professional approach to his sport "concentrated wholly on developing [his] own technique" and for hiring a professional coach to aid his efforts, which, they argued, betrayed the amateur code of sports favored at Cambridge. Abrahams responded with an angry outburst that ended the conversation: "You know, gentleman, you yearn for victory just as I do. But achieved with the apparent ease of gods. Yours are the archaic values of the prep school playground. . . . I believe in the relentless pursuit of excellence—and I'll carry the future with me!" W. J. Weatherby, *Chariots of Fire* (New York: Dell, 1981), 91–92.

13. Nicholas Dixon, "Canadian Figure Skaters, French Judges, and Realism in Sport," *Journal of the Philosophy of Sport* 30:2 (2003): 108.

14. Members of the relevant athletic community could be mistaken regarding the status quo view on, for example, ethical coaching. But that would be a descriptive failure. So it turns out that this version of conventionalism has an error theory after all, but hardly a very useful one.

15. Strictly speaking, however, most social conventions, to include those of sports, are not products of simple agreement. David Lewis's classic book, *Convention,* which spurred serious philosophical interest in this topic, was based on his attempt to disarm Quine's claim that language can't be conventional because, in Lewis's words, it "could not have possibly originated by agreement, since some [language] would have been needed to provide the rudimentary language in which the first agreement was made." *Convention* (Oxford: Blackwell, 2002), 2. So conventions of this wide-ranging kind can't be reduced to social agreements either owing to special features of the

practices they are supposed to govern, as in the case of language above, or because of the large numbers of people that, *per impossible*, would have to sign on to them in order for them to function as conventional norms. Theorists of conventions, instead, attempt to explain the emergence of conventions by appealing to forms of common practical reasoning that allow people to identify, for instance, "salient" features of the situations they find themselves in that make it possible to coordinate their behavior. For an insightful account of such common practical reasoning, see Gerald Postema, "Salience Reasoning," *Topoi* 27 (2008).

16. Leslie Howe, "Gamesmanship," *Journal of the Philosophy of Sport* 31 (2004): 212–225.

17. Pine tar is a sticky substance applied to baseball bats for better gripping purposes.

18. I think MacPhail is on the right side of this issue—gamesmanship looks more like a vulgar trick than a legitimate strategic skill. Had the officials been privy to Martin's calculated decision to call the pine tar violation to their attention at that precise moment, it might well have provoked them to deliberate more carefully about how to rule. That's not to say, however, as Berman has astutely pointed out, that there are only two possible ways this argument could turn out: either MacPhail was right and the umpires wrong, or the other way around. There are two other possible outcomes as well, that both MacPhail and the umpires were wrong, or that they were both right, that MacPhail was right to prevent an injustice given his executive oversight role and the umpires were right to limit their officiating to the rule rather than its underlying principles given their adjudicative role. Mitchell Berman, "On Interpretivism and Formalism in Sports Officiating: From General to Particular Jurisprudence," *Journal of the Philosophy of Sport* 38 (2011): 190.

Chapter 6

1. See, for example, R. Scott Kretchmar, *Practical Philosophy of Sport* (Champaign, IL: Human Kinetics, 2005).

2. Frank Reynolds, "Developing a Formal Coaching Philosophy," *Coaches Report* 12:2 (2005): 10–12; David Parsh, "Eight Steps to a Coaching Philosophy," *Coach and Athletic Director* 76:9 (2007): 56–57.

3. Parsh outlines the following questions: What do you want to accomplish? What are your priorities? What are the responsibilities? What are your teaching methods? How do you define success? How will practices and games be organized? What are your team rules and consequences? How will you communicate your philosophy?

4. Carol Dweck, *Mindset: The New Psychology of Success* (New York: Random House, 2006).

5. Henry Bugbee, *The Inward Morning: A Philosophical Exploration in Journal Form* (Athens: University of Georgia Press, 1999).

6. Alun R. Hardman and Carwyn Jones, eds., *The Ethics of Sports Coaching* (London: Routledge, 2011), 2.

7. Sigmund Loland, "The Normative Aims of Coaching: The Good Coach as an Enlightened Generalist," in *Ethics of Sports Coaching*, 15–22.

8. Oyvind Standal and Liv Hemmestad, "Becoming a Good Coach: Coaching and *Phronesis*," in *Ethics of Sports Coaching*, 45–55.

9. Gary Walton, *Beyond Winning: The Timeless Wisdom of Great Philosopher Coaches* (Champaign, IL: Leisure, 1992), xi.

10. John Lyle, "Coaching Philosophy and Coaching Behavior," in *The Coaching Process: Principles and Practice for Sport*, ed. N. Cross and J. Lyle (Oxford: Butterworth & Heinemann, 1999), 25–46.

11. This concept of *technē* comes from the Greek tradition and is understood as a particular skill or craft. The fulfillment of *technē* requires both *episteme* (theoretical knowledge) and *phronesis* (practical wisdom). Coaches need to acquire and develop the capacity for both aspects of *technē*.

12. Legendary college football coach John Gagliardi provides an unusual example in this regard by using coaching methods that have been described as "winning with no's," as in no tackling in practices, no wind sprints, no whistles, and more. Despite the seemingly odd methods, Gagliardi and his St. John's University team have consistently reached the national playoffs in NCAA Division III. See Austin Murphy, *The Sweet Season* (New York: HarperCollins, 2001), for more on Gagliardi and St. John's football.

13. Harry Sheehy, the author of *Raising a Team Player: Teaching Kids Lasting Values on the Field, on the Court, and on the Bench* (North Adams, MA: Story, 2002), coached men's basketball at Williams College for seventeen years before serving as athletic director. While coaching, he compiled a record of 324–104 (.757), and while he was lead administrator the Ephs won the NCAA Division III Directors' Cup every year. Most recently, Sheehy became director of athletics and recreation at Dartmouth College.

14. Bugbee, *Inward Morning*, 77.

15. Noted in Douglas Anderson, *Philosophy Americana: Making Philosophy at Home in American Culture* (New York: Fordham University Press, 2006).

16. Bugbee, *Inward Morning*, 36–37.

17. Anderson, *Philosophy Americana*, 67.

18. Bugbee, *Inward Morning*, 37.

19. Ibid., 141.

20. Ibid., 36.
21. Ibid., 37, 22.
22. Ibid., 170.
23. Ibid., 35.
24. For example, see Jeff Fry, "On Playing with Emotion," *Journal of the Philosophy of Sport* 30 (2003): 26–36.
25. Bugbee, *Inward Morning*, 49.
26. Ibid., 129.
27. Anderson, *Philosophy Americana*, 54.
28. Bugbee, *Inward Morning*, 164.
29. Anderson, *Philosophy Americana*, 71.
30. William Warren, *Coaching and Control: Controlling Your Team, Your Program, and Your Opponents* (Upper Saddle River, NJ: Prentice-Hall, 1997).
31. Anderson, *Philosophy Americana*, 173.
32. Bugbee, *Inward Morning*, 232.
33. Harold Heie, *Learning to Listen, Ready to Talk: A Pilgrimage Toward Peacemaking* (Lincoln, NE: iUniverse, 2007), 91.
34. As an example, while ranked the number one golfer in the world, Tiger Woods changed his swing coach and, perhaps more surprisingly, his swing. While many criticized his decisions, the changes also illustrated an openness to change and a humble recognition that his game could be improved.
35. Petrino achieved notoriety and success at Arkansas, attaining an 11–2 record in the 2011 season, including a 2012 Cotton Bowl victory. In the spring of 2012 the university dismissed Petrino, however, following an embarrassing series of events. Petrino sustained injuries from a motorcycle crash, carrying a rider (Jessica Dorrell) who was an athletic department employee. After some time, Petrino admitted having an extramarital relationship with Dorrell and providing Dorrell with an undisclosed $20,000 gift. In addition, Dorrell had received preferential treatment in the hiring process for her university job. Arkansas athletic administrators went on to fire Petrino.
36. Bugbee, *Inward Morning*, 49.
37. Ibid., 53.
38. Anderson, *Philosophy Americana*, 62–63.
39. I am grateful to Robert Simon for providing this very astute and fitting example. Those who follow college basketball remember the tremendous success Princeton coach Pete Carril had with his patented "backdoor" cutting offensive system, one that matched well with the type of student athletes at Princeton.
40. Standal and Hemmestad, "Becoming a Good Coach," 53.

41. Paul Davis, "Objectivity and Subjectivity in Coaching," in *Ethics of Sports Coaching*, 56–71.

Part Three: Coaching and the Ethics of Competition

Chapter 7

1. On the general relationship between distributive justice and scarcity, see John Rawls, *A Theory of Justice* (Cambridge: Harvard University Press, 1971), 127–129. On scarcity and inherently or necessarily scarce goods, see "Scarcity," Wikipedia, http://en.wikipedia.org/wiki/Scarcity. On the varieties of justice, see Aristotle, "The Varieties of Justice," in *Justice: Alternative Political Perspectives*, ed. James Sterba (Belmont, CA: Wadsworth, 1980).

2. See Janean Chun, "Bank Deposit Error in Your Favor? Give It Back," *Daily Finance,* December 9, 2009; and Ben Jailler, "Can You Keep Money Accidentally Paid into Your Bank Account?" www.money.co.uk/article/1005023-can-you-keep-money-accidentally-paid-into-your-bank-account.htm, for reviews of the law in the United States and the United Kingdom respectively. See also the US Treasury Department, "Answers and Solutions for Customers of National Banks," http://www.mymoney.gov/content/answers-and-solutions-customers-national-banks.html.

3. Robert L. Simon, *Fair Play: The Ethics of Sport*, 2nd ed. (Boulder, CO: Westview, 2004), 27.

4. William J. Morgan, *Why Sports Morally Matter* (New York: Routledge, 2006).

5. J. S. Russell, "Competitive Sport, Moral Development, and Peace: Skeptical Reflections," in *A Companion to Sport Philosophy*, ed. Cesar Torres (forthcoming). See also John Russell, "The Moral Ambiguity of Coaching Youth Sport," in *The Ethics of Sports Coaching*, ed. Alun R. Hardman and Carwyn Jones (London: Routledge, 2011).

6. I am applying Midgley's suggestion that games are ritualized conflicts. Mary Midgley, "The Game Game," in *The Ethics of Sports: A Reader*, ed. Mike McNamee (London: Routledge, 2010).

7. Quoted in Russell, "Competitive Sport."

8. Immanuel Kant, *Lectures on Ethics* (New York: Harper Torchbooks, 1963), 215–217.

9. See Alister Browne, "Violating Rules of Rationing," *Canadian Journal of General Internal Medicine* 3:3 (2008): 127–128, for a succinct review of these issues.

10. See Mitchell N. Berman, "Replay," *California Law Review* 99 (2011): 1683–1743; Harry Collins, "The Philosophy of Umpiring and the Introduction of Decision-Aid Technology," *Journal of the Philosophy*

of Sport 37:2 (2010): 135–146; and Richard Royce, "Refereeing and Technology: Reflections on Collins' Proposals," *Journal of the Philosophy of Sport* 39:1 (2012), for discussions of the role of replay and other decision aids in sport. For a discussion of umpire discretion regarding calls and rules in some other contexts, see J. S. Russell, "The Concept of a Call in Baseball," *Journal of the Philosophy of Sport* 24 (1997): 21–37; Russell, "Are Rules All an Umpire Has to Work With?" *Journal of the Philosophy of Sport* 26 (1999): 27–49. None of these discuss the role coaches or participants may have in overturning erroneous decisions.

11. I am indebted to Alister Browne for years of discussion on this topic and for comments on an earlier draft of this chapter.

Chapter 8

1. I mention Rudy because it was the fact of his being on the field in a real game that validated his project and served as the dramatic climax in the movie version of his story. Had Rudy just made the team, it would have produced a feel-good narrative. But getting into an actual game was the epiphany event—what the fans wanted . . . and of course, what Rudy wanted as well.

2. Sports like cross-country running effectively acknowledge rights of substitutes to play by allowing some of them to compete. Even though only a subset of runners' scores will count, nobody knows for sure who that will be when the race begins. So, one could say that cross-country is an example of a benchwarmer-friendly sport.

3. See, for example, concerns raised about ESPN television and the potential exploitation of young athletes, http://itsaboutthemoney.net/archives/2011/08/16/does-espn-exploit-little-leaguers. Also, I realize that one can read such must-play regulations with cynical or supportive eyes. In the former case, these rules are seen as hypocritical covers for underlying business motives or adult agendas. In the latter case, such rules would indicate that competition in these contexts is truly about the athletes and transcendent values like education and fun.

4 These concerns about premature judgments or decisions are elevated when one considers the fact that some coaches may not be good judges of talent. Because many junior high school coaches are young and inexperienced, the chances for these kinds of mistakes are increased.

5. When I cluster these values or emphases into two categories, I do not see that elements of each one necessarily entail one another. Rather, these are rough-and-ready groupings. Excellence, for example, does not entail public performance and even less, commercialization. But excellence is something

that typically attracts public interest. And public interest is one factor in commercial viability.

6. I use the terms "technician" and "instrumentalist" advisedly. They connote expertise but also a kind of value-free approach to problem solving. MacIntyre (1984), for example, roundly criticizes such an approach when he introduces the stock character of the manager. The worry is that many coaches operate too frequently in the amoral atmosphere of seeking maximal efficacy.

7. These nonschool settings I have in mind would include organizations like American Legion Baseball, AAU competitions, sport camp experiences, and the like.

8. This is stage 2 moral reasoning, according to Kohlberg. It is based on high degrees of self-interest (What is in it for me?) and fails to tap into universal principles that might govern human relationships—principles like loyalty and justice.

9. It is interesting that a nod is given in the direction of the importance of playing time at both high school and college levels by traditional "senior night" games. This is when all seniors get a chance to start and play for a short time. One wonders if this gesture is taken by some graduating players as more an insult than an honor.

10. In Division III, Bylaw 14.1.11.1 (NCAA 2011) limits the use of male practice players to one day a week, to the traditional playing season for the team in question, and to half the number of starters for that sport.

11. Limitations in Divisions I and II have more to do with normal eligibility requirements than practice restrictions. Practice guys have to be bona fide students.

Chapter 9

1. Stephen Potter, *The Theory and Practice of Gamesmanship* (New York: Bantam, 1947), 4.

2. Leslie Howe, "Gamesmanship," *Journal of the Philosophy of Sport* 31 (2004): 212.

3. The constitutive rules are considered the written rules that define a game.

4. Howe, "Gamesmanship," 213.

5. Included in this understanding of the manipulation of rules are questionable forms of performance enhancement that may not be cheating but could test the rules. This could include such examples as equipment advances that are unavailable to others or nontherapeutic surgical enhancement.

6. Howe, "Gamesmanship," 213.

7. Potter, *Theory and Practice of Gamesmanship.*

8. Ibid, 70.

9. Howe, "Gamesmanship," 214.

10. The regulative nature of the game is defined as the rules that regulate the activity, including "supporting the constitutive rules by explaining behaviors that aid in successful occurrences of the games . . . . [T]hey specify strategies, techniques, procedures and natural facts," as described in Chad Carlson and John Gleaves, "Categorical Shortcomings: Application, Adjudication, and Contextual Descriptions of Game Rules," *Journal of the Philosophy of Sport* 38:2 (2011): 199. They are the way the game should be played beyond its constitutive rules.

11. Howe, "Gamesmanship," 219.

12. Ibid., 214.

13. Ibid., 221.

14. Ibid., 215.

15. As to when this age appropriateness occurs there is room for debate, but for argument's sake this author will suggest at least the early teenage years. By then the young athlete may be sophisticated enough to deal with the weak forms of gamesmanship. There is no place for "icing" a ten-year-old.

16. Merriam-Webster dictionary, http://www.merriam-webster.com /dictionary/intimidate.

17. "Bullying Prevention," http://education.alberta.ca/teachers/safeschools /bullying-prevention.aspx.

18. Reprinted with the permission of Simon and Schuster, Inc., from *InSideOut Coaching: How Sports Can Transform Lives*, by Joe Ehrmann, with Paula Ehrmann and Gregory Jordan. Copyright © 2011 by Building Men and Women for Others, Inc. All rights reserved.

19. Ibid., 80.

20. Knight quotes: http://www.therxforum.com/archive/index.php /t-19832.html.

21. http://www.bullyingonline.org/cases/case97.htm.

22. Ehrmann, *InSide Out Coaching,* 77.

23. Howe, "Gamesmanship," 215.

24. To "work" an official is a colloquial term for "work over" or irritate an official so the referee will feel intimidated and thus be less eager to call a foul or penalty on the team making the complaint.

25. Some of the most outrageous examples of horrific sportsmanship occur when coaches direct players to harm opponents, even offering bounties for hits. Two such examples are provided in the article "Zeal Can Cloud Judgment," http://www.usatoday.com/sports/college/mensbasketball/2005 –02–28-chaney-sportsmanship_x.htm.

26. Ehrmann, *InSideOut Coaching,* 18.

27. Ibid.

28. Dermot Moran, *Introduction to Phenomenology* (New York: Routledge, 2000), 241.

29. Ibid.

30. Ehrmann, *InSideOut Coaching,* 76.

31. Ibid., 64.

32. Fyodor Dostoevsky, *Notes from Underground* (New York: Bantam, 1974), 88.

33. Moran, *Introduction to Phenomenology,* 241.

34. Ibid.

35. Ehrmann, *InSideOut Coaching,* 47.

36. Ibid., 12.

37. Ibid., 81.

38. Chris Stankovich, "Coach-Player Intimidation, Humiliation, and Physical Aggression Is Never Warranted," http://blog.drstankovich.com/blog/2011/02/coaching/coach-coercion-intimidation-and–humiliation.

39. Howe, "Gamesmanship," 221.

40. A comment made in my college sports ethics class by Elizabeth Patrick, February 2012.

41. I have written of this in the chapter "Hardwood Dojos," in *Basketball and Philosophy* (Lexington: University Press of Kentucky, 2007).

Chapter 10

1. The idea that the Copernican revolution lowered the standing of human beings has been called into question. See Alvin Plantinga, *Where the Conflict Really Lies: Science, Religion, and Naturalism* (New York: Oxford University Press, 2011), p. 6 n. 4.

2. Ramachandran discusses the first three revolutions in *A Brief Tour of Human Consciousness* (New York: Pearson, 2004), 1–2. Lone Frank attributes a discussion of four prior revolutions (the fourth being the discovery of DNA and the attendant possibilities of genetic engineering) to Ramachandran in *Mindfield: How Brain Science Is Changing Our World* (New York: Oxford University Press, 2009), 12–13.

3. Ramachandran, *Brief Tour,* 2.

4. For suggestions of the prior inertia of the National Football League in this regard, see Bennett Omalu, *Play Hard, Die Young: Football, Dementia, and Death* (Lodi, CA: Neo-Forenxis, 2008), chap. 4.

5. Alun R. Hardman and Carwyn Jones, eds., *The Ethics of Sports Coaching* (London: Routledge, 2011), 2.

6. The word "neuroethics" predates my usage. Neil Levy explains that neuroethics "has two main branches." He writes: "The *ethics of neuroscience* refers to the branch of neuroethics that seeks to develop an ethical framework for regulating the conduct of neuroscientific inquiry and the application of neuroscientific knowledge to human beings; *the neuroscience of ethics* refers to the impact of neuroscientific knowledge upon our understanding of ethics itself." Neil Levy, *Neuroethics: Challenges for the 21st Century* (Cambridge: Cambridge University Press), 2007, 1.

My topic is related to *the ethics of neuroscience*. I extend this notion by drawing on the newly developing fields of social and affective neuroscience to illuminate how we affect one another's brains and thereby the quality of one another's life experiences, in everyday life and in sporting contexts. In addition, what I say is also related to *the neuroscience of ethics*. This is particularly the case insofar as this discussion bears on the nature of human agency and its development through social interactions. Thus in the way that I approach the topic of neuroethics and sport, the two branches of neuroethics are two sides of a coin.

7. I have borrowed this phrase from John Kekes, *The Enlargement of Life: Moral Imagination at Work* (Ithaca, NY: Cornell University Press), 2006.

8. Martha C. Nussbaum, *The Fragility of Goodness: Luck and Ethics in Greek Tragedy and Philosophy* (Cambridge: Cambridge University Press, 1986).

9. I am indebted here to Susan Blackmore, *Consciousness: An Introduction*, 2nd ed. (New York: Oxford University Press, 2011), 156.

Some philosophers of mind and neuroscientists are confident of a causal relationship between brain states and putative mental states, even if the causal influence is unidirectional and mental states turn out to be epiphenomenal in nature, or lacking in causal efficacy. This confidence is due in part to the capability of neuroscientists to stimulate areas of the brain in laboratory settings and to record the accompanying bodily sensations and other experiences reported by subjects. Thus a somato-sensory area of the brain is stimulated and a person reports a sensation in a hand, or a motor area of the brain is stimulated and a body part moves. Stimulation of the brain can even produce movements without an accompanying sense of conscious willing of the movement. See a recounting of the well-known Wilder Penfield experiments in Sandra Blakeslee and Matthew Blakeslee, *The Body Has a Mind of Its Own: How Body Maps in Your Brain Help You Do (Almost) Everything Better* (New York: Random House, 2008), chap. 2.

10. For a discussion and attempted refutation of what he takes to be ontologically reductionistic, materialist views of mind, including

functionalism, see John R. Searle, *Mind: A Brief Introduction*, Fundamentals of Philosophy Series (New York: Oxford University Press, 2004), especially chaps. 2–4. Searle's own view, which he calls "biological naturalism," attempts to avoid both reductive materialism and dualism.

11. For an argument as to how conscious states might be causal in nature without presupposing dualism, see Searle (above), especially chap. 7.

12. Norman Doidge, *The Brain That Changes Itself: Stories of Personal Triumph from the Frontiers of Brain Science* (New York: Penguin, 2007).

13. Ibid., 132–163.

14. Ibid., xx.

15. See Ramachandran, *Brief Tour*, 10–18.

16. Ibid., 13.

17. Ibid.

18. Ibid.

19. Daniel Goleman, *Social Intelligence: The New Science of Human Relationships* (New York: Bantam, 2007), 4.

20. Ibid., 5.

21. Ibid., 11.

22. Cited in Doidge, *Brain*, 63.

23. Goleman, *Social Intelligence*, 12.

24. H. Richard Niebuhr, *The Responsible Self: An Essay in Christian Moral Philosophy*, Library of Theological Ethics (Louisville, KY: Westminster John Knox, 1999).

25. See Giacomo Rizzolatti and Corrado Sinigaglia, *Mirrors in the Brain: How Our Minds Share Actions and Emotions*, trans. Frances Anderson (Oxford: Oxford University Press, 2008). A group led by Rizzolatti discovered mirror neurons in the 1990s.

26. Goleman, *Social Intelligence*, 57–59.

27. Ibid., 42.

28. Ibid., 43.

29. Marco Icaboni, *Mirroring People: The Science of Empathy and How We Connect with Others* (New York: Picador, 2009), 5.

30. Ibid., 270–271.

31. Thomas Metzinger, *The Ego Tunnel: The Science of the Mind and the Myth of the Self* (New York: Basic, 2009), 233.

32. Ibid.

33. Ibid., 236.

34. See Barbara Strauch, *The Primal Teen: What the New Discoveries About the Teenage Brain Tell Us About Our Kids* (New York: Anchor, 2004).

35. Ibid., 14.

36. Ibid., 13.
37. Quoted in Ibid., 13.
38. See Ibid., 15–18.
39. Ibid., 17.
40. Ibid., 21.
41. See also Barbara Strauch, *The Secret Life of the Grown-Up Brain: The Surprising Talent of the Middle-Aged Mind* (New York: Viking, 2010).
42. John J. Ratey with Eric Hagerman, *Spark: The Revolutionary New Science of Exercise and the Brain* (New York: Little, Brown, 2008).
43. Andre Agassi, *Open: An Autobiography* (New York: Vintage, 2010).
44. Ibid., 38.
45. Ibid., epigraph.
46. On the significance of different "levels of description" see Searle, *Mind,* 49.
47. See Icaboni, *Mirroring People,* 268–272.
48. Robert Leamnson, *Thinking About Teaching and Learning: Developing Habits of Learning with First Year College and University Students* (Sterling, VA: Stylus, 1999), 14.
49. Quoted by Leamnson, *Thinking,* 14.
50. Carol S. Dweck, *Mindset: The New Psychology of Success* (New York: Ballantine, 2006), 202–211. Whether Dweck's characterizations of Knight and Wooden are accurate or not, the general point that coaches exemplify mindsets may still be salient.
51. Ibid., 203.
52. Ibid., 205.
53. Ibid., 207.
54. Goleman, *Social Intelligence,* 42–43.
55. Roland Lazenby, *Mindgames: Phil Jackson's Long, Strange Journey* (Chicago: Contemporary, 2002), 11, 32–33.
56. Clifford Craig and Randolph Feezell, *Coaching for Character: Reclaiming the Principles of Sportsmanship* (Champaign, IL: Human Kinetics, 1997).
57. See the notion of "bracketed morality" in David Lyle Light Shields and Brenda Jo Light Bredemeier, *Character Development and Physical Activity* (Champaign, IL: Human Kinetics, 1995), 120, 122.
58. I am indebted to an anonymous reviewer who raised the concern, and to Robert Simon, who suggested a response along the lines that I have offered. Note also that if one acknowledges that learning and the memory formation involve changes in one's brain, then it seems reasonable to suggest that coaches at least to some extent contribute to brain change in athletes.

59. See M. R. Bennett and P. M. S. Hacker, *Philosophical Foundations of Neuroscience* (Malden, MA: Blackwell, 2003), and the contributions of Bennett and Hacker in Maxwell Bennett et al., *Neuroscience and Philosophy: Brain, Mind, and Language* (New York: Columbia University Press, 2007). I am indebted to Leon Culbertson, who called my attention to Bennett's and Hacker's critique.

60. See Andy Clark and David J. Chalmers, "The Extended Mind," in *Philosophy of Mind: Classical and Contemporary Readings*, ed. David J. Chalmers (New York: Oxford University Press, 2002), 643–651.

61. Again I am indebted to Leon Culbertson, who called my attention to a version of this critique.

62. Steven Pinker, "The Riddle of Knowing You're Here," in *Your Brain: A User's Guide* (New York: TIME Books, 2009), 12–19.

63. See Plato's *Apology* in *The Last Days of Socrates: Euthyphro, The Apology, Crito, Phaedo*, rev. ed., trans. Hugh Tredennick (New York: Penguin, 1969).

64. I have borrowed the term "social brain" from Goleman, *Social Intelligence*.

65. Anthony Skillen, "Sport Is for Losers," in *Ethics and Sport*, ed. M. J. McNamee and S. J. Parry (London: Routledge, 1998), 181.

66. I would like to thank Elizabeth Agnew and Robert Simon for their helpful comments as I was writing this chapter. Material from this chapter was presented at the 38th annual meeting of the International Association for the Philosophy of Sport, Rome, Italy, September 2010, and at the 7th annual conference of the British Philosophy of Sport Association, Cardiff, Wales, March 2010. I am grateful for the feedback I received at those presentations.

Chapter 11

1. See David K. Wiggins, "A History of Organized Play and Highly Competitive Sport for American Children," in *Advances in Pediatric Sport Sciences*, 2 vols., ed. Daniel Gould and Maureen R. Weiss (Champaign, IL: Human Kinetics, 1987), 1:1–24; Wiggins, "A History of Highly Competitive Sport for American Children," in *Children and Youth in Sport: A Biopsychosocial Perspective*, ed. Frank L. Smoll and Ronald E. Smith (Madison, WI: Brown & Benchmark, 1996), 15–30; and Ronald B. Woods, *Social Issues in Sport*, 2nd ed. (Champaign, IL: Human Kinetics, 2011), 97–98. For simplicity's sake, throughout the chapter we refer to organized youth sports simply as youth sports.

2. Woods, *Social Issues in Sport*, 101. All statistics in this chapter refer to the United States.

3. Ibid.
4. Ibid.
5. Christina Theokas, "Youth Sport Participation: A View of the Issues: Introduction to the Special Section," *Developmental Psychology* 45:2 (2009): 303.
6. See Mark Hyman, *Until It Hurts: America's Obsession with Youth Sports and How It Harms Our Kids* (Beacon: Boston, 2009).
7. New York State Public High School Athletic Association, *2010–2012 Handbook* (Latham, NY: New York State Public High School Athletic Association, n.d.), 25. The handbook is available at http://www.nysphsaa.org.
8. See, for example, Wiggins, "History of Organized Play"; Wiggins, "History of Highly Competitive Sport"; and B. M. Sayre, "The Need to Ban Competitive Sports Involving Preadolescent Children," letter, *Pediatrics* 55:4 (1975): 564–565. Recent condemnations of competition in organized youth sport could be seen as part of a larger condemnation of competition in society. Alfie Kohn is among the most ardent opponents of competition. See Kohn, *No Contest: The Case Against Competition*, rev. ed. (Boston: Houghton Mifflin, 1992). For a summary of the reforms, see Cesar R. Torres and Peter F. Hager, "De-emphasizing Competition in Organized Youth Sport: Misdirected Reforms and Misled Children," *Journal of the Philosophy of Sport* 34:2 (2007): 194–210.
9. R. Scott Kretchmar, *Practical Philosophy of Sport* (Champaign, IL: Human Kinetics, 1994), 99.
10. Ibid.
11. See Alasdair MacIntyre, *After Virtue*, 2nd ed. (Notre Dame, IN: University of Notre Dame Press, 1984), 187–196, for an in-depth discussion of social practices and the distinction between internal and external goods.
12. Kretchmar, *Practical Philosophy of Sport*, 100.
13. Ibid., 101–102.
14. For a discussion of these reforms, see Torres and Hager, "De-emphasizing Competition."
15. Robert L. Simon, "Internalism and Internal Values in Sport," *Journal of the Philosophy of Sport* 27 (2000): 7. See Simon's chapter in this volume for more on broad internalism.
16. Simon, "Internalism," 8.
17. Ibid., 8–9.
18. Nicholas Dixon, "Canadian Figure Skaters, French Judges, and Realism in Sport," *Journal of the Philosophy of Sport* 30:2 (2003): 110.
19. See Bernard Suits, *The Grasshopper: Games, Life, and Utopia* (Toronto: University of Toronto Press, 1978), 22–41; and William J. Morgan, *Leftist*

Theories of Sport: A Critique and Reconstruction (Chicago: University of Illinois Press, 1994), 210–234.

20. Cesar R. Torres, "What Counts as Part of a Game? A Look at Skills," *Journal of the Philosophy of Sport* 27 (2000): 84–90.

21. J. S. Russell, "Broad Internalism and the Moral Foundations of Sport," in *Ethics in Sport*, ed. William J. Morgan, 2nd ed. (Champaign, IL: Human Kinetics, 2007), 55.

22. Ibid.

23. See, for example, Dixon, "Canadian Figure Skaters"; William J. Morgan, "Moral Anti-Realism, Internalism, and Sport," *Journal of the Philosophy of Sport* 31:2 (2004): 161–183; Russell, "Broad Internalism"; Russell, "Are Rules All an Umpire Has to Work With?" *Journal of the Philosophy of Sport* 26 (1999): 27–49; Simon, "Internalism and Internal Values in Sport"; Cesar R. Torres, "What Is Wrong with Playing High?" *Journal of the Philosophy of Sport* 36:1 (2009): 1–21; and Cesar R. Torres and Peter F. Hager, "The Desirability of the Season Long Tournament: A Response to Finn," *Journal of the Philosophy of Sport* 38:1 (2011): 39–54.

24. William J. Morgan, "Metaethical Considerations of Sport," in *Ethics in Sport*, ed. William J. Morgan, 2nd ed. (Champaign, IL: Human Kinetics, 2007), 4.

25. Russell, "Broad Internalism," 56.

26. Ibid.

27. See Cesar R. Torres, "Furthering Interpretivism's Integrity: Bringing Together Ethics and Aesthetics," address delivered at the 39th annual congress of the International Association for the Philosophy of Sport, Rochester, NY, September 8–11, 2011.

28. See Jesús Ilundáin-Agurruza and Cesar R. Torres, "Embellishing the Ugly Side of the Beautiful Game," in *Soccer and Philosophy: Beautiful Thoughts on the Beautiful Game*, ed. Ted Richards (Chicago: Open Court, 2010), 185–196.

29. Torres, "Furthering Interpretivism's Integrity."

30. Russell, "Broad Internalism," 57. See also Nicholas Dixon, "On Winning and Athletic Superiority," *Journal of the Philosophy of Sport* 26 (1999): 10–26; Warren P. Fraleigh, *Right Actions in Sport* (Champaign, IL: Human Kinetics, 1984); R. S. Kretchmar, "From Test to Contest: An Analysis of Two Kinds of Counterpoint in Sport," *Journal of the Philosophy of Sport* 2 (1975): 23–30; Kathleen M. Pearson, "Deception, Sportsmanship, and Ethics," in *Philosophic Inquiry in Sport*, ed. William J. Morgan and Klaus V. Meier, 2nd ed. (Champaign, IL: Human Kinetics, 1995), 183–184; Robert L. Simon, *Fair Play: The Ethics of Sport*, 3rd ed. (Boulder, CO: Westview, 2010), 24–37; and

Cesar R. Torres and Douglas W. McLaughlin, "Indigestion? An Apology for Ties," *Journal of the Philosophy of Sport* 30:2 (2003): 144–158.

31. Russell, "Broad Internalism," 58.

32. See, for example, the World Health Assembly resolution WHA64.78, May 24, 2011, "Youth and Health Risks," http://www.who.int/mediacentre/factsheets/fs345/en/index.html.

33. United Nations, Youth: Frequently Asked Questions, http://social.un.org/index/Youth/FAQs.aspx.

34. Ibid.

35. Ibid. This is the conventional view on children. See also Tamar Schapiro, "What Is a Child?" *Ethics* 109:4 (1999): 734.

36. Schapiro, "What Is a Child?" 729.

37. Ibid., 730.

38. Ibid., 735–736.

39. Ibid., 737.

40. Russell, "Broad Internalism," 57.

41. Simon, *Fair Play*, 27.

42. Edwin J. Delattre, "Some Reflections on Success and Failure in Competitive Athletics," *Journal of the Philosophy of Sport*, 2 (1975), 135.

43. Ibid.

44. Ronald Dworkin, *Taking Rights Seriously* (Cambridge: Harvard University Press, 1977), 272.

45. Torres and Hager, "De-emphasizing Competition," 198.

46. Simon, *Fair Play*, 196.

47. Ibid., 195–197.

48. William J. Morgan, "Sport, Wholehearted Engagement, and the Good Life," *Sport, Ethics, and Philosophy* 4:3 (2010): 241.

49. Ibid., 242.

50. Ibid., 251.

51. Dennis Hemphill, "Sport-Smart Persons: A Practical Ethics for Coaching Young Athletes," in *The Ethics of Sport Coaching*, ed. Alun R. Hardman and Carwyn Jones (New York: Routledge, 2011), 107.

52. Morgan, "Sport, Wholehearted Engagement, and the Good Life," 241.

53. Ibid., 242.

54. MacIntyre, *After Virtue*, 190.

55. See Torres and McLaughlin, "Indigestion?" 148–150.

56. Ibid., 148.

57. Ibid.

58. Hemphill, "Sport-Smart Persons," 104.

Part Four: Coaching, Compliance, and the Law

1. Hart's own influential views as well as his critiques of earlier versions of positivism are most famously developed in his book, *The Concept of Law* (New York: Oxford University Press, 1997).

2. An example of a purported game that collapses under its own arbitrariness is "Calvinball" from the cartoon strip *Calvin and Hobbes.* In Calvinball, each player can change the rules simply by declaring them changed in some particular way. Consequently there are no rules and therefore no game.

3. As noted in the introduction to Part 1, readers interested in Dworkin's legal theory might start with chapters 2 to 4 of his book *Taking Rights Seriously* (Cambridge: Harvard University Press, 1978). A fuller treatment is provided in his book *Law's Empire* (Cambridge: Harvard University Press, 1988). His most recent views on ethics and interpretivism are developed in *Justice for Hedgehogs* (Cambridge: Harvard University Press, 2011). For an excellent overview and critical discussion of these positions in legal philosophy, see Jules Coleman and Jeffrie G. Murphy, *Philosophy of Law: An Introduction to Jurisprudence* (Boulder, CO: Westview, 1989).

Chapter 12

1. "The Olympic movement does its greatest work by instilling values of sport into the hearts and minds of young people everywhere. Sport is a universal language. It teaches us how to strive for excellence in all that we do. How to live in friendship and peace. How to respect ourselves, each other and the rules. Excellence, friendship and respect are the fundamental Olympic values. They anchor all our activities." Jacques Rogge, speech before the Chicago Council on Global Affairs and Economic Club of Chicago, 2007.

2. For a thorough discussion of the hurdles to asserting the right to a sports opportunity, see Welch Suggs, *A Place on the Team: The Triumph and Tragedy of Title IX* (Princeton: Princeton University Press, 2006); Susan K. Cahn, *Coming on Strong: Gender and Sexuality in Twentieth-Century Women's Sport* (Cambridge: Harvard University Press, 1995); Kristen Galles and Jocelyn Samuels, "In Defense of Title IX: Why Current Policies Are Required to Ensure Equality of Opportunity," 14 *Marq. L. Rev.* 11 (2003); and Nancy Hogshead-Makar and Andrew Zimbalist, *Equal Play: Title IX and Social Policy* (Philadelphia: Temple University Press, 2007).

3. The NCAA embraced the concept of sports as education when Walter Byers coined the term "student athlete." Walter Byers, *Unsportsmanlike Conduct: Exploiting College Athletes* (Ann Arbor: University of Michigan Press, 1995), 69.

4. Some have debated whether this equity principle may mean different things to different people and urge the following definition: that gender equity would make no unjustified distinctions based on gender. Robert Simon, "Gender Equity in Athletics," in *Sports Ethics: An Anthology,* ed. Jan Boxill (Malden, MA: Blackwell, 2003).

5. A. M. Jaggar, "Feminist Ethics," in *Encyclopedia of Ethics,* ed. L. Becker and C. Becker (New York: Garland, 1992).

6. Ellen Staurowsky et al., *Her Life Depends on It II: Sport, Physical Activity, and the Health and Well-Being of American Girls and Women* (2009), 13–15, 28, 32–33, 37, http://www.womenssportsfoundation.org/home/research/articles-and-reports/mental-and-physical-health/her-life-depends-on-it.

7. Ibid.

8. As reported by Tara Parker Pope, "As Girls Become Women, Sports Pay Dividends," *New York Times,* February 15, 2010, http://well.blogs.nytimes.com/2010/02/15/as-girls-become-women-sports-pay-dividends.

9. Alun R. Hardman and Carwyn Jones, eds., introduction to *The Ethics of Sports Coaching* (London: Routledge, 2011), 2.

10. Ellen Staurowsky and Erianne Weight, "Title IX Literacy: What Coaches Don't Know and Need to Find Out," *Journal of Intercollegiate Sport* (December 2011): 190–209.

11. 20 U.S.C. Sections 1681–1688. The law was renamed as Patsy T. Mink Equal Opportunity in Education in 2002, after the death of Representative Patsy Mink, one of the authors of the law. The law is still referred to as Title IX.

12. Senator Birch Bayh, address to the Secretary's Commission on Opportunity in Athletics, August 27, 2002, www.ed.gov/about/bdscomm/list/athletics/transcript-082702.pdf.

13. "More Hurdles to Clear: Women and Girls in Competitive Athletics," Clearinghouse Publication no. 63 (Washington, DC: U.S. Commission on Civil Rights, 1980), 3. The data from 2007 can be found at www.nfhs.org/custom/participation_figures/default.aspx.

14. Richard H. McAdams, "An Attitudinal Theory of Expressive Law," 79 *Or. L. Rev.* 339 (2000).

15. The company has numerous sites throughout the western and midwestern states of the US.

16. See, for example, Title IX Legal Manual, http://www.justice.gov/crt/about/cor/coord/ixlegal.php; *Breaking Down Barriers: A Legal Guide to Title IX and Athletic Opportunities*; and Kristen Galles and Jocelyn Samuels, "In Defense of Title IX: Why Current Policies Are Required to Ensure Equality of Opportunity," 14 *Marq. L. Rev.* 11 (Fall 2003).

17. The initial adoption of gender-neutral admission standards resulted in some men (who otherwise might have been admitted) being denied entry to

some institutions. For example, the 1964 *Report of the Virginia Commission for the Study of Educational Facilities* found that 21,000 women were denied admission to that state's higher education system—versus not one male applicant being rejected. When men had to compete for admission to institutions of higher education with a larger group of applicants, which included more women, many were denied admission. In contrast, Title IX does not reduce or eliminate athletic opportunities for men; it simply requires equality between the men's and women's programs, which can be done by expanding men's and women's opportunities.

18. S. Conf. Rec. No. 1026, 93d Cong., 2d sess. 421 (1974).

19. See 34 C.F.R. §§ 106.41 Athletic scholarships regulation: 34 CFR 106.37(c).

20. Ibid.

21. *Cohen v. Brown Univ.* (1997).

22. 44 Fed. Reg. at 71413 (1979). Interestingly, the three-part test was created, proposed, and promoted by the NCAA. At the time, males were the majority of students in higher education. They knew it would give schools a long time to add sports gradually, and it was presumed that females were less interested in playing sports than males were.

23. 44 Fed. Reg. at 71413 (1979). For ease of reading, I have substituted "female athletes" instead of the verbiage in the regulations that refer to protecting the "underrepresented gender." While a few women's colleges apply the test to men, the overwhelming majority of schools apply the test to women.

24. See *Chalenor v. University of North Dakota*, No. 00–3379ND (8th Cir. May 30, 2002); *Pederson v. Louisiana State University*, 213 F.3d 858, 879 (5th Cir. 2000); *Neal v. Board of Trustees of the California State Universities*, 198 F.3d 763, 770 (9th Cir. 1999); *Horner v. Kentucky High School Athletic Association*, 43 F.3d 265, 274–75 (6th Cir. 1994); *Kelley v. Board of Trustees, University of Illinois*, 35 F.3d 265, 270 (7th Cir. 1994), *cert. denied*, 513 U.S. 1128 (1995); *Cohen v. Brown University*, 991 F. 2d 888 (1st Cir. 1993) [*Cohen I*], and 101 F.3d 155, 170 (1st Cir. 1996), *cert. denied*, 520 U.S. 1186 (1997) (this case was before the 1st Circuit twice, first on Brown University's appeal of a preliminary injunction granted by the district court (*Cohen I*), and the second time after a trial on the merits [*Cohen II*]); *Roberts v. Colorado State Board of Agriculture*, 998 F.2d 824, 828 (10th Cir. 1993), *cert. denied*, 510 U.S. 1004 (1993); and *Williams v. School District of Bethlehem*, 998 F.2d 168, 171 (3d Cir. 1993).

25. Galles and Samuels, "In Defense of Title IX."

26. Nancy Hogshead-Makar, "Hurricane Warning Flags for All Olympic Sports: Biedieger v. Quinnipiac," *Boston Coll. L. R.*, Spring 2011. (Given these

small percentages of spots to play sports, it would be almost impossible for these schools to prove that they were meeting the interests and abilities of either men or women students.)

27. It is easy to presume that girls are uninterested in sports, particularly when women's athletic achievements are practically ignored by the mainstream media. See Michael A. Messner and Cheryl Cooky, "Gender in Televised Sports; News and Highlights Shows, 1989–2009," Center for Feminist Research, University of Southern California, June 2010. Researchers found that women's sports accounted for less than 2 percent of network news and ESPN Sportscenter. Although more women than ever participate in all levels of sports, coverage of their gender is drastically declining. In 2004 network affiliates dedicated 6.3 percent to women's sports. Last year it dropped to 1.6 percent.

28. See 34 C.F.R. §§ 106.

29. Galles and Samuels, "In Defense of Title IX."

30. John Cheslock, "Who's Playing College Sports? Trends in Participation," 2007, www.womenssportsfoundation.org/~/media/Files/Research%20Reports/Whos%20Playing%20College%20Sports/fullreport.pdf; "Intercollegiate Athletics: Recent Trends in Teams and Participants in National Collegiate Athletic Association Sports," www.gao.gov/new.items/d07535.pdf.

31. *Sports Sponsorship and Participation Rates Report,* 1981–82–2008–09 NCAA, www.ncaapublications.com/productdownloads/PR2010.pdf National Federation of State High School Federations, "High School Sports Participation Tops 7.6 Million, Sets Record," www.nfhs.org/content.aspx?id=4208&terms=sports+participation. NCAA sports sponsorship and participation rates: www.ncaapublications.com/Uploads/PDF/ParticipationRates2009c2f40573–60aa-4a08–874d-1aff4192c5e4.pdf.

32. *Neal v. Bd. of Trs.* (1999).

33. Sex Discrimination Regulations: Hearings Before the Subcomm. on Postsecondary Educ. of the House Comm. on Educ. and Labor, 94th Cong. 1 (1975). Statement by Representative O'Hara, chair of the subcommittee.

34. 2003 clarification letter, paragraph 11.

35. *Chalenor v. Univ. of N.D.* (2002).

36. Ibid. An outside funder that contributes to a particular team is giving to either men or women, due to the sex-segregated nature of athletics. A funder could no more give microscopes to only the men in a classroom while the school gives women magnifying glasses.

37. Budgets are increasing at a feverish pace, particularly in Division I athletics, where growth has been over 7 percent per year over the last ten

years. Knight Commission on Intercollegiate Athletics, *College Sports 101*, www.collegesports101.knightcommission.org.

38. *Palmer v. Thompson*, 403 U.S. 217 (1971).

39. *Clark v. Thompson*, 206 F. Supp. 539 (S.D. Miss. 1962), aff'd per curiam, 313 F.2d 637 (5th Cir.).

40. *NCAA Gender Equity Report*, 2004–10, 37.

41. *NCAA Gender Equity Report*, 2009–10, 35.

42. Theoretically schools could offer one sport to men, football, with one hundred athletes, and seven sports to women, with soccer at twenty-five athletes, golf at five athletes, tennis at ten athletes, swimming at twenty athletes, cross-country at ten athletes, basketball at fifteen athletes, and lacrosse at fifteen athletes. Thereby the school would be choosing to offer one hundred athletics opportunities to males and one hundred to females.

43. Peter Keating, "The Silent Enemy of Men's Sports," http://espn.go.com/espnw/title-ix/7959799/the-silent-enemy-men-sports

44. *Oncale v. Sundowner Offshore Servs., Inc.*, 523 U.S. 75, 81 (1998). "A professional football player's working environment is not severely or pervasively abusive . . . if the coach smacks him on the buttocks as he heads onto the field, even if the same behavior would reasonably be experienced as abusive by the coach's secretary (male or female) back at the office."

45. Nancy Hogshead-Makar and Shelden E. Steinbach, "Intercollegiate Athletics' Unique Environments for Sexual Harassment Claims: Balancing the Realities of Athletics with Preventing Potential Claims," 13 *Marq. Sports L.J.* 173 (2003). Sexual harassment can, of course, occur in athletics in ways that are similar to other contexts. See, for example, *Norris v. Norwalk Pub. Schs.*, 124 F. Supp. 2d 791, 792–93 (D. Conn. 2000). A coach pinched a student athlete, grabbed her ponytail, and hit her legs and head.

46. Hogshead-Makar and Steinbach, "Intercollegiate Athletics' Unique Environments."

47. "Quid pro quo" sexual harassment occurs when a position, raise, continued employment, or promotion is conditioned on the receipt of sexual favors. "Hostile environment" sexual harassment occurs when a worker is subject to a pattern of exposure to unwanted sexual behavior from persons other than an employee's direct supervisor, and supervisors or managers do not take steps to stop such behavior. The objectionable actions must be frequent, severe, or pervasive.

48. See pages 210–211 for the United States Olympic Committee coaching ethics policy.

49. 36 U.S.C. 220501 *et seq.*

50. 36 U.S.C. 220522 (8) provides an equal opportunity to amateur athletes, coaches, trainers, managers, administrators, and officials to participate in

amateur athletic competition, without discrimination on the basis of race, color, religion, sex, age, or national origin, and with fair notice and opportunity for a hearing to any amateur athlete, coach, trainer, manager, administrator, or official before declaring the individual ineligible to participate.

51. "Recognizing, Reducing, and Responding to Misconduct in Sport: Creating Your Strategy," *USOC Safe Sport Handbook*. http://pressbox.teamusa.org.

52. Ibid. Sexual Misconduct:

(1) Any touching or nontouching sexual interaction that is (a) non-consensual or forced, (b) coerced or manipulated, or (c) perpetrated in an aggressive, harassing, exploitative or threatening manner;

(2) Any sexual interaction between an athlete and an individual with evaluative, direct or indirect authority. Such relationships involve an imbalance of power and are likely to impair judgment or be exploitative.

(3) Any act or conduct described as sexual abuse or misconduct under federal or state law (e.g. sexual abuse, sexual exploitation, rape).

Note: An imbalance of power is always assumed between a coach and an athlete.

Safe4Athletes.org was founded to address the need for a stronger response to the issue. Organizers noted that little punishment was meted out to coaches who violate ethical policies, and there was rarely a designated person to whom abused athletes could address their concerns, without fear of an all-powerful coach.

53. Mariah Burton Nelson and Deborah Brake, "Staying in Bounds," http://www.nacwaa.org/sites/default/files/images/Staying%20in%20Bounds.pdf; see also the Women's Sports Foundation's policy: www.womenssportsfoundation.org/Content/Articles/Issues/Coaching/S/Sexual-Harassment—Sexual-Harassment-and-Sexual-Relationships-Between-Coaches-Other-Athletic-Personn.aspx.

54. See, e.g., University of Colorado at Boulder, https://www.cu.edu/policies/policies/HR_COI-Amorous.html.

55. *Jackson v. Birmingham* (2005).

56. *USA Today*, May 12, 2008, www.usatoday.com/sports/college/2008–05–12-titleix-cover_N.htm.

57. *USA Today*, May 12, 2008, www.usatoday.com/sports/college/2008–05–12-title-ix-qanda_N._htm.

58. Public Justice Foundation, 2008.

59. Nancy Hogshead-Makar, "Attitudes, Platitudes, and the Collegiate Sports Arms Race: Unsustainable Spending and Its Consequences for Olympic and Women's Sports," *Journal on Intercollegiate Sports* (2010).

60. When efforts were under way in Congress to exempt football and men's basketball from Title IX, the arguments were rebuffed. The implication was that sex discrimination is acceptable when someone profits from it and that money-making propositions should be given congressional absolution from Title IX. Sex Discrimination Regulation Hearings Before the House Subcommittee. on Post-Secondary Education of the Commitee on Education and Labor, 94th Cong. 166 (1975). Statement by Representative Mink.

61. Twenty-two school athletic departments in the country are operating at a profit. Knight Commission on Intercollegiate Athletics, *Restoring the Balance: Dollars, Values, and the Future of College Sports* (Miami, FL: John S. and James L. Knight Foundation, 2010), www.knightcommissionmedia.org/images/restoring_the_balance_2010.pdf.

62. Ibid.

Chapter 13

1. 1376 P.2d 406 (Ore. 1962).

2. Glenn M. Wong, *Essentials of Sports Law,* 4th ed. (Santa Barbara, CA: Praeger, 2010).

3. 613 N.Y.S.2d 660 (N.Y. App. Div. 1994). See also *Larson v. Cuba Rushford Central School District,* 912 N.Y.S.2d 827 (N.Y. App. 2010) (coach's failure to provide proper supervision of cheerleading activities unreasonably increases risks of injury to participants and creates potential negligence liability to cheerleader injured during practice session).

4. 2011WL2329216 (La. App. 2011).

5. 301 N.W.2d 1 (Mich. Ct. App. 1980).

6. 239 So.2d 456 (La. Ct. App. 1970).

7. *Gahan v. Mineola Union Free Sch. Dist.,* 660 N.Y.S.2d 144 (N.Y. App. Div. 1997).

8. 568 N.E.2d 914 (Ill. App. Ct. 1991).

9. 600 So. 2d 1389 (La. Ct. App. 1992).

10. 2006 WL 1587101 (Cal. Ct. App. 2006).

11. 679 N.W.2d 198 (Neb. 2004).

12. 75 P.3d 30 (Cal. 2003).

13. *Wilson v. O'Gorman High School,* 2008 WL 2571833 (D. S.D. 2008) (concluding that "the South Dakota Supreme Court would not adopt the Kahn standard, but rather would apply the general negligence standard" in connection with coach's alleged negligent instruction and supervision of high school gymnast during practice).

14. *Morales v. Beacon City Sch. Dist.*, 44 A.D.3d 724, 726 (N.Y. Sup. Ct. 2007) (holding that "plaintiff raised a triable issue of fact as to whether the coach failed to properly train and supervise the plaintiff, and whether this failure unreasonably increased the plaintiff's risk of injury").

15. *Avenoso v. Mangan,* 2006 WL 490340 at *6 (Conn. Super.) ("[T]he normal expectation of young children and their parents is that adult coaches will conduct themselves in such a way as to avoid injury to the children. . . . In short, the normal expectations of those involved, in the coaching of young children, including the children and their parents, are more consistent with a standard of care that would require coaches to avoid acting negligently.")

16. 884 N.E.2d 122 (Ill. 2008).

17. 42 U.S.C. § 14501, et seq.

18. 2006 WL 490340 (Conn. Super.)

19. N.H. Rev. Stat. §508:17.

20. M.G. L. A. 231, § 85V.

21. *Welch v. Young,* 950 N.E.2d 1283 (Ind. App. 2011) (coach who is an employee of Indiana public high school is immune from negligence liability while acting within the scope of his employment pursuant to Indiana Code § 34–13–3–5[b]).

22. 450 N.W.2d 226 (S.D.1990). See also *Schnarrs v. Girard Bd. of Education,* 858 N.E.2d 1258, 1265 (Ohio App. 2006) (coach's "determination to use male players during girls' basketball practices demonstrated a positive exercise of judgment and a considered adoption of a particular course of conduct to achieve an object, viz., improving skills for upcoming games. Thus, the school district cannot be held liable, because [the coach], by virtue of his position, had the discretion to plan and conduct practices."); *Starkey v Hartzler,* 1997 WL 197202 (Ohio App.) (coach immune from negligence in connection with discretionary discipline that injures eighth grade football player).

23. 741 So. 2d 207 (Miss. 1999).

24. In a dissenting opinion, Justice Banks argued: "In *Womble v. Singing River Hosp.*, 618 So.2d 1252 (Miss.1993), this Court removed a then relatively recently discovered blanket immunity for 'discretionary' medical decisions. We concluded that medical treatment decisions, however discretionary, were not governmental policy decisions and, therefore, no immunity attached. Womble put medical personnel back on an even footing with all other governmental personnel, where they had always been and where they belonged. Today's decision elevates athletic coaches to the same perch from which we removed medical personnel. . . . In my view the football coach and trainer in the instant case owed a duty of reasonable care to the player, the

breach of which should incur liability from which there is no immunity. That is not to say that they were, in fact, negligent in breach of their duty. Perhaps what they did was fully in keeping with reasonable care under the circumstances. All I say is that there should be no immunity."

25. 867 So.2d 188, 193 (2003). See also *Covington County Sch. Dist. V. Magee*, 29 So.3d 1 (Miss. 2010) (public school district immunized from negligence liability relating to the heatstroke death of a high school football player during practice because the coach's decision to hold practice under the weather conditions is a discretionary act).

26. *Elston v. Howland Local Schools*, 865 N.E.2d 845, 852 (Ohio 2007).

27. 736 A.2d 1229 (N.H. 1999).

28. 65 S.W.3d 510 (2002).

29. 2010Vt. Super. Ct. LEXIS 1.

30. 574 S.E.2d 258 (2003).

31. 769 N.E.2d 738 (2002).

32. 758 P.2d 968 (Wash. 1988).

33. *Zides v. Quinnipiac Univ.*, 2006 WL 463182 (Conn. Super.) (coach negligently provides defective L-screen that did not adequately protect pitcher from risk of severe head injury during batting practice).

34. *Sorey v. Kellet*, 849 F.2d 960 (5th Cir. 1988) (a college head football coach's general authority over the football program provides qualified immunity under Mississippi law from negligence liability in exercising discretionary functions); *Lennon v. Petersen*, 624 So. 2d 171 (Ala. 1993) (a college head football coach has qualified immunity under Alabama law).

35. *Zides v. Quinnipiac Univ.*, 2006 WL 463182 (Conn. Super.) (refusing to enforce liability waiver which does not expressly state that college baseball assumes risk of injury caused by university or its coaches' negligence).

36. 683 N.E.2d 706 (Mass. App. 1997).

37. 924 N.E.2d 906 (Ohio App. 2009).

38. 131 P.3d 383 (Cal. 2006).

39. 795 N.E.2d 1170 (2003).

40. 989 F.2d 1360 (3d Cir. 1993).

41. 850 P.2d 401 (Or. Ct. App. 1993). See also *Searles v. Trustees of St. Joseph's College*, 695 A.2d 1206 (Me. 1997) (coach may be liable for insisting that a student athlete with knee problems play basketball contrary to the medical advice of the college's athletic trainer).

42. 108 F.3d 1388 (10th Cir. 1997).

43. Complaint, *Gathers v. Loyola Marymount Univ.* (Los Angeles Cal. Super. Ct., filed April 20, 1990) (No. C759027). In defense of these claims, issues were raised regarding whether Gathers was taking his medication in

the prescribed dosage and/or engaging in pregame running on his own initiative to reduce its side effects of making him feel sluggish and preventing him from playing to his full potential.

Chapter 14

1. Robyn L. Jones, "How Can Educational Concepts Inform Sports Coaching?" in *The Sports Coach as Educator,* ed. Robyn L. Jones (London: Routledge, 2006), 1–3.

2. Felicity Wikeley and Kate Bullock, "Coaching as an Educational Relationship," *in Sports Coach as Educator,* 14. "Coaches are educators in that their role is to work with one or more athletes in order to move the latter's performance to an improved level." Stanley D. Eitzen, "Social Control and Sport," in *Handbook of Sports Studies,* ed. Jay Coakley and Eric Dunning (London: Sage, 2000), 376.

3. Eitzen, "Social Control and Sport," 376.

4. Sigmund Loland, "The Normative Aims of Coaching," *in Sports Coach as Educator,* 19.

5. Alun R. Hardman and Carwyn Jones, eds., introduction to *The Ethics of Sports Coaching* (London: Routledge, 2011), 2.

6. Ibid.

7. Loland, "Normative Aims of Coaching," 19. Coaching "affects the attitudes, values and behaviours of athletes towards each other how they play sport. Most, if not all, coaching exchanges have a moral dimension to them."

8. Hardman and Jones, introduction, 2.

9. Alun R. Hardman and Carwyn Jones, "Sports Coaching and Virtue Ethics," in *Ethics of Sports Coaching,* 2.

10. Stanley D. Eitzen and George H. Sage, *Sociology of North American Sport,* 8th ed. (Boulder, CO: Paradigm, 2009), 53.

11. Loland, "Normative Aims of Coaching," 19.

12. Hardman and Jones, introduction, 2.

13. Robyn L. Jones and Mike Wallace, "The Coach as 'Orchestrator,'" in *Sports Coach as Educator,* 55.

14. Ibid.

15. Ibid., 71 (noting calls for shared leadership).

16. Eitzen, "Social Control and Sport," 376–377 ("with few exceptions, coaches impose their will over athletes").

17. Mike McNamee, "Celebrating Trust: Virtues and Rules," in *Ethics of Sports Coaching,* 35.

18. Eitzen and Sage, *Sociology of North American Sport,* 58.

19. McNamee, "Celebrating Trust," 35.

20. Ibid.

21. See, for example, *Kavanagh v. Trustees of Boston Univ.*, 795 N.E.2d 1170, 1179 (Mass. 2003) (stating that "a coach's ability to inspire players to compete aggressively is one of a coach's important attributes"); *Kahn v. East Side Union High Sch. Dist.*, 75 P.3d 30, 43 (Cal. 2003) (finding that in his or her role as an instructor, a coach must challenge students to achieve their athletic potential, even if this may involve pushing them beyond their existing capacities).

22. See, for example, *Tennessee Secondary Sch. Athletic Assoc. v. Brentwood Academy*, 127 S.Ct. 2489, 2495 (2007) (noting the influence that coaches exert over middle school students can negatively affect "informed and reliable decision making").

23. National Collegiate Athletic Association, *Examining the Student-Athlete Experience Through the NCAA GOALS and SCORE Studies*, January 13, 2011, 12.

24. Ibid., 10.

25. Timothy Davis, "Student-Athlete Prospective Economic Interests: Contractual Dimensions," *Thurgood Marshall Law Review* 19 (1994): 585, 599.

26. Harry M. Cross, "The College Athlete and the Institution," *Law and Contemporary Problems* 38 (1973): 151, 155.

27. Davis, "Student-Athlete Prospective Economic Interests," 599.

28. Barry Temkin, "Suit Could Chill Recruiters' Pledges," *Chicago Tribune*, September 5, 1993, 20C.

29. Ibid.

30. Davis, "Student-Athlete Prospective Economic Interests," 601.

31. Heather J. Lawrence, Anastasios Kaburakis, and Christina Merckx, "NCAA Division I Recruiting, Identifying, and Mitigating Institutional Risk Associated with the Official Visit," 18 *J. Legal Aspects Sport* 18 (2008): 89, 92–93.

32. *Southern Methodist University, NCAA Public Infractions Report*, February 24, 1987, 3.

33. See University of Kansas, *NCAA Public Infractions Report*, October 12, 2006; Millersville University of Pennsylvania, *NCAA Public Infractions Report*, January 19, 2006.

34. The NCAA Division I manual defines a secondary violation as a "violation that is isolated or inadvertent in nature, provides or is intended to provide only minimal recruiting, competitive or other advantage and does not include any significant impermissible benefit." National Collegiate Athletic Association, Article 19.02.2.1, *2011–12 NCAA Division I Manual* (hereafter NCAA Manual), 319. All other violations are considered major violations. Article 19.02.2.2, NCAA Manual.

35. For an example of such an infractions case, see NCAA Division I Committee on Infractions, *California State Polytechnic University, Pomona, Public Infractions Report,* December 16, 2011.

36. NCAA rules prohibit a coach and other institutional representatives from directly or indirectly giving or offering to give financial or other benefits to a prospective student athlete and his or her relatives and friends unless the NCAA specifically permits the offering or giving of such benefits. Article 13.2.1, NCAA Manual.

37. NCAA Division I Committee on Infractions, *Baylor University, Public Infractions Report,* June 23, 2005.

38. Ibid., 2–3.

39. Article 19.7 Restitution, NCAA Manual.

40. For an example of a case involving the negative implications for student athletes of a coach's violations of NCAA recruiting rules, see NCAA Division I Infractions Appeals Committee, *University of Memphis, Public Infractions Report,* March 22, 2010. There the NCAA deemed a student athlete recipient of the improper recruiting-related inducements as ineligible to participate in intercollegiate competition. The NCAA required the student athlete rendered ineligible to participate in intercollegiate athletics to apply for reinstatement in order to have her eligibility restored.

41. NCAA Division I Committee on Infractions, *Boise State University, Public Infractions Report,* September 13, 2011.

42. Ibid., 60.

43. NCAA Manual, 45.

44. Article 10.1 Unethical Conduct, NCAA Manual, 45.

45. Articles 15.3.3.1 and 15.3.3.1.2, NCAA Manual; see also Doug Segrest, "The One-Year Itch: Some Athletes Lose Their Single-Year Grants to Better Players," *Birmingham News,* October 23, 2011.

46. Michelle B. Hosick, "Multiyear Scholarship Rule Narrowly Upheld," www.ncaa.org/wps/wcm/connect/public/NCAA/Resources/Latest+News/2012/February/Multiyear+scholarship+rule+narrowly+upheld.

47. Alfred C. Yen, "Early Scholarship Offers and the NCAA," *Boston College Law Review* 52 (2011): 585.

48. Ibid., 606.

49. Ibid., 606–607.

50. Ibid., 607.

51. See Jamie U. Nomura, "Refereeing the Recruiting Game: Applying Contract Law to Make the Inter-Collegiate Recruiting Process Fair," *University Hawaii Law Review* 32 (2009): 275.

52. See, for example, Bruce Pascoe, "UA Rescinds Scholarship Offer," *Arizona Daily Star,* September 30, 2008 (examining allegations that the

University of Arizona revoked a scholarship offer to a recruit); Jeff Call, "BYU Football: Cougars Rescind Scholarship Offer to Hawaiian Prep Star," *Desert News,* January 29, 2010 (one week prior to the date when an NLI could be signed, BYU allegedly revoked a scholarship offer to football recruit Kona Schwenke, because he visited Notre Dame).

53. See Mike McGeeney, "Freshman Sues Davidson over Retracted Scholarship," *Amherst Student News,* http://amherststudent-archive.amherst.edu/current/news/view.php?year=2002–2003&issue=12&section=news&article=04.

54. See Nomura, "Refereeing the Recruiting Game," 275 (providing a detailed discussion of the claims an athlete would likely assert and how a court would like rule).

55. 985 F.Supp. 782, 796 (N.D. Ill. 1997).

56. *Accord, Federation Internationale Du Sport Universitaire v. Greater Buffalo Athletic Corporation,* 1994 WL 411908 at *2 (W.D.N.Y. 1994).

57. See *Weaverton Transport Leasing, Inc. v. Moran*, 834 A.2d 1169, 1174 (Pa. Super. Ct. 2003).

58. *Smith v. University of Hawaii,* Circuit Court of the First Circuit, Hawaii, Civil No. 08–1–0250–02 (Feb. 5, 2008).

59. Ibid., 10–11.

60. Fred Lewis, "Football Player's Case Costs Thousands," *Star Advertiser,* June 12, 2011.

61. Ibid.

62. 985 F.Supp. 782, 796 (N.D. Ill. 1997). Although it did not involve a promissory estoppel claim, the court in *Fortay v. University of Miami,* 1994 WL 62319 (D. N.J. Feb. 17, 1994) lends support for such a claim. There the court held that oral promises made by a coach during his recruitment of a student-athlete could provide a basis for imposing liability on an institution. Fortay alleged the coaches promised to provide guidance that would enable the athlete to develop his football skills, not to recruit other quarterbacks, and that Fortay would be the starting quarterback by his third year.

63. *Williams v. University of Cincinnati,* 752 N.E.2d 367, 377 (Ohio Ct. Cl. 2001).

64. See Jonathan D. Bateman, "When the Numbers Don't Add Up: Oversigning in College Football," *Marquette Sports Law Review* 22 (2011): 7 (discussing oversigning in detail).

65. Hannah Karp and Darren Everson, "SEC Coaches Defend Oversigning," *Wall Street Journal,* March 1, 2011.

66. Hannah Karp and Darren Everson, "Alabama's Unhappy Castoffs," *Wall Street Journal,* September 24, 2010 (reporting that some athletes have

complained that they were forced to take medical red shirts even though the athletes were not so incapacitated that they could not compete).

67. John Infante, "Ovesigning and NCAA Federalism," www.ncaa.org/blog/2011/06/oversigning-and-ncaa-federalism (describing the practice of oversigning as unethical in part because a coach is making a promise that he can't keep).

68. Bateman, "When the Numbers Don't Add Up," 7.

69. Karp and Everson, "Alabama's Unhappy Castoffs."

70. J. Bernard Machen, "Florida President: Grayshirting Is Morally Reprehensible Practice," SI.com, February 1, 2011.

71. Gregg Doyle, "Bad Guys Utilize Over-signing, and It Has to Stop," CBSSports.com, April 8, 2010.

72. Bateman, "When the Numbers Don't Add Up," 7.

73. Ibid.

74. Article 13.9.2.3, 2012–13, NCAA Manual.

75. NCAA Division I Proposed Bylaw Amendments 13.9.2.3; 15.5.1.10.1 (2011).

About the Contributors

Robert L. Simon (editor) is Bartlett Professor of Philosophy at Hamilton College in Clinton, New York. He is the author (with Norman E. Bowie) of *The Individual and the Political Order*, and sole author of *Neutrality and the Academic Ethics* and *Fair Play*. He is editor of the *Blackwell Guide to Social and Political Philosophy* and the author of numerous articles in political philosophy and ethical issues in sports. He is a past president of the International Association for the Philosophy of Sport and received its Distinguished Scholar Award in 2004. Simon coached men's golf at Hamilton College from 1987 to 2001; several of his teams were nationally ranked in Division III of the NCAA.

Jan Boxill is senior lecturer and director of the Parr Center for Ethics at UNC–Chapel Hill. She is editor of *Sports Ethics* and *Issues in Race and Gender*, and has written articles on ethics in sports, Title IX, and affirmative action. Currently, she is working on a book, *Front Porch Ethics: The Moral Significance of Sport*. Jan played basketball at UCLA and coached at both the high school and the collegiate level, serving as the head women's basketball coach at the University of Tampa. She has served as the public address announcer for women's basketball and field hockey, and now serves as the radio color analyst for women's basketball at UNC.

Timothy Davis, John W. and Ruth H. Turnage Professor of Law at Wake Forest, is one the country's best known sports law scholars. He has coauthored a casebook on sports law, *Sports Law and Regulation*, and coauthored *The Business of Sports Agents*. Tim serves on the review board for the U.S. Anti-Doping Agency and is a member of the advisory board for the National Sports Law Institute.

Jeffrey P. Fry is an associate professor in the Department of Philosophy and Religious Studies at Ball State University, Muncie, Indiana. Jeff has served as associate editor and book review editor of the *Journal of the Philosophy of*

Sport and has been a member of the editorial board of *Sport, Ethics, and Philosophy: Official Journal of the British Philosophy of Sport Association.*

Peter F. Hager is currently an associate professor of sports studies at the College at Brockport, State University of New York, where he has taught since 2000. Peter has coauthored articles in the *Journal of the Philosophy of Sport* and *Journal of Physical Education, Recreation, and Dance* with Cesar Torres.

Mark Hamilton is a graduate of Wittenberg University, where he studied philosophy and religion and was captain of the baseball team. He has been teaching philosophy at Ashland University since 1981 and has also served as the assistant baseball coach. Hamilton teaches courses in ethics, philosophy of religion, and general philosophy, as well as a popular course in sports ethics. He is also a teaching pastor/elder in Providence Church, near Ashland, Ohio. He has published numerous journal and magazine articles as well as chapters in books, including *Baseball and Philosophy, Poker and Philosophy, Basketball and Philosophy,* and *Theology, Ethics, and Transcendence in Sport.*

Doug Hochstetler, associate professor of kinesiology, teaches at Penn State University, Lehigh Valley. His research interests include sports ethics, meaning, and physical activity, as well as historical aspects of sportsmanship and fair play. He has published in a variety of disciplinary journals, both theoretical and applied.

Nancy Hogshead-Makar, a former Olympian and Gold Medal winner, is one of the nation's foremost exponents of Title IX of the Education Amendments of 1972, particularly in the context of intercollegiate sports. She has testified before Congress numerous times on the topic of gender equity in athletics, has written numerous scholarly and lay articles, and has been a frequent guest on national news programs, including *60 Minutes, Good Morning America,* CNN, and ESPN. In 2007 *Sports Illustrated* magazine listed her as one of the most influential people in the thirty-five-year history of Title IX. She is the coauthor of *Equal Play, Title IX, and Social Change.*

Scott Kretchmar is professor of exercise and sports science at Penn State University. He has been editor of the *Journal of the Philosophy of Sport* and has authored a popular text in the philosophy of sport: *Practical Philosophy of Sport and Physical Activity.* He has written numerous articles on ethics, the nature of sports, and the operation of human intelligence in physical activity. He is founding editor of the *Journal of Intercollegiate Sport.*

Matthew J. Mitten is a professor of law and the director of the National Sports Law Institute and the LL.M. (Masters in Law) in sports law program for foreign lawyers at Marquette University Law School (Milwaukee). He teaches courses in amateur sports law, professional sports law, and torts as well as a sports sponsorship workshop. He has authored *Sports Law in the United States*, coauthored *Sports Law and Regulation: Cases, Materials, and Problems*, and has published several articles in leading law reviews and medical journals. He has presented at more than one hundred law or medical conferences throughout the United States and in Australia, Canada, China, England, Korea, and Turkey.

William J. Morgan is a professor in the Division of Occupational Science at USC. He has served as editor and published extensively in the *Journal of the Philosophy of Sport*. He has authored two books, *Why Sports Morally Matter* and *Leftist Theories of Sport: A Critique and Reconstruction*, and edited several anthologies focusing on the philosophy of sports and sports ethics.

Heather Reid is professor and chair of the Philosophy Department at Morningside College in Sioux City, Iowa. Reid's first book, *The Philosophical Athlete*, was published in 2002. In 2010, while a visiting scholar at the University of Rome, she completed her new book, *Athletics and Philosophy in Ancient Greece and Rome: Contests of Virtue.*

J. S. Russell chairs the Department of Philosophy at Langara College in Vancouver, British Columbia. He has published extensively in philosophy of sports, philosophy of law, social and political philosophy, and applied ethics. He has been editor of the *Journal of the Philosophy of Sport* since 2006.

Cesar R. Torres is a professor in the Department of Kinesiology, Sport Studies, and Physical Education at the College at Brockport, State University of New York. A philosopher and historian of sports, he has published over forty pieces in peer-reviewed journals and edited collections and another forty-plus pieces in newspapers and magazines. With an interest in the diffusion of sports philosophy in the Spanish-speaking world, he authored *Gol de media cancha: Conversaciones para disfrutar el deporte plenamente*, edited *Niñez, deporte y actividad física: Reflexiones filosóficas sobre una relación compleja*, and coedited *¿La pelota no dobla? Ensayos filosóficos en torno al fútbol*. He is associate editor of the *Journal of the Philosophy of Sport* and reviews editor of *Soccer and Society*.

Index

For Product Safety Concerns and Information please contact our EU
representative GPSR@taylorandfrancis.com
Taylor & Francis Verlag GmbH, Kaufingerstraße 24, 80331 München, Germany

www.ingramcontent.com/pod-product-compliance
Ingram Content Group UK Ltd.
Pitfield, Milton Keynes, MK11 3LW, UK
UKHW021502240926
475702UK00035B/221
* 9 7 8 0 3 6 7 0 9 7 5 3 0 *